The Pen and the Faith

THE PEN

AND

THE FAITH

*Eight Modern Muslim Writers
and the Qur'ān*

by

Kenneth Cragg

London
GEORGE ALLEN & UNWIN
Boston   Sydney

**George Allen & Unwin (Publishers) Ltd,
40 Museum Street, London WC1A 1LU, UK**

George Allen & Unwin (Publishers) Ltd,
Park Lane, Hemel Hempstead, Herts HP2 4TE, UK

Allen & Unwin Inc.,
Fifty Cross Street, Winchester, Mass 01890, USA

George Allen & Unwin Australia Pty Ltd,
8 Napier Street, North Sydney, NSW 2060, Australia

First published 1985

British Library Cataloguing in Publication Data

Cragg, Kenneth
    The pen and the faith: eight modern Muslim
writers and the Qur'an.
1. Koran——Commentaries
I. Title
297'.1226   BP130.4
ISBN 0-04-297044-X

Set in 10 on 11½ Plantin by
Phoenix Photosetting, Chatham
and printed in Great Britain by
The Anchor Press Ltd, Tiptree, Essex

Foreword

The substance of this book formed the Ian Douglas Memorial Lectures delivered by Kenneth Cragg (D.Phil Oxon.) in three major cities of India in October and November 1984 at the invitation of the Henry Martyn Institute of Islamic Studies, Hyderabad, India.

The Ian Douglas Memorial Lectures Series was established by the Henry Martyn Institute of Islamic Studies in recognition of the significant contribution which the Revd Dr Ian Henderson Douglas (1920–75) made during the years of his association with the Institute. He is well remembered as a leading spirit in the development of Christian Muslim dialogue and for his careful and honest scholarship. These lectures are seen as a fitting way in which his dedication to scholarship and dialogue can continue to find fulfilment.

A special fund has been established to enable the Institute from time to time to invite some scholar from India or overseas to deliver a series of lectures which will then be available for publication. It is intended that the lectures shall address issues of religious concern within the general purpose of seeking better understanding among people of different faiths, especially between Muslims and Christians.

It was largely the imagination and dedication of Ian Douglas as Director from 1962 to 1967 that revitalised the Institute and gave shape and direction to its expanding programme. Through his tireless efforts support for the Institute was broadened among the churches in India and beyond. He worked constantly to bring together and sustain a strong staff, inspiring them to work together as a team. He reached out to establish friendships with the Muslims of India and good relationships with Muslim institutions, all of which still continues. His vision and efforts laid the foundations for a building programme which has resulted in the present facilities of the Institute in Hyderabad.

Dr Douglas left India in 1968 and settled in the USA, where he worked as co-ordinator of the Syracuse branch of the Empire State College, University of New York. He suffered a sudden heart attack on February 18, 1975 which proved fatal.

The Board of Management of the Henry Martyn Institute was unanimous in inviting Bishop Cragg, a gifted and thoughtful writer, to be the first guest lecturer in the series. He is widely recognised as a leading Christian scholar of Islam. His book *The Call of the Minaret* (1956), shortly to be re-issued in a revised edition, marked a turning point in this field of study. It moved away from a merely academic approach to Islam and pointed the way towards a new understanding and a positive encounter within the deep themes of Muslim religious thought and experience. It has influenced a whole generation of Christian students who have become increasingly aware of the significance of the Islamic world and of the need to know more about their Muslim neighbours.

Kenneth Cragg has had a deep and varied experience living and teaching in Arab countries and also in the United States, the United Kingdom and West Africa. He spent fourteen years resident in the Middle East, apart from numerous visits while resident elsewhere. He taught philosophy at the American University of Beirut. The research for which he received his doctorate at the University of Oxford was entitled: 'Islam in the 20th Century: The Relevance of Christian Theology to its Problems.' From 1951 to 1956 he was Professor of Arabic and Islamics at Hartford Seminary, Connecticut. During those years, and until 1960 he was editor of *The Muslim World*, a journal devoted to the study of Islam and Christian-Muslim relationships. His teaching and pastoral work in Jerusalem and Egypt kept him in close contact with current developments. During this time he served as assistant bishop in the Archbishopric (Anglican) in Jerusalem.

In *The Pen and the Faith* the reader will find a selection of contemporary, or near contemporary, Muslim writers and a study of their 'way' with the Qur'ān, how their concerns move with and from their Islamic Scripture. The writers selected serve well to illuminate the diversity of Quranic understanding and to indicate how Quranic guidance is discerned and applied to critical situations in the modern world, as seen by politicians, academics or men of letters. The works from which the lectures are drawn, it is important to stress, are not only those of textual exegesis but also of imaginative literature, sociology and political science. Faith and theology are always, in some degree, biographical. Their meaning and expression must be sought in the life-story of the faithful in every area of action and reflection. The survey as a whole is intended to help to ventilate serious issues facing us all, as well as attempting a solid, academic presentation for its own sake. The lectures awakened warm interest at the time of their delivery and I am happy that they are now available in book form and in more detailed format than the oral situation allows.

The inaugural function was held on October 27, 1983 at Vidyajyoti, a Catholic Institute of Religious Studies, in Delhi. The first two lectures took place at that venue, the third and fourth at the Ghalib Academy, Basti Hazrat Nizamuddin, New Delhi. The fourfold sequence was also given in Hyderabad, Andhra Pradesh, and at Bangalore. Different chairmen presided on each occasion. The list of these indicates the reach and quality of the interest and participation.

1 Dr Rafiq Zakaria, MP and member Secretary, High Power Panel on Minorities, Scheduled Castes and Scheduled Tribes and Weaker Sections, Government of India, Ministry of Home Affairs, Lok Nayak Bhavan, New Delhi.

2 Syed Shahabuddin, IFS (retd), former Ambassador of India to Algeria and Mauretania, Editor of *Muslim India, Monthly Journal of Reference, Research and Documentation*, New Delhi.

3 Dr Christian W. Troll, SJ, PhD (London), Department of Islamic Studies, Vidyajyoti Institute of Religious Studies, Delhi.

4 Syed Ausaf Ali, Director, Indian Institute of Islamic Studies, Associate Editor, *Studies in Islam*, New Delhi.

5 Mir Akbar Ali Khan, former Governor of Uttar Pradesh and Orissa, President of Abul Kalam Azad Oriental Research Institute, Hyderabad.

6 Rt Revd Kariappa Samuel, Bishop of the Methodist Church in India, Hyderabad Episcopal Area, Chairman of the Board of Management Henry Martyn Institute, Hyderabad.

7 The Rt Revd Victor Premsagar, Bishop in Medak Diocese, Church of South India, Medak.

8 The Most Revd Arokyaswamy, Archbishop of Bangalore.

9 Mr S. M. Yahya, former Minister for Finance, Government of Karnataka, Bangalore.

10 Justice Mir Iqbal Hussain, former Judge, High Court of Karnataka, Bangalore.

11 The Rt Revd Solomon Doraiswamy, former Moderator of the Church of South India, Bangalore.

We enjoyed the co-operation of Vidyajyoti, the well-known Jesuit Centre of Religious Studies, Delhi; the Maulana Abul Kalam Azad Oriental Research Institute, Hyderabad; the United Theological College, Bangalore; and Dharmaram College, a Catholic Centre for the Study of World Religions, Bangalore. I offer my deep gratitude to the heads of these institutions for their unfailing kindness and generosity.

The thought of Sayyid Qutb and Ali Shariati was also presented in a lecture at the Aligarh Muslim University, under the chairmanship of its Vice-Chancellor and with the co-operation of its Head of Islamic Studies, Dr Muhammad Iqbal Ansari. The theme of Ali Shariati alone was the topic at an invitation lecture at Osmania University, Hyderabad, by invitation of the Islamic Studies Department. Again the Vice-Chancellor presided, in the person of Mr Hashim Ali Akhtar. The Consul-General of the Islamic Republic of Iran in Hyderabad graced this occasion and presented an extended commentary on the role of Ali Shariati, which prefaced a lively discussion.

Among the other sessions during Dr Cragg's visit were a Faculty discussion at Jawaharlal Nehru University, New Delhi (West Asian Studies Department), a lecture on 'Sufism and the Spread of Islam' to the Anjuman-e-Islam, Bombay, at the Akbar Pirbhoy Hall, and sessions in Leonard Theological College, Jabalpur, Andhra Christian College, Hyderabad and St John's Regional Seminary, Hyderabad.

The Church in India in general and the Henry Martyn Institute in particular have profited greatly from the occasions from which this book has grown. Royalties are vested in the Henry Martyn School for the support of an ongoing ministry within the field of human relationships and the spiritual issues with which *The Pen and the Faith* is concerned. With gratitude for all who made the sessions possible, and to the present publishers, George Allen & Unwin, I am happy to commend it to 'the ken and the faith' of its readers.

April 1984
Hyderabad
Andhra Pradesh
India

SAM. V. BHAJJAN, PHD
DIRECTOR
HENRY MARTYN INSTITUTE OF ISLAMIC STUDIES

Contents

Author's Note

Diacritical marks and vowel signs have been used in transliteration only for Islamic terms and titles of works. Personal names have been left bare since spellings here often vary, especially in respect of modern people. Unless otherwise indicated, translations are by the author.

Acknowledgements

Grateful acknowledgement is made to the following publishers for use of material cited from their publications as footnoted:

The Academy of Islamic Sciences, Hyderabad, India, for a passage from Syed Abd al-Latif's translation of Maulana Azad's *Tarjuman al-Qur'ān*.
The American University Press in Cairo for extracts from *The Hallowed Valley* of Muhammad Kamil Husain.
Bibliotheca Islamica, Minneapolis for quotations from *Major Themes of the Qur'ān* by Fazlur Rahman and from Roger Allen's translation of Najib Mahfuz: *Marāyā*.
Editions Beauchesne, Paris, for passages from Hasan Askari drawn from their *Verse et Controverse, Les Musulmans*.
The International Journal of Middle Eastern Studies.
Mizan Press, Berkeley, California for sentences from *Islam and Revolution: Writings and Declarations of Imam Khomeini*, and from Ali Shariati: *Sociology of Islam* and *Marxism and Other Western Fallacies*.
Modern Persian Literature Series, No. 4, New York, for an extract from Jalal e Ahmad's *Gharbzadegi*.
MWH publishers, London for passages from *In the Shade of the Qur'ān*, Vol. 30, by Sayyid Qutb.
Les Nouvelles Editions Africaines, Dakar, for sentences from Mamadou Dia: *Essais sur l'Islam*.
Orbis Books, Maryknoll, New York, for a quotation from José P. Miranda: *Marxism and the Bible*.
Oxford University Press for a sentence from Denys Johnson Davies' translation of Najib Mahfuz' *Zaabalawi* in *Modern Arabic Short Stories*.

1

Introduction

I

The sense of possessing a Scripture – a Scripture which finalises all others – is the very making of the Muslim. It follows that there is nothing more important than the sense the Scripture possesses. The word 'Qur'ān' means literally 'reading' as 'recital'. It is a Book to be heard in chant and transcribed in calligraphy. But these arts of possession await the art of interpretation. Only wise exegesis, attending on recitation and perusal, fulfils in the soul and in society what is cherished on the lips and in the memory. The text in the reciter's sequences passes into the context of the reader's world. The Qur'ān is precious and crucial as given to the one. It is no less so as received in the other.

In this passage from page to life, from authority inhering to meaning applied, responsible Muslim faith has both its vocation and its tests. In what is widely identified as the first revelation (Surah 96.4), the Qur'ān celebrates the pen of the writer. Mankind is taught by that which is at once the lesson and the instrument. The pens first inscribing the Qur'ān, in its collection through the years of Muhammad's mission and into its recensions after his death, bequeathed to the pens of commentators the tasks of its interpretation as the Book of its people. The sacred Scripture acquired its margins of reception. *Tafsīr*, or exegesis, within Islam is at once the token of loyalty and the arena where loyalty must work. Calligraphy is the first sacred duty of the pen, commentary the second.

The aim of this book is to take stock of Quranic reading on the part of eight outstanding writers in their context of time and place this century. It is to appreciate how they were guided by the Qur'ān and how awareness of their Muslim setting affected their discernment of what its guidance might be. For discernment is vital in reading any Scripture, not only because any text requires thought and scholarship but because fidelity has to be resourceful and situations are perplexing.

Moreover, both mind and spirit are subject to the hazards of emotion or impulse, or the interests of causes and conflicts which may distort or obscure the intention of the Scripture – an intention which, in the human situation for which revelation itself is given, must necessarily engage with the intentions of the reader.

These may be caught up in what the Qur'ān, in several passages, sees as 'supposition' (ẓann) (e.g. 49.12): 'O you who believe, steer well clear of supposition.' Nowhere is the business of integrity with meaning more exacting than where, as in Islam, a faith once and for all documented has to be interpreted and obeyed in a world now and ever in flux and transition. By its own rubric, the Qur'ān contains both things categorical and things metaphorical, meanings that are absolute and meanings that are similitudes (3.7). Faced with these, it warns, there are those of deviant heart desiring to strain the interpretation in line with their own deviance, so putting themselves in a state of *fitnah*, or disputatious rebellion against the true word.

Both *ẓann* and *fitnah* are terms of high reproach in the vocabulary of the Scripture and tradition of Islam. Though we meet them in political issues and communal history, the fact that they may lurk in the ink-wells and the sacred margins means that the Scripture itself is not immune from the partisanship of its own custodians in its very name. The ultimate interpretation, Surah 3.7 warns, is known only to God. Yet precisely because that is so and He has, nevertheless, committed it to human readerships, these must aspire to interpret consonantly with Him even when properly disclaiming any assurance that they do so. The will to such consonance may take many forms and seek many aids, rational, mystical, traditional, and intuitive. But, at best, we may only be encountering the meaning on the lowest of the seven, or the seventy, 'levels' the Qur'ān possesses, the one, that is, on which it addresses our finitude. Mere personal opinion (*ra'y*) is quite inappropriate to the elucidation of such sanctity. Yet, in measure, personal 'opinion', duly disciplined and chastened, is all that the believer possesses when, pen in hand, he addresses mind and heart to a revelation that finds him in document and language, which invites him to 'recite' and 'read'. Chant and calligraphy could not well undertake, in sound and shape, the artistry of worship, without mind and heart having their due role, however circumspect, in the reception of their meaning.

What will such role require in the tangled circumstances of contemporary Islam? Answer is sought here by a study of eight representative thinkers whom we assess in their use of the Qur'ān. The hope is to elucidate their attitude to the major themes in which conviction and conjecture are at issue within Islamic loyalty. The names fall roughly into four pairs, two being men of affairs of state, two activists of revolution, two primarily academics or men of scholarship, and two men of letters and imaginative literature. These categories, however, are not rigid or exclusive. The subcontinent of India is represented by three writers, Egypt by three, Iran and Senegal by one each. The reasons for their selection will be clear from the presentation. Broadly comparable positions could, in most cases, have been studied in other minds and sources.

Only two, Sayyid Qutb and Maulana Azad, have in fact published commentaries on the actual text of the Qur'ān, the former a monumental one. Fazlur Rahman has a thorough work on *Major Themes of the Qur'ān*, while Mamadou Dia and Kamil Husain wrote essays in which they evaluate the use of the Qur'ān by others and outline their own attitude. With Ali Shariati and Hasan Askari intriguing angles on Islamic Scripture emerge, in the one case that of social revolution and, in the other, that of response to religious pluralism. As for the novelist Najib Mahfuz, with whom we conclude, there is in his writing almost no direct comment on the Qur'ān or quotation from it. But his whole stance involves the most radical exploration of all into the viability of a contemporary theism and of the faith about prophethood which almost all Islam sees as the fundamental core of religion. It is he who invites all commentary – though by implication only – to the most exacting dimensions of its duty. For he raises a haunting spectre of the futile and the absurd which threatens all credence in 'prophets' with pointlessness historically and all assurance about God with emptiness essentially. That he can only do so in the form of the novel is itself significant. Elsewhere, in the Christian tradition, the major disturbers of dogmatic confidence have been in the realm of imaginative literature, with its elusiveness to censure and its power to delineate anxiety without requiring to reassure it.

It will be useful to preface the individual studies with some brief review of the main areas of thought and life preoccupying all eight exponents chosen here. To do so will also serve to indicate the rationale of the selection. For there are still many thinkers and exegetes within Islam not evidently preoccupied with one or other of the anxieties and concerns here evident and operative. Such commentators may be significant in historical study. They are less relevant in probing issues of continuity and change.

II

There are four dimensions of faith and of its definition and renewal within Islam exercising these writers today. Though India presents

them in distinctive form, they are evident elsewhere even where the
first of them does not obtain. They are: (1) minority condition, (2)
secular pressures, (3) interrelations among Muslims, and (4) interrelations among religions. One can see at once how these are the arena
of varying opinion, of personal and public judgement, of verdicts to be
reached, and so of suppositions that arouse suspicion and the wisdom
which knows how to resolve them. All these resort to the Qur'ān as the
definitive norm by which they must be proved, thus drawing exegesis
and interpretation into their stresses and anxieties.

Minority condition has been the major factor in Indian Islam since
the collapse of the Mughal splendour in the early nineteenth century
and more sharply still since the 1948 partition of the subcontinent. But
Sayyid Qutb and Ali Shariati, in different terms, saw themselves in an
Islamic minority in the Egypt of Abd al-Nasir and in the Iran of the
Shah. Indeed Qutb characterised his setting as a Muslim *Jāhiliyyah*
and resolved on political revolt as the only valid option for a true
Muslim. A *de facto* Muslim state may be far from being an Islamic one.
The distinction between the two adjectives can be held to warrant
revolution. In some senses the minority situation of (in his own eyes)
the 'true' Muslim under an ostensible Islam may be worse than that
under a non-Muslim majority.

Even so, it is the situation prevailing in Indian Islam which most
expressly contains the stresses in which the Qur'ān has to be read. The
career of Maulana Azad exemplifies what they entail. They belong
much further back last century and are well illustrated in the campaign
of Sayyid Ahmad Khan to reconcile Indian Muslims to a continuing
British Raj after the events of 1857–8. Should they continue sullenly
regretful of the forfeiture of Mughal glory and see themselves effectively
disqualified of *Dār al-Islām*? Or should they identify the latter in their
unimpaired religious rights and rituals, and meanwhile recover poise
and assurance by a lively imitation of the West via education? The
strain such an advocacy involved, both for a true self-esteem and for the
sure political instincts of Islam, was too great for its wide acceptance,
salutary though its orientation was in the immediate context.

After the turn of the century, the Khilafatist Movement sought to
fulfil the political security of Islam by linking the Indian segment with
the larger 'pan-Islamic' expression embodied, at least theoretically, in
the fact of the Ottoman Caliphate. But the demise of that *imperium* after
the First World War, by decision of the Turks themselves, made that
hope sterile. In the emotional vacuum which followed for Indian
Muslims came the crucial and ultimately divisive issue of how, in
Hindu harness or otherwise, to expedite the departure of the British.
The final verdict meant the decision for partition, for Islamic statehood

where majority population could sustain it, and so for permanent non-majority condition for those whom partition excluded. The long and ardent labour of Maulana Azad for the contrary decision which would have ensured a united India measures how deep and searching that option was. Once the decision was taken, the very existence of Pakistan – as a state created in the name of the sole, alleged, circumstance of Islamic survival – spelled a perpetual disclaimer both of the position and the chances of Muslims beyond its borders. It became their vocation to survive without benefit of the condition which fellow religionaries in their majority areas affirmed to be the political *sine qua non*. Moreover, the presence over the border of the embodiment of that disclaimer of the Indian Muslim condition served for years as an active symbol working against the effort to defy and transcend it.

How many and fierce temptations to *zann* were here! No minority settling down to survival and participation within a secular state had a more exacting condition for Islam than had Indian Muslims. Gone beyond recovery was the traditional essential of power wielded by, and identified with, faith – not gone yet hopefully recoverable (as under the British Raj), but gone in perpetuity by a transition which both denied it and argued it as indispensable. To prove its dispensability was the long travail of Maulana Azad both before and after the die was cast. It is this which makes him so significant a figure in the counsels of Islam. Some of the aspects of his case will arise in section IV below concerning the Muslim and 'alien' religions. Here the salient point is his conviction that Muslims could appropriately participate in a statehood they did not dominate, that *zann* to the contrary harboured against Hindus and others could and should be repudiated in the creative taking of risk.

Minority condition even for those faiths which do not assume politicisation as Islam does holds strenuous temptations. The martyr complex is all too readily assumed. The dominant community always has to be suspected of designs to dominate, their will to 'neutrality' constantly doubted by those who find, or think, themselves on the receiving end of disadvantage. Yet acceptance, by Muslims, of the risks of a 'secular' statehood is the only way to prevent a Hindu one. Communal interests and institutions have to forfeit privileged sanctuaries no longer compatible with inclusiveness. They struggle to retain them as a second line of defence and so strain the mutual trust on which a larger, but still precarious, security depends.

These themes are all too familiar in India today. 'Steer well clear of suspicion' is an injunction hard indeed to fulfil when it has somehow to obtain across the frontier of 'believers', and relate to fellow nationals of another faith and worship. The situation is taxing both to mind and psyche. For it seems to place religion altogether outside the power realm. Absolute beliefs have to be sustained in a setting that relativises them. The guidance of religious authority and its exercise by the '*ulamā*' have to proceed in an order of things which disallows their normal Islamic assumptions of what is proper to the faith. It is hard even to express in Urdu the idea of 'secular' statehood,[1] and to persuade Muslims that such a state need not necessarily be inimical to religion. Still more difficult is it to recognise in secular statehood an invitation to a humbler posture on the part of religion, a call to serve society from within and not from above, a destiny to achieve and prove one's mettle only amid diversity. In the loss of triumphalism and in a condition of orphanhood, inhibiting occasions of *ẓann* are all too plentiful. It is in the light of this experience over many years that Quranic reading must be set, if we are to discern how its authority obtains in an order of things so contrasted with those of its first time and place.

III

But the minority condition, in political terms, is only part of the equation. When we distinguish the 'secularity' of the state in the political sense of its legal tolerance of religious diversity (as we must certainly do) from the 'secularisation' of the mind and of society, we recognise an even sterner theme for commentary. Many of our writers, Najib Mahfuz most incisively of all, are reacting to the sense of religion on the defensive against what they see as the erosion of faith. Some, like Jalal Al-e-Ahmad of Tehran, in his *Westitis*, castigate the West as the source of all evils, the breeding ground of world-wide plague. Sayyid Qutb decides that the only defence is a total repudiation of the secular factor, and reserves his sharpest antagonism for those he identifies as its agents within – and traitors to – Islam. Kamil Husain, in his temperate way, fears only that the young will fail to distinguish the essence of religion from its dogmatic forms, approves the latter on psychological grounds only if they suit, and is sanguine about a ready compatibility of Islam and secularity provided both are rightly understood. For Ali Shariati the problems are almost wholly taken up into the political and social campaign where alone, in his view, they can be duly faced and resolved.

Exegesis has endless and taxing occasions here also, with opinion hardening into fear or distorted by resentment. Mental or institutional vested interests all too often preclude the kind of patient, perceptive response the situation requires and which, freed from panic and emotive anxieties, a Qur'ān exegesis should be well able to offer. Modernity, it is true, as Fazlur Rahman shows in his concern for a right reading of it, does present an unprecedented challenge to Islamic theism. The intellectual and spiritual aspects are compounded for many by the fact that, though empirical science owes much historically to Islamic civilisation, its current technological impact is almost entirely alien in its provenance and origin. The wise Muslim finds himself in a double battle to be objective and sober about the West while maintaining his proper quarrel with its political and economic relationships.

It is as necessary as it is difficult for Muslim thought and Quranic commentary to make proper reckoning with the travail of western spirituality in face of secular pressures which, though their impact may be delayed or blunted for a time, are liable to be universal in their incidence. There is no final answer here in the fundamentalist triumphalism which holds itself proudly exempt or in the purely defensive reassertion of traditional attitudes. Only Najib Mahfuz, it may be said, among our eight writers, has really penetrated the core of the issue about – shall we call it? – the credibility of God within the current seeming *imperium* of man. It is he who is the Kafka or the Camus of the Arab Muslim world and, like such writers in the West, he can only be so in the idiom not of 'theology' but of the novel.

Elsewhere, responses, whether of educationists or jurisprudents or theologians, tend to be marginal to the real issues. *Ẓann* may identify 'the great Satan', always externally, dub all doubters as evil, or dismiss the sharp problems of faith and ethics in the contemporary scene as somehow already within the prescripts of a dogmatic morality whose only duty is to be ever more insistent. One may well call many recent secularisers 'teachers of suspicion',[2] that is to say people who generate what the Qur'ān calls *raib*, or doubtfulness, and filch the confidence of theists. But those who suffer from them must beware of being themselves, in turn, 'teachers of suspicion', presuming to counter others only by calumny, censure, or disdain. It is urgent for all to face how far man does appear to be in charge, to be left alone, where even his nuclear terror is of his own making and his positive imperialism into space is by his own resources of intelligence and will. That there is, via technology, a deepening recession in the sense of the need for God, or the centrality of prayer, or the instinct for worship, can hardly be gainsaid.

The right response, however, is not to suppose that the issue is confined to the West and that other faiths are immune to its meanings. Nor is it to reiterate a defensive assertiveness which takes no account of its actual thrust within society, especially among the young and the educated. Nor is it, again, to suggest, as some have done, that the works of technology can be serenely accepted while blandly decrying or discarding the mind-set which has produced them.[3]

The sure response must come from the Quranic sense of the *khilāfah*, or 'dominion' of man, and the sacramental nature of all human experience, whether ecology, chemistry, physics, aeronautics, sexuality, culture, and the rest. All, within the Quranic purview of the *āyāt*, or 'signs', of God, are an entrustment about which we must say: 'What have we that we did not receive?' All human competence to control, to organise, to recruit and enlist the powers and procedures of the natural order is to be seen as the *amānah* from God to mankind, which makes us tenant-trustees, accountable beyond ourselves for the mastery between ourselves. This movement, as it were, *from* the human dignity *to* the divine beneficence, whereby mastery is responsibility and 'empire' must be gratitude, is both entirely congruent with what our technological experience indicates *and* properly and authentically 'religious' in its quality. The resources of the Quranic vocabulary and directive to instil and sustain this reading of the divine–human situation are manifest to any reader who will refuse both panic and obscurantism in face of the secular challenge. This will be the secure and sound way to make good a theist's faith that God, as Surahs 56.60 and 70. 41 have it, 'is not among the outdated'.

How far this pattern of response, via the Qur'ān and its understanding of man, is active must be gauged in the chapters below. Technology in its works – and their economic fruits – can be so preoccupying that its implications are ignored or assumed to be other than they truly are. A further problem is how to translate trusteeship, gratefulness, and consecration in the handling of 'signs', from the sphere of true perception to that of actual conduct, from the conceptual to the operative. A further duty is to lift the issue above the rancour of east/west, Muslim/Christian, them/us disparities and to appreciate its global, human quality through all the diversities of degree and locale. There is no theme in which avoidance of idle *ẓann*, from whatever quarter whether of believers or unbelievers, is more urgent.

IV

Both of the foregoing, the minority condition and the burden of secularisation, mean that there is between Muslim and Muslim the kind of *ẓann* which Surah 49.12 was most at pains to rebuke and terminate. The issues being so vital and concerning both past and future, they could hardly fail to entail controversy within Islam about Islam. Sayyid Qutb, as we will note, goes so far as to coin the paradox of a Muslim *Jāhiliyyah*, a condition among Muslims like to that of the Quraish before Islam. Fazlur Rahman, in his very different idiom, finds it necessary to disavow a variety of Qur'ān commentary as having quite failed to translate its there-and-then content into the context of the present day. Without such translation, he insists that its guidance is nullified and its meaning obscured. Other Muslims, for their part, deny that any there-and-then applies to the Qur'ān, since it is a timeless message saying for all times exactly what it says. For such minds the notion of any 'translation' from then to now is abhorrent and perilous to truth. Does not the Book avoid being chronological for just that reason?

Discussion about the exegesis of this or that exegete tends to revolve around the charge of *tafsīr bi-l-ra'y* – commentary by private notion or idea. But it is sometimes hard for those who decry this in others to absolve themselves convincingly of the same charge. Short of a sacrosanct exegesis uniformly acceptable, all commentary must proceed in measure by private decision, however reverent. And no such monumental authority exists. Indeed the dethronement of punditry, old or new, that pretends to it is the first order of the day for *tafsīr bi-l-ra'y*.

There is nothing unique to Islam and the Qur'ān about this situation. It can even be a sign of health and vigour, but only if it generates a tolerance of diversity and a realisation that there are levels of meaning in the Qur'ān and that its interpretation must be open-ended. But, for minds of passion and fixed loyalties, this posture has little to commend it. Moreover, there are strenuous matters at stake here about the role of Muhammad in the incidence of *Waḥy*, about the interpretation of the principle of 'repugnance' to the Qur'ān, and about the application of *Ijmā'* and *Ijtihād*, or 'consensus' and 'enterprise', in this connection. One of the results of technological change is an increasing laicisation among Muslims and a weakening of the competence of the *'ulamā'* vis-à-vis modern problems. This means, in turn, a shift in the location of prestige and influence within Islam and so of the gravitational centre of *Ijmā'* and *Ijtihād*. The organs to which appeal for authority has to be made are themselves subject to query and become a ready arena for debate about it. Each of our contributors illuminates, or at least illustrates, this problem.

Another aspect of the inter-Muslim issues stems from the ancient fission between Sunnī and Shī'ah and particularly from their respective views of the manner in which the Qur'ān's authority and meaning are perpetuated through the generations, whether in the custody of community and scholarship, or through the Imāms and – in their 'hiddenness' – the *Mujtahids* who speak in their name. Further to this is the Shī'ah doctrine of *taqiyyah*, or prudential acquiescence in a regime which is inwardly, even adamantly, disapproved, pending the time when it can be successfully unseated. This concept clearly leaves in essential 'supposition' (*ẓann*) an outward conformity and precludes the sort of forthright dependable participation which citizenship ought normally to be expected to bring. The passionate signal to end *taqiyyah* explains much of the power of Ayatollah Khomeini, in bringing to a climax the ripeness for destruction of the Shah's regime and enabling the Ayatollah to unfrock those rival '*ulamā*' who still supported *taqiyyah*. Dissimulation as a policy may be a means of surviving adversity unscathed. But, as an ingredient in the body politic and religious, it is a fertile source of perennial misgiving and the 'suspicion which is an evil'. These militate against the integration without which states and societies cannot flourish. So doing, they raise the related question about the obligation of religious conviction to social cohesion. We will find our authors presenting a variety of positions in that regard.

V

The tensions, however, within the body of Islam merge into those which exist between diverse faiths and the communities they inhabit. Here the Indian context is a central focus of the stakes involved. In discussing above the political aspects of the minority situation we were involved in spiritual dimensions deferred until now. The career and thought of Maulana Azad enshrines them all. What should the Muslim think of the Hindu, not simply as a fellow national in a unitary state but as adherent of a faith alien to Islam, polytheist perhaps, much given to images and representation and on many counts antithetical to Islamic genius? How should he see not merely his political security in such a partnership but his spiritual fidelity in such a context? If he abjures political separatism how will he survive religious cohabitation, weakened as he must be numerically and emotionally by the departure of those who go for separate statehood and thereby read doom in his cohabitation? How should the Muslim interpret religious pluralism when his theory has to be married with his survival?

These are the questions involved for the Muslim within political India. Remembering that he left a few months later for Pakistan, it is interesting to recall a speech of Maulana Abu-l-Ala al-Maududi in May 1947 at Pathankot:

We would request you [the Hindus] to study the lives and teachings of Ramachandra, Krishna, Buddha, Guru Nanak and other sages. Please study the Vedas, Puranas, Shastras and other books. If you cull out any divine guidance from these, we would ask you to base your Constitution on this guidance. But if you do not find any detailed guidance in your own sources it does not mean that God has never given it to you. It means that you have lost all or part of it. . . . We are presenting to you the same guidance sent by the same God. Don't hesitate to accept it. It is your own lost treasure coming back to you through another channel. Recognise it.[4]

Plainly Maududi found reliance on this thesis too tenuous to allow a unitary state in India. But the thesis is familiar. We find in some of our writers the same conviction that all valid content of faith elsewhere is 'anonymous' Islam. Where it cannot be so identified it is not valid. Azad held this position but in a temper ready, nevertheless, to coexist. Such thinking, however, fails to measure the degree of disparity between doctrines, sanctioned and ritualised as they are, by symbol systems which all too often obtrude their diversities even painfully.

Kamil Husain tended to resolve the inter-religious issue by relegating doctrines to the margin and applying the purely pragmatic test of efficacy in the quest for soul-purity. His desire to neutralise the potential of doctrines for negative antipathy was sound. But he urged it at the expense of the positive role doctrine must play in the crisis of the self. Only Mamadou Dia and Hasan Askari among our writers venture a reciprocal relation with the convictions of people outside Islam. The latter urges that a concern with other faiths is a vital part of the integrity with which any is held. Such voices, however, are rare, and it is not difficult to sense both distance and imperception in the comments of other writers here. It is as if the temper characteristic of Islam, by dint of the circumstances of its origin, continues to shape its assessments of faiths which see the world and man and God through perspectives of a different provenance.

Increasingly, it would seem, within the claims of nationhood, that Indian Islam must pioneer those tasks of faith-relation which dominance, fanaticism, or inertia elsewhere within the household of Islam are liable to impede or reject. For their measure there is no more searching reflection than that suggested by Najib Mahfuz. This is the reason for his inclusion here and for his being placed at the end. In his elusive manner and in the covering of his traces he resembles very closely some of the disturbers of European believing. These throw an aura of wry conjecture over the human faith in God and hint, through episode and character, that 'the Lord of the Great House', hidden away in his seclusion, an absentee seemingly real only in the human credence – and that a despairing, puzzled one – is virtually, if not actually, a fiction. Mahfuz, too, has ably depicted, somewhat after the manner of Bertolt Brecht, the sinister doom implicit in the captivity of the science-magician to the corrupt politician. It is almost as if Mahfuz aims to set *ẓann* at the very centre of his vision of the human scene – not the petty, breeding, transient *ẓunūn* of frail and private folk, but the inclusive supposition that all the props of our faith and worship may themselves have no higher status. It is to such radical awareness of its own engagement with doubt that faith must be called today. What are the Islamic resources for response?

VI

We must let our chosen speakers say. For some the Qur'ān does not admit of such points of departure and will yield its guidance only to those who do not question its source. Such a position has a long authority also in Christianity and in respect of Biblical Scripture and has been strenuously renewed this century. Others in Christianity have seen that stance as virtually a faith in faith, and have wanted instead a faith which, for its very integrity, left room within itself for doubt of itself. That thought may be remote from the first instincts of Islam. But, either way, do we not have to concede that belief depends upon believers and the faith upon the faithful? The faithful, to be sure, are identifiable by the faith, its content, its traditions, its rites, its code and practices. But these presuppose their adherence and their loyalty. 'God', said the old rabbis, 'is enthroned upon the praises of His people.' His throne is elsewhere too, or it could not be the place of praise. 'God IS, blessedly, divinely like Himself', as the English poet-preacher John Donne phrased it. But, being, He has also to be let be. His reality is such as to await recognition and believers, according to their understanding, are the community that brings it. Revelation and prophethood, within creation, all bear witness to the reality of God within the acknowledgement of man, an acknowledgement turning on faith and love. This does not make Him less sovereign: it only indicates how sovereign He is.

If faith be so, then it is appropriate that it should be neither arbitrary, nor pedestrian, nor contrived, nor routine, nor mechanical. The more consciously and honestly such faith wrestles with its problems the more duly relevant the acknowledgement will be. The liveliest awareness of itself and its task such faith can bring will mean the surest attainment of faith's vocation to be faithful. If 'suspicion', *zann*, aroused or harboured, is the bane of faith, will it not be the open, rather than the blind, faith which gives no cause to be suspected?

These are long thoughts. Meanwhile, there is the immediate business of how eight Muslims this century have explored, or are exploring, the faith issue, via the Qur'ān, within Islam.

NOTES: CHAPTER 1

1 *Lā dīnī* or *ghair mazhabī* or *na mazhabī* would mean 'having no religion'. It is difficult to render the idea of an indifference between religions which is not necessarily an indifference about religion. There is a similar problem in Arabic also: how to capture an attitude which is not worldly as such, nor atheist, nor irreligious, but cognisant of pluralism, ready to tolerate and be uncommitted.

2 See, for example, Marcel Neusch, *The Sources of Modern Atheism*, trans. from the French by M. J. O'Connell (New York, 1982), p. 225.

3 See the remarks of Ziauddin Sardar in *Science, Technology and Development in the Muslim World* (London, 1977), p. 177. See also 'The Qur'ān in the Inter-Faith Future' by the present writer, in *International Congress for the Study of the Qur'ān*, Series 1 (Canberra, 1982), pp. 161–81.

4 *Jamā'at-i-Islāmī ki Da'wat* (Delhi, 1964), pp. 29–31.

2

Maulana Abu-l-Kalam Azad of Delhi

I

The effort will involve . . . the exercise of deep insight into the meaning of things. It is only then that the forsaken reality of the Qur'ān may put in its appearance.[1]

Abu-l-Kalam Azad was writing in 1930 from the district jail, Meerut, in a preface to the first edition of the first part of his Commentary on the Qur'ān, one of the most celebrated in this century. With three other figures in the chapters to follow, he shared the dignity of political imprisonment and found it a rich occasion of prolonged reflection on the Scripture from which he drew the guidance directing and motivating his long career in letters and politics.

If we isolate from his prefatory words 'the effort', 'the exercise', and the 'reality', they may serve us as themes under which to study his biography and his significance. They belong with a dramatic and tragic era in Indian Islam, an era which raised decisive issues about the very meaning of Islam, and did so not in the abstractions of the academies but in the sharp actualities of life – and death – for multitudes of Muslims. There are few life stories, and no Qur'ān commentaries, more calculated to carry us to the heart of things Islamic than the faith and pen of Maulana Azad. The man who aspired to be *Imām al-Hind* while still a youth and found himself Minister of Education in the new secular state of India, who carried a compelling sense of personal mission through many crises both of thought and situation, deserves to be seen as a prime index to the Qur'ān and to what, retrieved from 'forsakenness', its reception ought to be.

It may be said that the context of his biography was characterised by three crucial factors, each of them a radical test of the resources of a faith, namely what is due from religion to politics, the obligation of a religion to the inter-religious situation, and the response to personal and corporate tragedy. In the history of Indian Islam Azad's name will always be linked with a spirited and costly verdict from within Islam on each of these exacting themes. He lived through a prolonged crisis on the way to Indian independence which confronted Muslims with a radical decision about themselves and power. It was a decision which turned on the role of Islam within nationhood and its understanding of nationalism. These, in the Indian context, entailed the entire thesis of Islam about itself among the human faiths. For Azad, resolving them as he did, they also entailed a sharp and long experience of calumny, vilification and inner loneliness. A complex personality, he carried these tribulations with a stoical dignity, pursuing his active role through stresses of inner disquiet. It was not simply that British imperial officers occasioned him, twice over, the harrowing loss of his precious Quranic translations and notes, traumatic as that desolation was. Fellow Muslims also tried his spirit sorely, with their ready surrender to populist passion, their incapacity for the perspectives he desired for them, their proneness to mass hysteria and their inability to perceive, as he saw it, their true destiny. Perhaps the final measure of his suffering is the paradox that a leader so authentically Islamic in devotion to the Qur'ān should have found himself so far disillusioned with Muslims. In all these ways, immersed in political action, among communal religions, and dogged by adversity, Azad's story sifts Islamic issues in revealing thoroughness. His Commentary certainly kindled from his life experience. But this too was itself eloquent commentary.

II

There has long been a strong interaction between Arabia and the subcontinent, not only by the sea links between east Arabia and west India, but by the kinships within, for example, the Wahhābī movements, between Indian Muslim theology and Arabian counterparts. By his birth in Mecca and his Indian-Arab parentage, Abu-l-Kalam Azad inherited that association, though his career gave to it a character quite contrasted with the conservative, Wahhābī, form it historically followed. His father, Muhammad Khair al-Din, had emigrated to Mecca after the uprising in British India in 1857 and had married the daughter of an Arab shaikh, Muhammad Zahir Witri. His earliest years were spent in the immediate locale of the Qur'ān. The family returned to India when he was a boy of ten and Calcutta became his home. There he passed his adolescent years, experiencing a sharp, if in some ways normal, variety of emotions and strains.

He was the youngest of five children. His mother died a year after the move to Calcutta. She knew only Arabic, which was the language of the household along with Urdu. Undoubtedly his father was the major influence in his development, a man of deep Islamic piety, a preacher of repute, and a well equipped theologian who had crossed with Meccan pundits over *Sharī'ah* matters, and a strong lover of the Mughal heritage. He inculcated in his younger son a lively interest in the Mughal past and in their own family share in its pride. Azad gained from his father at least an exemplification in life, piety and letters, of what an Indian Islam could mean in personal terms.

In his intense individualism, Azad was minded often to depreciate these influences and insist that his personal convictions had all been hard won by his own lonely efforts. He had from his early years a prodigious ability of mind and memory but developed with it, and perhaps because of it, a will to independence of spirit. This instinct was abetted by political and psychological factors obtaining for Indian youth at the turn of the new century. The Aligarh Movement of Sayyid Ahmad Khan had responded to post-Mutiny trauma by proposing a positive Westernism, a Muslim will to accept and promote modern education and claim its 'enlightenment' as an Islamic prerogative. But, in Ahmad Khan's case, this entailed an Anglophile stance, an apparent eulogy of all things British and Oxonian, which Azad instinctively rejected.

He had, indeed, no access to Western thought and culture throughout his growing years and had later to absorb these self-taught and, in measure, against the grain. For they might well run counter both to his blossoming loyalty to all things Urdu and to his incipient Indian nationalism – emotions which could hardly, at that point, if at all, coincide with Ahmad Khan's logic of a necessary Muslim recruitment of Western norms and attitudes.

For a time, in his teens, as he became more conversant with Western literature, which he read avidly, that logic did assert itself, only to be followed by a disconcerting sense of lostness and unease. Ahmad Khan's *nechari* rationalism, with its political corollaries, gave him no secure assurance. But, along with other factors, it had parted him from a simple continuity in his father's Islam, with its sure theology, its meticulous *Sharī'ah* and its strong emotional piety. He queried and then rejected the habit of rote memory and citation of past authorities (*taqlīd*) which was instinctive to his father's world, and he also found dubious the adulation which his father could command, as an *'ālim*, from disciples. His own short near infatuation with Ahmad Khan's views came to seem to him yet another sort of *taqlīd*, a blind cult of 'authority', a new style of *'ālim* mentor. Though it stimulated his first interest in journalism and propagation of ideas, it could not supply a home for his heart and intellect. 'Disturbance of mind', he wrote, 'began all over again of a different kind, as if the intermediate peace which Sir Sayyid's *taqlīd* had brought was only a delusion, and underneath the heart had never really found peace.'[2]

What is of interest here for Azad's later approach to his own work on the Qur'ān is the problem of reconciliation between authentic religious conviction and genuine openness of mind. There are several points in his mature exegesis, having to do with the finality of prophethood and the meaning of theological language, at which he makes such reconciliation, as we must see, in too facile or elusive a fashion. The dilemma is apparent in his youthful reaction against Ahmad Khan. He tended to see in Ahmad Khan's questioning of dogma a stance in which there was no halfway house, so that to question at all left him with no ground of conviction whatsoever. In this, he did a grave injustice to the positive content of Ahmad Khan's thought. In his mingled youthful confusion and assertiveness of mind, Azad underwent a deep crisis of unbelief in the wake of his briefly enamoured encounter with Khan's rational Islam, a crisis in which he persuaded himself that atheism was the only final destination to which such liberties of thought could lead.

What elsewhere might have been a normal incidence of adolescent uncertainty was accentuated in his case by his loneliness and mental intensity. Ruminating during his adult imprisonment, he used that analogy of prison to describe his experience of being confined to unbelief, under sentence of seclusion from the converse of familiar faith. He seems also to have been puzzled by the diversity of religions, as well as by the varieties within his own Islam. Beneath an outward loyalty there lay a degree of tension within the family and between the ritual claims of Muslim practice and his inner state of mind. The strong personalism which throughout characterised Azad's experience explains much in his reading of the Qur'ān.

The stress of this faith crisis during his first years in Bombay, and then in travels to Lucknow and elsewhere, did not preclude preliminary ventures in literary work and political action. Indeed, it was these which provided the context of his chastened recovery of religious faith soon after he entered on his twenties. The most significant of his early editorships was that of *Al-Hilāl* in 1912. Hindu nationalists in Bengal kindled his sympathies and, from the outset, he took the view that Muslim action alongside them was due and right. They seem, in fact, to have inspired him to travel, in 1907–8, to Arab countries and Turkey to make contact with nationalist fervour in those countries. His own childhood and his father's rapport with Arab Islam facilitated these contacts which helped to develop in Azad the deep pan-Islamic feeling which was the necessary balance to his readiness for Hindu–

Muslim co-action in the Indian context. They also made him *au fait* with the thinking of Jalal al-Din al-Afghani and Muhammad Abduh, those pioneers of Arab Muslim 'modernism', and with the inadequacies of Al-Azhar.

But perhaps the salient lesson was the sense of national sentiment subduing religious division in a common cause. But, notably, this political factor in the religious equation did not tend in Azad's case to the sort of easy indifferentism to which it is often liable. On the contrary, he experienced around 1909 some deep emotional recall to religion which, though it did not resolve or even involve his intellectual questions, did restore him to conviction and devotion, following what appears – though his poetic references to it are somewhat elusive – an occasion of self-accusation. The experience left him with a strong instinct to hold the ultimate areas of religious truth neither amenable nor responsible to reason, but standing in mystical assurance and what he called *jadhbah*, or attraction. The thought seems akin to one we shall note, independently, in Kamil Husain. Those who come with it to religious scriptures are likely to respond to the text, as we shall find Azad doing, by identifying there what they see as its religious relevance and intention, wisely excluding pseudo-rational reading but also tending, less wisely, to ignore real intellectual issues, assuming them transcended in spiritual significance.

Azad's sense of religious conviction embraced not only an assurance about the inner truth of the Qur'ān and Islam but a powerful belief in his personal destiny in which Islamic renewal and Indian independence would go hand in hand. The prophets of the Qur'ān, and Muhammad most of all, seemed to him to imply a summons to their emulation in the active service of a cause that was both religious and political. For the decade before his first imprisonment this was his driving impulse and writing and speaking and organising were its main channels. He had as his mouthpiece *Al-Hilāl*, an Urdu journal in which his articles proved a powerful tonic to a growing constituency of Muslims who relished the satire and rhetoric and the other literary skills he had at his command. It helped to galvanise the dormant sentiments of ordinary Muslims while impressing the intelligentsia with a religious fervour often lacking among them. On both counts it pioneered a new vital quality at odds with both imitative Westernisers and traditional obscurantists.

It would seem that he was consciously trying to give Indian contemporary form to the Quranic theme of a *Ḥizb-Allāh*, a 'party of God' (Surahs 5.56 and 58.22). He wrote a sort of *Fātiḥah*, or Prelude, in Arabic in some issues, in deliberate cultivation of the aura of a scholar interpreter, a political *'ālim*, and he was active in sponsoring a *Dār al-Irshād* for educating Muslims in their faith and devotion. When the permit for *Al-Hilāl* was withdrawn by the British authorities – itself a tribute to its political effectiveness – Azad started another journal, with the title *Al-Balāgh*. His moods of self-deprecation alternated with supreme self-confidence in which he saw himself as symbolising a leadership which the '*ulamā*', though it was their proper role, were unfitted to provide and to which Westernised figures, like Amir Ali, were unsuited because of their physical or mental aloofness from the masses. His advocacy was in line with his own emotive and political reading of Surah 13.11: 'God only transforms a people's case when they transform their inward selves.'

III

Controversy about Abu-l-Kalam Azad's position from the days of *Al-Hilāl* onwards, about political action, co-operation with Hindus and the nature of the Muslim community in India, has resulted from subsequent debates about the Pakistan story. While insisting on the total self-sufficiency and finality of Islamic principles, so that, in taking up Indian 'liberation' alongside Hindus, Muslims were not somehow abandoning their integrity, Azad saw their actual situation as demanding common action with non-Muslims. Islamic self-assurance, he argued, ought to banish that minority complex which made them fear and hate Hindus. He believed that just when Muslims were being roused to action it should not be to an aggressive communalism which mistook the real goal.

In this he was sustained, as was the whole Khilafatist Movement before and after the final collapse of the Ottomans, by a sense of pan-Islam. Indian Muslims could afford to be in league with Hindus and others in the cause of independence from the British Raj, by virtue of their solidarity with the whole household of Islam in the wider world. During his imprisonment in Ranchi, from 1916 to the end of 1919, Azad pondered further the lessons of his first foray into political journalism and the burning question of Hindu–Muslim co-operation. His autobiographical reflections demonstrate his search for mentors both in the medieval theologians and legists and among the recent leaders in Arab renewal. He ruminated on the effect of British strategy with Muslims in India, decrying the advocacy of education as a decoy away from political activism, yet acknowledging that emancipation could not ignore it. He was imprisoned again in 1922, emerging a year later into the growing disarray and dismay of the Khilafatist hope in the light of developments in Turkey itself. When Kemalist nationalism gave the *coup de grâce* to the Caliphate the brothers, Muhammad and Shawkat Ali, who had been so closely associated with its significance for

Indian Muslims, had to concede their frustration. It was in the aftermath of that disappointment that Azad's championship of Hindu–Muslim co-operation came still more to the fore, and with it his distinctive blend of communal revivalism and unitary freedom, as a political *jihad*.

Azad presided in 1923 over the Delhi session of the Indian National Congress. The twenties and early thirties were the heyday of his policy of national unity. Muhammad Ali Jinnah himself, the creator of Pakistan, was not converted to the Pakistan idea until 1938. But the Muslim League and its mentors never held the decisive convictions about India as a nation which Azad drew from his interpretation of Islamic community. Their Islam did not equip and fortify them to withstand the divisive logic of Hindu extremism and the gathering temptation to counter it with an irreconcilability of their own. Nor were they ready for the kind of suffering to which Azad was exposed by his very resistance to populist vulgarity. As the tensions sharpened between the advocates of separatism and Azad's case for unity, between the ideology that made Muslims a separate 'nation' in their majority areas and that which reckoned with the future of an entire Indian Islam outside these, he became increasingly in himself the symbol of the issue, and thereby the subject of deepening controversy. His capacity to gain the confidence of moderate Hindus and to weather the provocation of the fanatical ones, his sensitivity to the quality of Gandhi and his mentor, Tolstoy, and his ability to comprehend such attitudes within the rubric of the Qur'ān were vital factors in the shaping of his leadership and the interaction with it of the movement of his mind and spirit.

It is fitting, then, in midstream of his career, to explore their matrix in the Qur'ān, the chequered production of his Commentary coinciding with this juncture in his biography.

IV

The genesis of the idea of a translation, annotation and commentary of the Qur'ān goes back to the days of *Al-Hilāl*. But, through the vagaries of imprisonment and the unhappy miscarriages of the first two drafts at the hands of his captors, his own ideas underwent some change. The first volume, finally published in 1930, was a long disquisition on the *Fātiḥah*, which he held to be the quintessence of the whole, and included material on Surahs 2 to 6. A second edition appeared in 1940. The second volume of the *Tarjumān*, dealing with Surahs 7 to 23, was published in 1936. The fact that no further volumes appeared is often attributed to Azad's political preoccupations. But the likelier truth is that he believed he had covered the basics in the *Fātiḥah* exposition and that, essentially, his Urdu translation itself was the primary element in the public education of Muslims to which his project was committed.

One might begin an assessment of his handling of the Qur'ān with the broad injunction (to Muhammad) of Surah 50.45: *Fadhakkir bi-l-Qur'ān* – 'So let the Qur'ān be your admonition' or 'By the Qur'ān alert [them] to remember', where the verb in the imperative yields one of the Qur'ān's titles, namely *Al-Dhikr*, the Reminder. This principle might mean many things, or even by a circuitous thought 'Quranise by the Qur'ān.' But Azad saw it as a principle of simplicity, of letting the Qur'ān explain itself. It clearly suggested also a vigorous repudiation of exegesis believed to introduce extraneous ideas, that is *tafsīr bi-l-ra'y*, though of course what is held 'extraneous' may well be a subjective judgement and what is intrinsic still a matter of the reader's 'opinion'.

Like Sayyid Qutb and Kamil Husain among our eight exegetes, Maulana Azad was sure that pseudoscientific attributions to the Quranic text were indeed extraneous. It was completely against the grain of his thought to allow that the Qur'ān curiously anticipated modern techniques and identified them in cryptic ways only understood once science had invented what it had foreseen. This offended crudely his law that the Qur'ān was a spiritual text having to do with God and man and conduct and obedience, the enjoining of good and the prohibition of evil.[3]

But he was also sure that medieval pundits like Fakhr al-Din Razi had lost their way in minutiae and niceties of grammar, parsing and syntax. He wrote: 'Had Imam Razi chosen to represent what exactly the Qur'ān stood for, at least two thirds of what he wrote would have been left unwritten.'[4] This may be a harsh verdict on a monumental writer who, moreover, represented and drew from a long tradition of commentary. Choosing what the Qur'ān stands for is a criterion which can scarcely be distinguished from *tafsīr bi-l-ra'y*, unless its application takes up more explicit formulation with reasons to justify it.

Azad's intention was 'to appreciate a simple thing for its simplicity' and so let the Qur'ān 'disclose its own reality'.[5] He recognised that in appealing to simplicity he must dissociate himself from the Islam of many of his co-religionaries, past and present. Indeed, he affirmed in *Al-Hilāl* that 'We cannot take a single step towards the truth by starting from those ideas and beliefs which are actually found in the minds of the followers of any inculcated religion.'[6] This seems a rather magisterial view, the more so as Azad's whole political concern was with the minds of followers and the inculcation of Islam. But it no doubt reflected the strain of lofty vocation which recurred throughout his conflict with himself and his destiny. It also sprang, too, from his distrust of institutionalisation in religion. Essentials, for him, were spiritual and it was these, no doubt, which he meant by 'the simplicity of the Qur'ān'. Like many other idealists he was bound to reserve the truth of faith from the compromises of actuality, though it was with these that politically he had to work. It is always difficult for purists to reckon adequately with the unworthy side of religion in its historical manifestations. But to fail to do so risks exempting faith from radical tasks within itself.

It is possible to illustrate the problems entailed in his criterion of simplicity and perspective by a closer look at an area vital to Azad's whole orientation, namely the relation of the Qur'ān's finality to other religious scriptures and beliefs. In his *Tarjumān* Azad recalls that there is no people to whom a prophet or messenger is not sent, which may be taken to authenticate other founders and leaders of faiths. Further, he holds that all faiths are essentially one when in their pure, original form. The aspects that differ are those that have accrued to them in the aberrations of their history and through the compromises of human nature. Both theses are, of course, familiar in Islamic writing and can be sustained from the Qur'ān. They allow it to be assumed that Islam is the right, or at least the best, form of the unadulterated original. All other faiths would be Islamic if they purged themselves of distorting accretions.[7]

The difficulty with this attitude is that it ignores the disparities which belong to the basic doctrines of the various faiths and which are both original and crucial to their identity as understood by themselves. Developments and changes there have certainly been – though Azad too credulously accepts the theory of W. Schmidt in *The Origin and Growth of Religion*, which fascinated him and suited his view.[8] But such flux in the content and stance of the historical religions in no way warrants a neglect of their original and inherent distinctiveness, the measure of how far they are apart. His position led him into some highly superficial judgements about other faiths in his effort to illustrate his case, among them his characterisation of Christianity as 'the spectacle of a form of monotheistic polytheism'.[9]

It would have been sounder to posit some transcendental 'goal' or *quṭb* of all religions, without affirming an initial single character belonging in their history, from which their historical developments had been deviant and retrograde. How would the Sufi dimension in Islam itself emerge by such criteria? And are there not implications about the original in the nature and consequence of the changes it undergoes? These may well indicate issues belonging to the origins the blame for which, if there is blame, these origins cannot escape. Militarism, superstition, and schism would clearly be such aspects of declension arguably latent in the origins themselves. How a faith handles its own dynamic and dialectic can hardly be separated from what it is supposed to have been at the outset. At least on the theoretical level Azad's view of how religious diversity can be weighed, broadly Islamic as it is, fails to suffice. That, however, does not diminish the deep practical importance of his will for coexistence and mutual forbearance.

V

In his discussion of transcendence and anthropomorphism, Azad's plea to let the Qur'ān simply be heard for what it says likewise falls short of what the issue involves. He recognises that an absolute transcendence would mean the impossibility of worship and prayer. For language could never then relate or denote. There must be, for Islam as for any theism, an operable 'nameability' of God if the devotion and the faith are to find expression. But this sound observation is hedged by a somewhat evasive reproach of anthropomorphism in theology. In this he is characteristically Muslim both in his sharp quarrel with anthropomorphism and his assumption that, somehow, the Qur'ān is free from it.

He looks for a middle way and claims that the Qur'ān attains one. While cruder forms of superstitious and insensitive humanising of language about God are to be repudiated, their healthy exclusion in no way means that the problem of language is solved.

If we lean towards transcendentalism we end in negation. If we go forward in the affirmation of attributes, we lose ourselves in anthropomorphism. Safety lies in proceeding cautiously along a middle path. We have neither to give the reins to transcendentalism, nor let affirmation slip out of hand. Affirmation will effect a pleasing display of attributes. Transcendentalism will prevent the shadows of similitude to cloud our vision. The one will let the beauty of the Absolute appear in the glow of attributes. The other will hold back all similitude from throwing thereon its cloudy dust.[10]

But what is this middle path in which, Quranically, 'all the veils of anthropomorphic similitudes are lifted and transcendentalism glows in Perfection'? For we 'have to look at the beauty of Reality through the veil of positive attributes'.[11] The Qur'ān itself (3.7) acknowledges that it contains the *mutashābihāt* – similitudes and metaphors. 'The hand outstretched' and 'seated upon the throne' are familiar examples (5.64 and 10.3, etc.), and 'the face of God' is a frequent usage. It would be difficult to justify the summary differentiation Azad makes in this context between the Biblical and the Quranic situation in respect of this perennial problem.

Within the Qur'ān alone, he cites a similitude but quotes its negation following: 'Nought is there like to Him.' The negation, however, must not nullify, nor the ascription affirm. Azad certainly formulates the issue squarely but his solution hardly resolves it. For solution only 'houses' what it has to resolve. It is good that he yields so readily the necessity of imagination and meaning, in the context of faith. For 'non-attributive concept . . . cannot quench the human thirst'. It is good, too, that he wants to avoid the subtleties of the old theologians. But is he, like so many in Islam, unduly captive to the circumstances of original Islam and its necessity to resist all similitude, however watchful, in the overriding obligation to repudiate idolatry? Is the solution to the problem, rather to comprehend the divine–human relation as *not* such as to prejudice transcendence but to fulfil it? Need we imagine, given this sacramental creation, a reluctant creating Lord? Would an absolute transcendent ever be putting the question of Surah 7.172: 'Am I not your Lord?'

These two important examples of Azad's instinct to circumscribe issues he treats, by ending so, lead us into one of his favourite topics, *Al-Rubūbiyyah*, the divine Lordship. In his own spirituality he lived very much in the sense of Surah 7.172.

VI

In his commentary on the *Fātiḥah* Azad concentrates the whole meaning of transcendence within the term *Allāh*, where all attributes indeed belong but where they designate an ineffable reality which eludes designation. He reserves the term *Rabb al-'ālamīn* for divine provision somewhat after the sense of *Al-Razzāq*, rather than for the more strict Semitic connotation of sovereignty. Like Muhammad Iqbal, he prefers 'nurture' to 'lordship' or 'ownership' as the root meaning. God nourishes, fosters, sustains all things. Unlike Iqbal, however, who grafted a Bergsonian evolutionary scheme on to this reading whereby God presides over a dynamism in the order of things, Azad interprets the *Rubūbiyyah* on lines familiar from the old cosmological and teleological arguments for the existence of God. God as 'Lord' disposes the seasons and the rains, the planets and the winds. He matches need to supply throughout nature and fits all creatures, by instinct and organs, to occupy the world and fulfil their lifespan, in the harmony of *taqdīr*, or ordainment, and *hidāyah*, or guidance, which responds to it.

What might be called the 'religious' quality here is one of the most significant elements in the Qur'ān, as Azad shows by numerous quotations calling upon mankind to register, in cognisant praise and gratitude and awe, the endless panorama of nature's course in rocks and seas and soils and harvests. Here he is deeply within the ethos of the Scripture. But should this authentically 'religious' sense of *Rubūbiyyah* be quite so unmindful of the intellectual aspects as Azad appears to be? For it has often been the burden of other minds, as ardent as his about nature's beneficence, to account for the tragic waste, the hostilities to man, that obtain within the physical universe. It is right to note and enthuse about the positive wonders of *Rubūbiyyah* but also to take honest stock of all that has been, and could be, read as giving the lie to it. The teleological argument (or, better, posture of soul) must be ready for all the oppressive non-teleology which accompanies its case.

Further, the partial parallel with Iqbal's philosophy points up the question whether the evidences of design in the order of things, the contrivances Azad observes in *taqdīr* and *hidāyah*, may not be simply attributed to natural factors. It is possible to appreciate tides, clouds, rainfall, irrigation, or the hawk's eye and beak, or the worm's contribution to landscape, as superbly calculated as means to ends, and yet to find no need, or ground, to connect them to divine workmanship. Natural causes might suffice. If they did, it would leave *Rubūbiyyah* as no more than an optional acknowledgement for those so minded. But to leave it so, no honest Biblical or Quranic faith could be content.

This leads into a further issue about the amenability of humanity to these attitudes of reverence and devotion. Here, too, Azad is fully in the stream of Muslim estimates of man as fundamentally responsive to divine goodness and ready for the goodness of conformity. He sees a fittingness between the divine intention for man and the human readiness for God, in line with the familiar interpretation of Surah 30. 30, where the very *fiṭrah*, or 'nature' of man, means also the 'religion' of a right submission for which God 'natured' man. Thus Azad's exposition of the *Fātiḥah*, with its vivid and ample quotations from the Qur'ān, brings together all that is congruent in the human condition with the divine rule and providence. But the order of nature, yielding into man's response, also underwrites the economies of men, and these in turn their politics and policies. When he comes, at the close of the *Fātiḥah*, to comment on 'those who go astray' and 'those upon whom anger rests', he understands the reference to be to 'man-made groupism', the tribal aberrations refusing the universal *Dīn*, which incur their due nemesis by natural consequence.

His whole career, doubtless, was taken up with the menace of communalism and its divisive effects. But does not the phenomenon of self-interest, within and behind communal tensions, the unruliness and acquisitiveness of mankind and the tyranny of the structures to which they give rise, deserve a deeper exploration than Azad makes? His own bitter experience of sectarian passion, which he bore with such fortitude, witnesses to more radical evil than he penetrates in his commentary. The urges which led to partition sprang from motives which made precisely the same praise of *Al-Sirāṭ al-Mustaqīm* as he did, and believed they were following it in the very pursuit of a separatism which he deplored.

This is not to say that communal harmony is not the way of true religion but that the claim to the latter all too confidently destroys it. The perversity of man, even of man in ostensible possession of final truth, needs to be more firmly related to faith about his amenability to *Dīn* under God. 'The urge to find the straight road and to walk therein', writes Azad, 'is inherent in human nature.'[12] Success, he avers, naturally follows those who find and take it, whereas retribution and failure overtake those who reject it. Warning and admonition constantly give notice of the difference. The alert and responsive temper is the mind the Qur'ān 'aims to build'.

VII

In assessing the significance of Azad's work on the *Fātiḥah* it is important to remember that he regarded the Urdu translation of the text as no less vital to his concern to have the ordinary Muslim apply the basics of Islam to his daily life. The notes which he wrote in the further volume went some way to meet the objections of the *'ulamā'* who, among other points, raised the question why the Prophet himself was not more in evidence in the *Fātiḥah* discourse. Here Azad gave some attention to the occasions of *Tanzīl*, without developing any extended exposition of them. To some of Surahs 7–23, with which the second volume was concerned, he appended studies of particular items, the most extended of which was a lengthy theory about *Dhū al-Qarnain* in Surah 18. His aim may have been to counter the *'ulamā'*s suspicion that he was not learned in minutiae. It was in the only extant form of his *Muqaddimah*, or introduction to the whole project, that Azad dealt with the phenomenon of prophetic experience. He avoided philosophical discussion of *waḥy* as some sort of participation in divine wisdom and sought to comprehend it by metaphors like the breaking out of the life in a seed or like the breaking of the dawn to flood the world with sunlight. Azad's implicit confidence in the Qur'ān as the result of *waḥy* did not require, from him, any curious disquisition into its manner of incidence. It may also have been that his stress on the oneness of religion moved him to give priority to their common theme rather than see the prophets in separate case. That incorporation of Muhammad, albeit the instrument of final revelation, in the whole fraternity of prophethood was in line with Azad's will to curb the 'groupisms' he deplored.

That the full project to which he had first committed himself in his work on the Qur'ān was never completed was due to the increasing preoccupations of the political struggle. During the thirties, with the hope of Khilafatism killed and the tensions of communal factors within the independence movement sharpening, Azad became increasingly the symbol of a Muslim policy that the majority of his fellow Muslims were hardening to reject. As the leading Muslim within the Congress Party the commitment, in the Lahore Resolution of 1940 of the Muslim League to a separate Pakistan, ensured for him a personal travail in which his own ardent view was set against a gathering contrary campaign. It became an unequal battle for the mind and soul of Islam. For the Pakistan objective of the Muslim League demanded to be recognised as the sole voice of Islam. Such exclusivist claims are characteristic of nationalist movements which cannot tolerate alternative views of their cause. What was at stake concerned the viability of Islam as a religious reality. Was separate statehood mandatory in those areas where population majorities made it feasible? Or could, and should, Islam see its authentic destiny as participating with Hindus and others in a free and united subcontinent? And ought the issue to be decided in terms only possible where Muslims predominated, thus assigning millions of other Muslims to a deprivation of the very condition which that statehood thesis declared to be insupportable? Should Muslims follow a logic for independent statehood which divided them by a political frontier and rescued some only by excluding others, in an exclusion highly prejudicial to their future?

There can be no doubt that Azad's courageous decision on these questions represented a verdict about the very nature of Islam and about how the Qur'ān should be read. While advocacy of Pakistan might claim that the power equation within Muhammad's own mission and so within the rubrics of the Scripture entirely sustained the statehood cause, Azad and the Muslim strivers for unity could invoke those other aspects of the Qur'ān which urge a wise and sincere participation in the human condition and commend the sort of *Tadabbur* about its contents which can appreciate changing situations and respond dynamically. The horrendous human cost of partition, easily foreseeable, also argued against it on any ground of Quranic

compassion. The unseemly scramble for the supposed security of
Pakistan reflected little confidence in that *tawakkul*, or trust in God,
which the Qur'ān frequently enjoins, as in 39.38: 'Say: "God suffices
me: it is in Him that those who entrust themselves do trust."' That
God knows all that men hide in their bosoms – of motives, interests and
purposes – might arguably imply that the integrity of these was beyond
merely political attainment and that the drive for their political
attainment might itself prove the more corrupting. A sense of the feel of
the Qur'ān in changed times might indicate that *Hijrah* could be a
spiritual vocation within humanity rather than a physical migration.
Certainly Pakistan carried all the vital problems with it, many of them
accentuated by the fact of partition. The often latent, always crucial,
question during the years of debate and conflict prior to partition was
'whether moral values could be asserted in the form of political
principles'.[13] The historian may conclude that through those years and
in those that followed within India Azad exemplified what a reading of
the Qur'ān for spiritual priorities should mean, in no way abandoning
things political but conceiving them within a wider human and
religious field of reference.

Ideologues for partition and Pakistan might reply that they, by their
lights, were doing the same and that the very availability of Islam for
the human scene turned on their interpretation of its self-interest.
Theirs would follow closely the Judaic analogue, whereby conscious
and even fiercely restrictive identity becomes the *sine qua non* of any
wider human relation or relevance. As Zionists would say, one has to be
politically and nationally particularist if one is to have any feasibly
universal meaning.[14] That this is true of nations is self-evident.
Whether it has to be true of faiths remains the doubtful question. Azad
from within Islam proclaimed that it has not. This, beyond all explicit
written commentary, is his reading of the Qur'ān.

Of course, he corroborated his case by practical considerations. But
for him, making a territorial 'country of the pure' (*pak*) was a symbol of
defeatism, 'a sign of cowardice', a question mark around Islamic
capacity to survive without frontiers and among religions. Moreover,
within the Islamic state, language and cultural distinctions would
persist which Islam would have to unify, if at all, in other than political
terms. In this foresight the history of Pakistan confirms him.

His own narrative of the climax of partition and the aftermath in
India Wins Freedom[15] underlies the pains and perplexities of the events,
the personal dereliction and sense of defeat. Of all the major
participants, Hindu and Muslim, Azad seems to have been the most
dismayed and desolated. Others accepted the inevitability more
philosophically. In his earlier days he had struggled to bring Muslims,

not least the '*ulamā*', into politics for their own good, rather in the way in which blacks in America are urged to register for elections. But he had not been able to inject into their political participation, when it came, his own vision of a common nationality for which he wanted them to be politicised against the British Raj. The Muslim League, with its anti-thesis of separate independence, had become the beneficiary, as also the distortion, of his political concern. Given the proud and introspective pattern of his character. Azad's experience has something of the aura of a martyrdom.

His reading of how the Islamic and the political should interact differs sharply from that of Sayyid Qutb and of Ali Shariati. A free India was as important to him as an Islamic Egypt or an Islamic Iran was to them. But with the long Mughal tradition in his veins, and his natal links with Mecca itself, Azad could envisage an Islam not of sectarian belligerence but of confident partnership in a cultural and spiritual diversity where a strident divisiveness would be its betrayal. There was a hidden intensity behind his activity but he was relaxed enough to be cosmopolitan.

His role within the politics of India after partition expressed a continuing loyalty to his ideals. He survived only a decade into the new order and served as Minister of Education, an intriguing role inasmuch as education is a crucial factor in the well-being – and the suspicions – of minorities. There was now no possibility of any *Ḥizb Allāh* except in spiritual terms of integrity, service and compassion. 'Azad', writes Aziz Ahmad, 'became the bridge between the nationalist '*ulamā*' of Deoband and liberal modernists' like A. A. A. Fyzee and Zakir Husain.[16] He shared in the effort to align Islam in India with Hinduism and Buddhism (where his warmest sympathies lay in respect of pluralism) as far as loyalty allowed, and to give the lie to the steady charge, or implication, from Pakistan, that living without benefit of statehood would inevitably entail a slow assimilation of Muslims into the dominant ethos of Hinduism.[17] His readiness to be carefully eclectic equipped him for both tasks, but was safeguarded by the fact that – in contrast to thinkers like Fyzee and, earlier, Iqbal – his hold on the characteristic doctrines of divine sovereignty and revelation was more firmly traditional.

The most impressive feature of the Islam Azad personified was the dignity with which he carried the wound of partition. Once the die was cast he treated the concerns of Pakistanis with courtesy and without rancour, despite the built-in vested interest their vindication had in his dilemmas. One of his long-standing friends wrote:

If by chance old memories were revived for him, he would simply say with a sigh: 'Why expose the scar on one's heart? No one is to blame. I alone am to blame. I was so incompetent that I could not succeed in keeping back the Muslims of India from committing deliberate suicide.[18]

Comparably, one of his persistent opponents, Abd al-Majid Daryabadi, declared:

Towards his opponents, particularly the Muslim League, there was not a trace of complaint or criticism in what Maulana said. References to all were equally well-mannered. With regard even to Pakistan, instead of complaints or sneers, there was goodwill and some words like: 'Now that it has come into existence, everybody's interest lies in its being strong and stable.'[19]

Such magnaminity was the more generous inasmuch as advocates even of theocratic mind could cull from his *Hilāl* days sentiments which they could cite in their own cause, ignoring the tactical necessities of that time, when apathetic Muslims needed to be galvanised into action. Azad had to bear not only the trauma of 1947 but deliberate, even ruthless, distortion of his own personal Islamic sequences of thought on the part of others. Between 1912 and 1952 there were certainly developments in his programme for Muslims but these were within, and on behalf of, the massive changes in the times themselves. At mid-century there was a different task for Muslim leadership than that in its first decade. The consistency, in Azad, and through all the stresses of his personality, lay in his authentic inward piety, his living within the *Rubūbiyyah* he explored in the *Fātiḥah*. Just as he was ready to comprehend the whole Qur'ān within the verses of the first Surah, so he conceived and pursued the politics of Islam within the Qur'ān's dimensions of *taqwā* and *tawakkul*.

VIII

In the light of the final conclusion in discussion of the eighth thinker, Mahfuz, it may be fitting to leave Maulana Azad with a kindred perception of beauty.

The very nature of the universe is constituted of beauty. Even as the elements were created to give a form to the universe, even so it was invested with the qualities of colour, light, and shade, and of rhythm and beauty.[20]

Azad's comment here relates to Surah 32.6 and 7: '. . . the Almighty, the merciful One, who beautifies all things He has created, initiating the being of man out of clay'; and to 17.44: 'The seven heavens and the earth and all they comprehend yield Him praise. Nothing is that does not praise Him. But what that praising is will always be more than you [pl.] can grasp.'

Azad here is not simply echoing the Sufis. He relates the praise of beauty to the sombre shadows of tragedy and decay by an interpretation of these as within a process in which they stimulate a refining response. There is some kinship with the thought of Kamil Husain about the checks which halt a false direction and help eliminate the unworthy choice and conserve the right one. Ebb and flow, night and day, dark and light, weariness and renewal, in the natural order have their counterpart in the ethical calling of man. Falsehood may obtain but only to evoke the countering force of truth. Such is *itqān*, or 'bringing to perfection', the root which occurs in the Qur'ān only in 27.88: '. . . the work of God who has done all things to perfection'. The immediate context there is the dissolving mountains, falling away like clouds at the last day, when ethics passes into eschatology and the alternation of creation and judgement becomes final.

Perhaps this note of beauty in the order of divine providence suggests the wisest clue to the assessment of Maulana Azad's half-century of Muslim endeavour from eager youth to chastened age. As S. M. Ikram remarks, 'Azad saw much, suffered much and changed much.'[21] Through all, his dedication to Islamic piety, co-operatively with Indian pluralism, and his *gravitas* both in leadership and adversity drew their quality from the Qur'ān and, with his written exegesis, constitute effective commentary on its meaning as *Dīn* and *Īmān*.

NOTES: CHAPTER 2

1   Maulana Abu-l-Kalam Azad, *Tarjumān al-Qur'ān*, translated by Syed Abdul-Latif (Bombay, 1962), Preface to the first edition, p. xl.
2   Quoted from Ian Douglas; 'The Life and Religious Thought of Maulana Abu-l-Kalam Azad', unpublished thesis, Oxford, 1969, p. 37.
3   See *Tarjumān*, pp. xxxvi f.
4   ibid., p. xxxiii.
5   ibid., p. xxxiv.
6   Himayun Kabir (ed.), *Maulana Abu-l-Kalam Azad: A Memorial Volume* (New Delhi, 1959), p. 82.
7   See *Tarjumān*, p. 174.
8   Azad's fascination with W. Schmidt is clear in the *Tarjumān*, p. 102. There were some, too, within Christian theology, like Samuel M. Zwemer, who were enthusiastic about Schmidt's theory of an original monotheism and used it for a similar purpose. Schmidt's work appeared in English, in 1931, in summary form, translated by H. J. Rose, from the German, *Der Ursprung der Gottesidee*, 1926–55.
9   *Tarjumān*, p. 121.
10 ibid., p. 131.
11 ibid., pp. 128–9.
12 ibid., p. 187.

13   The words are those of M. Mujeeb, *The Indian Muslims* (London, 1967), p. 440.

14   This parallel was not lost upon Azad. See Leonard Mosley, *The Last Days of the British Raj* (London, 1961), quoting the *Hindustan Times* of 15 April 1946.

15   Humayun Kabir (ed.), *India Wins Freedom: An Autobiographical Narrative* (Bombay, 1959).

16   Aziz Ahmad, *Islamic Modernism in India and Pakistan* (London, 1967), p. 254.

17   Istiaq H. Qureshi, first Minister of Education in Pakistan, opined that Islam in India was destined to wither away. 'Nothing short of political independence could guarantee their [Muslims'] existence as a distinct entity'. See *Muslim World Quarterly*, vol. 44, no. 1 (Jan. 1954), p. 9.

18   In *A Memorial Volume*, p. 47.

19   S. M. Ikram, *Modern Muslim India and the Birth of Pakistan* (Lahore, 1950), p. 156.

20   Aziz Ahmad's translation from the *Tarjumān*, section 4; cf. Abd al-Latif, p. 53.

21   Ikram, op. cit., p. 156.

3

Mamadou Dia of Senegal

I

The city of Dakar stands proudly on the Atlantic shore at the westernmost reach of the Muslim world. Senegal, the state of which it is the capital, is unique among Islamic nations in having, through all its recent formative years, as President and ruler a Christian and world statesman, Léopold Sédar Senghor. His response to colonialism was not to repudiate the culture and heritage of the foreign regime but, appreciating and sharing its human traditions, to supersede its political dominance by a positive, reciprocal affirmation of African identity, a joy in *négritude*, as the surest foundation for the autonomy of African peoples. His leadership drew heavily from the economic doctrines of Karl Marx but interpreted them from within the perspectives of Teilhard de Chardin, whose understanding of man in history and in Christ has been a powerful theological incentive in Christianity this century.

In close collaboration with Senghor from the earliest days of their French tutelage and their work for independence was Mamadou Dia, a Muslim of the Tukulor tribe in Senegal, who was Prime Minister of Senegal from 1958 until 1962, when a radical break occurred with Senghor. Both the long partnership and the bitter quarrel are significant. Each involved revealing cross-currents of Muslim-Christian attitudes and action in face of sharp problems of policy and decision about economic objectives and political priorities, behind which were basic issues of faith and philosophy. A study of the career of Mamadou Dia opens up fascinating areas of Islamic thinking within urgent practical fields of statehood, as these were related to categories of society and man derived from Marx or inspired by de Chardin. Some of Dia's views supply an intriguing corrective to familiar Muslim assumptions about God and man, religion and life.

Born in 1910, Mamadou Dia was educated in local schools in the river region of the Tukulor people and became a local schoolteacher and then a headmaster. He studied economics and practised journalism. His political association with Senghor began when he was in his mid-thirties and they were close political colleagues for seventeen years. Dia was a founder member and subsequently Secretary-General of the *Bloc Démocratique Sénégalais* (BDS), which later became the *Union Progressiste Sénégalaise* (UPS). He was a Senator of the French Republic from 1948 to 1956 under the pattern of integration of colonial territories within the French system. This gave him wide experience of French culture and society. He proved himself a capable orator and a lively protagonist of Senegalese identity within the ideals of Senghor and the *Présence Africaine* concept of *négritude*, first voiced by Aimé Césaire and taken up by the BDS.[1] Whereas the central motto of Kwame Nkrumah in Ghana was 'Seek ye first the political kingdom and all else will be added to you', the stance of *négritude* was 'Seek ye first the cultural kingdom and all else will follow.' Decolonialisation was not to be sought, as Franz Fanon alleged,[2] by bitter, violent repudiation of the colonial factor, but by strong, confident, self-reliant reassertion of the local identity, in all its proper dignity, history and authentic quality. It is clear that Mamadou Dia shared fully this ideal made articulate in the poetry and thought of Senghor, who so remarkably exemplified what a double literacy, a bicultural existence, could be.[3]

'Seeking the cultural kingdom' did not mean neglect of the political. It meant an expectant, constructive expression of the political resolve, though – as we will see – it left serious occasions of dispute about economic decisions. When, in 1956, Senegal became independent, Mamadou Dia reaped with Senghor the fruits of their campaign. Senghor's was in no sense a titular presidency. He stood at the centre of power. But Dia rapidly advanced to the premiership and while the Mali Federation endured he was its Vice-President. For four years the two men enjoyed a close partnership. It foundered in the closing days of 1962, when conflict developed over the degree of feasible socialism and Dia was ousted after failing in a bid to override Senghor. The army, or the vital part of it, sided with the President. Dia was arrested in December 1962, after dissolving the Assembly. Five months later he was sentenced to life imprisonment, which was commuted, in 1972, to twenty years. He was released in 1974 and regained his political rights in 1976. But since that date his activities have been confined to journalism via the *Ande Soppi* newspaper in Dakar and his interests in the *Internationale Africaine des Forces pour Le Développement*, which he founded in earlier days.

The factors behind the quarrel between the two leaders had to do with the tactics and, essentially within tactics, the aims of Senegalese socialism, in respect of which Mamadou Dia's position was more radical than Senghor's. But this issue reached back into contention for the loyalty of Senegalese Muslims and for their interpretation of Islam.

The influence of the Sufi orders and of the marabouts remains strong in Senegal.[4] The main Sufi orders, the Qādiriyyah, the Murīdiyyah and the Tijāniyyah, are still significant politically. Their leaders exercise a powerful social control and there are few independent sources of Muslim leadership to challenge the authority of the marabouts. The cohesive discipline of the orders, the popular mystique which they enjoy, and their organisation are factors which no politician can ignore. The marabouts have agrarian economic as well as commercial interests to defend and enlarge and are often endowed to serve them with considerable political *sagesse*. As a Catholic Christian heading a state more than 80 per cent Muslim, Senghor needed to cultivate the orders and the marabouts sedulously and to observe their inner alignments carefully. In this necessity he proved more adept than his Muslim partner, Dia, perhaps by the very fact of his being non-Muslim. Senghor's line was that the basic issues of state and society did not arouse questions between this religion and that, but between good and bad religiousness.

Mamadou Dia, himself a Tijānī Muslim and closely connected with one of their *Murīds*, Abd al-Aziz, failed to win over the Tijānī *Khalīfah*, who backed Senghor. One of the charges against him in 1962 concerned his effort to unify the Islamic dimension in the country and symbolise this by building a central 'ecumenical' mosque, as a focus for all Muslims. This incurred the suspicions of the *Murīds*, who were jealous for their separate prerogatives. 'Unifiers' of religious loyalty, as activists for social action are wont to be, often fall foul of the susceptibilities of religion's official custodians. Dia was no exception. Just as Dia found radical allies in Christian quarters in Senegal, so Senghor found support for his pragmatic socialism from the dominant religious establishment. It is never safe for exponents to assume that religious frontiers will coincide with moral and ideological ones. The ability of 'religion' to deliver votes and so manoeuvre politicians is often more evident than its will, or ability, to guide them. So Mamadou Dia was to discover. His long imprisonment might perhaps be regarded as a casualty of religious traditionalism playing safe with its interests. That the casualty should have happened in the context of a reputation as high-minded as that of Senghor is the more suggestive not simply of the complexities of politics but also the tensions in religion.

However the major factors in Mamadou Dia's downfall were economic. His socialism was more insistent – opponents would say, more doctrinaire – than that of Senghor. His determination was to reduce what he called 'social, family and caste parasitism' so that each active citizen recovered his earning capacity. He realised that political independence was still impeded by economic 'neo-colonialism', by which European interests, operating through commercial middle-class Senegalese, continued to dominate and dictate the economy. His measures in 1962 were designed to limit the power of these interest groups. He aimed to give to rural co-operatives a monopoly in the importing of merchandise necessary to the rural sector. His rural 'animation' projects excited the suspicion and the opposition of the marabouts, who stood to lose heavily by the implementation of his measures.

He thus aroused resistance from all parties, commercial or traditional, whose vested interests were neo-colonialist. He was accused of thwarting European efforts to build up the private sector of the economy. His plans for the import monopoly in vital commodities set off a spate of money transfers back to Europe. Falling money confidence led Senghor to repudiate Dia and his pragmatic brand of socialism after Dia's fall brought confidence back to investors. While Dia languished in gaol in Kedougou in eastern Senegal, Senghor continued successfully on his presidential path, only giving way to the Muslim, Abdou Diouf, in 1980. He could plead that Dia's economic measures were unrealistic, too rapid, inoperable within the given constraints. But Dia had loyal support from organs of Catholic opinion such as *L'Esprit* and the advocates of the *Économie et Humanisme* group of Christian social action. All faiths have their pragmatists, all are capable of idealism.

II

Mamadou Dia's eleven years in prison set him in the noble company of those who, like Gandhi and Nehru and Azad, Qutb and Shariati, have been compelled, either by colonial regimes or their successors, to ponder their thoughts and mature their convictions in the detachment of enforced isolation from events. Such prolonged deprivation of physical liberty, and the inflicted status of suffering for a cause, give existential warrant to such convictions and should suffice to ensure their attentive study.

Three years after his release, and within a year of the restitution of his political rights, Mamadou Dia published his *Essais sur l'Islam*, Tome 1, *Islam et Humanisme*.[5] It may be read as an inner manifesto from those years of political incarceration, comparable to other documents of enforced seclusion in contemporary Islam, like the *Letters on Islam* of Fadil Jamali of Baghdad,[6] and Muhammad Ali's *My Life, a Fragment*, from Lahore.[7]

However, before exploring the contents of Dia's essays on Islam it may be well to summarise the association of mind between Senghor and Teilhard de Chardin. For ideas of the latter certainly appear in Dia's writing, drawn – it would seem – from Senghor's influence. It is part of the paradox of Dia's story that he should have been both the partner of Senghor's philosophy and at the same time the victim of his policy. The whole relationship between the two Senegalese leaders makes a fascinating study in parallel Muslim and Christian participation in the wake of one of the most arresting initiatives in twentieth-century theology.

Senghor's socialism was rooted in the Marxist diagnosis of human 'alienation' within the capitalist system. He accepts Marx in his critique of non-communal ownership of the means of production and recognises in colonialism the exploitative attack upon human dignity which Marx had found there. But, in a paper to a conference in 1961, which he was unable to attend, Senghor described how the thought of de Chardin had enabled him to redeem the necessary economic radicalism of Marx from its brutal materialism by that sense of *le milieu divin* which de Chardin kindled in his mind. He confessed that it was to this he owed the clue and the stimulus to *négritude*.[8] Man had to be seen as a cosmic phenomenon at the juncture of two infinities. Marxist 'futurism' was based solely on physical categories and a material dialectic. It required the necessity of 'the class war', and, therefore, the rejectionist stance in decolonialisation. On Marxist grounds, colonialism, being solely the manifestation of capitalist exploitation, was to be countered solely by a decolonialising repudiation of the entire historical experience. Nor, on Marxist premisses, could this be analysed on any other terms. For its *only* significance was economic. De Chardin's 'futurism', however, saw man, and therefore even the colonising–colonised encounter, in the larger context of organic spirituality, containing, indeed, the economic dimension, but in no way imprisoned in or monopolised by it.

On this count of a more fundamental, and transactable, inter-humanism, rooted in cosmic reality and destined towards a spiritual future of which God was 'the Omega point', Senghor was free to 'appreciate' the French and believe in his Serer people, his Senegalese nation, without apology and without exclusivist violence. Humanity must be understood as 'pan-humanity'. As such it was not simply a concept but an impulse. To hold it so was not merely a conviction, but a programme. Liberty was the ability to desire this forward movement of the human meaning. Contemporary crisis was our power to refuse or impede it.

So much for Senghor's acknowledged debt to the thought of Teilhard de Chardin. For both himself and his mentor its authenticity was inseparable from the fact of Christ, from what de Chardin called 'the

Christic'. It was a personalisation of man, made possible – both conceptually and effectively – by the personalisation of God. Senghor quoted Albert Camus: 'If man realises that the universe can love, he will be reconciled.' In Christ was the possibility of what he called *centréité*, 'union by love',[9] a faith which, as he put it, 'rectified' Marxist activism, saved it from both its harshness and its naïvety. He mused in his paper on whether he could add that one could include Islam also in this *centréité*, whether it could be Muslim also. His decision was: Yes.[10] God, he felt, was personal in Islam also, the convergent point of our particular loves. As we shall see, it was just here that the thought of Mamadou Dia, as expressed in his *Essais sur l'Islam*, affirms likewise from within Islam.

Some kinship is discernible here with the thought of Kamil Husain, though there is no evidence of mutual contact.[11] Both writers have a confidence that there is some continuity between those 'organic' truths that have to do with biology and the 'organic' truths which have do to with ethics. The way the universe of man *is* scientifically (that is to say its physical and biological *being*) sets the stage for how the universe of man has to *do* and to *choose* spiritually (its moral and spiritual fulfilment). The thought here is arguably akin, in the distinct idiom of de Chardin, with the frequent and more general theme of Muslim writers who move from an involuntary *islām* they see in the 'laws' of physics and chemistry and the like to a volitional *islām* in the moral and religious 'obedience' of man.

At all events, in so far as the exigencies of statecraft and politics allowed (on which, as we have seen, Senghor and Dia came sadly to differ), these were the thoughts which authorised both socialism and *négritude*. For socialism aimed to put all political, technological and cultural factors at the service of pan-humanism. The aim must be fully conscious nations for a total world. The wealth of negro energies must be confidently awakened, not in bitter unforgiving rejection of European humanity but in positive and hospitable self-respect. Comparably European humanity in post-imperial history must consent to belong within a pan-human mutuality. What brought Senghor and Dia to the parting of the ways in this common faith was the issue of translating it into honest realism *vis-à-vis* the economic facts of neo-colonialism. Both the two protagonists had support from within the other's religious community, and in the paper we have now summarised Senghor was confident that Muslim reformers in a parallel way were reaching a synthesis between scientific socialism and religious faith akin to that drawn by him from the de Chardin he admired.[12] We must now see how Mamadou Dia gave documentation to that confidence when his political rights were restored.

III

His quest is for a new Islamic humanism proper to the unprecedented needs of contemporary society. It is a quest in which he looked beyond traditional Muslim apologetics, and beyond what he saw as the too narrowly conceived verdicts of Western Islamicists whom he wished to enlist, to the transcendental reference of Islam and its divine metaphysic of man, made operative in prophetic action. Quranic revelation calls for 'submission to what God ordains, accepting to model life and the social order in accordance with transcendent norms'. The Muslim has 'to base history on a divine imperative, on an ethic dictated by God, not by men'.

> Revelation is a calling to mind: the Quranic message simply renews the same eternal message in face of the repeated failures of history . . . to restore history and redeem man. Islam, as a prophetic religion sets forth a vision of the world common to the great prophetic faiths – that of a kingdom of God on earth through the establishment of the justice of God. It is a new initiative of the Creator, witnessing once more to His supreme pity which neither error nor rebellion have been able to impair, to make human history at length a success for man. This is no longer by simple proclamation of a transcendent truth and justice, but by the putting of such truth and justice into effect in human history; no longer in leaving the moral order and the conduct of the world's affairs to secular powers unsubdued to celestial norms, but in putting in hand the development of society on a normative foundation that accords with the very structure of the universe which it sees as a harmony of divine order. Thus Islam offers itself as 'prophetism in act', religion engaging with history and taking hold of it . . . History is a necessary stage on the return to God.[13]

There is an almost lyrical quality about Dia's writing on the Qur'ān's perspectives as he sees them. History must be made 'sacred' by the sanctification of the temporal order. It was not by chance that Mecca and the Hijāz were chosen as the locale of the disclosure of the divine design. For the social and economic patterns there obtaining provided a setting well calculated to test and illuminate the task of prophetic mission in the service of the transcendent vision. Making commerce moral, fulfilling an eco-philosophy, replacing cupidity by sharing – in a word, subduing 'having' to 'being' – these were the vocation and the achievement of Muhammad. The Quraishī society Dia reads as perverse, exploitative, mercantilist, acquisitive, and – by all these –

atheist. It was criminally dominated by 'the trade mind', blindly
confident in money, and disruptive of the old *murū'ah*, or tribal loyalty
of the Arabs. The Qur'ān, he believes, attacks the love of wealth more
than it accuses the cult of idols. In the time and place of what Dia sees
as an 'international *Jāhiliyyah*', the Qur'ān's *kerugma* (he enlists the
New Testament term) was a sustained negation of materialism in the
name of the ethic of transcendence. In this cause Muhammad

> consecrated himself to temporal tasks, clothed himself in the tunic of
> the warrior, ordered raids and sometimes massacres, negotiated
> alliances and benevolent neutralities, signed armistices and separate
> peaces, in brief risked his whole reputation for sanctity in accepting
> to soil his hands. History . . . faced with the grandeur of the
> achievement is bound to do homage to the grandeur of the man.[14]

The *Hijrah*, and Islam's 'establishment' in Medina, gave concrete
expression to the doctrine of a distributive economy fulfilling equality,
fraternity and justice. What Dia calls interpersonalisation was central to
this economic/ethic, allowing private property but requiring mutual
enrichment. Capital was 'moralised', by *Zakāt*, by regulations relating
to booty in war and by patterns of inheritance. Callous usury gave way,
in concept, to calculated risk and involvement in enterprise, to mutual
help in pursuit of returns. Essentially, this metaphysic of wealth can be
translated into contemporary terms, since present-day technology is all
within that divine ordering of the human dominion which the Qur'ān
affirms. In this connection he notes how iron, as well as Qur'ān, is
credited to *Tanzīl* (cf. Surah 57). God is the source of the techniques
of metal and these are worthy to be dignified by the same term as the
Scripture. Thus all things are a gift and an entrustment. Technology is
in no way an end in itself, or a basis for human self-sufficiency.

Here the concept of the *Ummah* is invoked. Commodities do not
have a value in themselves. Value results from relation between
persons. It is 'inter-subjectivity', a transaction in solidarity, a
psychosomatic equilibrium agreed between persons,[15] in total contrast
to the exploitative mind of mercantilism and trust in sheer market
forces. The Islamic state exists to discipline and enforce this economic
of fraternity.

Inevitably this lyrical idealism has to concede that, historically,
Muslim societies have defaced and betrayed it. Dia reproaches not only
the worldliness of the Ummayyads in this context, but great names in
the later story. Ibn Khaldun preached an economic liberalism which
rejected collective control in the name of free enterprise. He is also
reproached for a pessimism born of eschatological ideas difficult to

reconcile with any dynamic view of creation or a real sense of historical continuity.[16] Al-Razi is also criticised for a static idea of the universe which precluded any economic dynamism towards a just society. Al-Ashari was too absorbed in doctrinal issues about revelation and reason. Ibn Hazm allowed himself to be recruited by the pursuers of private gain. The great Al-Ghazali lost all contact with the real world in his nebulous Sufism, despising the goods of the material order and the business of ordering them justly. In seeking the intimate religion of the ascetic, he ignored the subtle corruptibility of religion and, for all his prestigious influence, quite failed to give concrete content to the aspirations of mysticism and to root them in the patterns of society.[17]

Dia's conclusion about medieval Islam is that, instead of the spiritual determining the material, the reverse happened. Theologians withdrew into their doctrinal world and left the ordering of society to the lawyers, who in turn became mere collaborators with the ruling power. Theological orthodoxy constituted a privileged caste profiting, through *Awqāf* (religious endowments), from patterns of economy which it should have condemned. It became inseparable from an exploitative system within a 'despiritualised' Muslim legal authority which identified commerce with mercantilism and denied the economics of fraternity. Thus theology and philosophy alike abdicated their real role as custodians of the economic teaching of the Qur'ān and so became themselves distorted, bereft both of vision and vitality.

Medieval Islam, to be sure, generated impressive material development, as Mamadou Dia indicates in a rapid survey of a variety of territories and skills. But he finds it all vitiated by a vulgar 'nationalism' forsaking the universal vision, and by a compromising 'materialism' which sacrificed quality to rapacity. Sufism, however high-minded, was powerless to save it from capitalist and secular forces. The Islamic bond between the spiritual and the temporal, between profane and religious 'history', was slackened. Mughals, Ottomans, Safavids all failed to make actual a dynamic economy and a social ethic to realise an authentic Islam. The lesson of this historical retrospect is that the economy of the 'merchant' mind is merely opportunist, a matter of contrivance and conjecture, which quite fails to master history and to subdue the seductions and deceits of circumstance which are now, more than ever, intensified by the shape of events.

IV

Turning, in the third and fourth parts of his *Socio-Anthropologie de l'Islam*, to contemporary Islamic perspectives, Mamadou Dia pleads for

a revaluation of both Islamic theology and economics, for a defossilis-
ation of the *Sharīʿah*, and for an inspired engagement with development, guided by a laicisation of *Ijtihād*. Creative industry, facilitating
material development, reform of *Awqāf* or endowments and other
factors in maldistribution and a static society, and pan-Islamic
co-operation (an Afro-Asian, not merely an Arab, common market),
and a close association with the European spirit – these are the demands
of the hour. Muslims should not be deceived by their victory over
political colonialism. Without virile enterprise, technical and cultural
dependence persists within an accomplished 'independence'. The latter
is only psychological, not radical, victory. After a brief review of Islam
in Black Africa, Dia concludes that there, as elsewhere, the task is one.
The new *Fitnah* – or test, as he calls it, adopting a Quranic term – is
whether Islam can rise to technological change, faithful to Islamic
personalism, and renewing both doctrine and practice in institutional
rejuvenation.[18]

To do so, it must adapt to the necessities of the industrial world while
preserving its primordial vision. This means a rejection of Keynesian
economics, with its monetarism and its total reliance on market forces.
Dia demands state intervention against reliance on supply and demand,
manipulable as these are by economic interests and unsuited to the real
needs of developing societies. The aim must be to maximalise national
revenue and achieve full employment. By contrast with capitalism the
Marxist 'labour theory of value' is built on an authentic humanism, a
teleology. Its analysis of 'alienation' has a deeply ethical quality. But
doctrinaire rigidity in Marxist practice must be broken through by a
new Marxist *Ijtihād* taking due account of new situations and of the
developing world.

Calling for a will to garner the inexhaustible creativity of the
Qur'ān, Mamadou Dia outlines what he sees as 'a dynamic Muslim
economic theory'. It will cherish 'the fundamental notions of Islam' but
apply them dynamically, alive to historical change. Planning is basic. A
profit that is 'functional' must displace profit that is merely acquisitive
or brazenly monopolistic. Economic criteria in production and
investment must be those of public good and distributive justice,
identified by rational collective debate and enforceable by responsible
state power. They must also be alert to regional and world community.[19] Islamic economics must be dedicated to scientific reflection
on the problems of production and distribution. It must obey the vision
of a future of justice, interpersonal fulfilment, and genuine creativity,
the vision which is at once prophetic and Promethean.

While an *essai* is not a treatise, the average reader may conclude that
Mamadou Dia's presentation, strong on vision and aspiration, is short

on detail and specifics. There is no doubting the urgency and sincerity of his discussion. But one is surprised at the lack of explicit argumentation from the Qur'ān itself for the vision of an Islamic economic order which he presents. The sense of a *fitnah*, or crucible of spirit, in the challenge of modern technology and its economic discipline is the sole direct appeal to the Scripture, apart from the question of *riba'*, or 'usury'. His central emphases – the common good, personal values, state responsibility, economic justice, dynamic intention – can certainly be found there. But the outsider is bound to query an identification of any faith's significance which has to disown or disqualify long stretches of its history and its familiar exponents. Or, at least, such dissociation needs to take seriously the factors behind the disparity it alleges between what was and what should have been. For this larger task we must turn from Dia's economic thinking back to his theology, where the urge to a dynamic Islam – so evident in the practical sphere already reviewed – effectively belongs.

V

The evident readiness, even eagerness, of Mamadou Dia to relate to European thought, strong in his economic and social essay, marks his theological writing still more. He has no part in that exclusivism we find so crucial in Sayyid Qutb whereby Muslims must in principle insist on the absolute isolation of Islamic resources and Muslim truth. Dia happily cites among his mentors Louis Massignon, Jacques Berque, Henry Corbin, Georges Guénon, French orientalists, and Jean-Paul Sartre, Albert Camus and Gabriel Marcel, French men of letters. But the underlying factor seems primarily to be, as with Senghor, the stimulus drawn from Teilhard de Chardin, confidently associated, in Dia's case, with what he takes to be the mind of the Qur'ān. His confidence no doubt involves the question, vital for all scriptures, as to 'reading' and 'reader', the 'intention' of the text and the 'intentions' that invoke it. All the 'pens' with which we are here concerned bring differing interests to the one Qur'ān. There is no agreed criterion as to why an apparently innovative stance should defer to one which is allegedly traditional or 'loyal'. But, before closing that issue by any of the several options, it is well to explore just how Dia reads. With many of comparable temper of mind, he does so more by broad conviction than precise commentary.

His theme in *Islam et Humanisme* has to do with the theological bases of the Muslim view of man and their encounter with contemporary humanism. But he first devotes more than a third of his space to a discussion of Islamicists and how they have approached Islam. Islamic meanings, he insists, are very much the concern of non-Muslims,

whose expertise in the field he readily acknowledges. But his plea to
them is that they must transcend mere academicism, appreciate the
existential reality of what they handle and engage deeply with Muslims
religiously. Only in this way can either keep faith with the other or
serve the common future. For common it must be.

Western Islamic study is itself under scrutiny. It can no longer be
pursued in some academic pride, or immunity. Its prejudices, from the
'positivism' of Renan onwards, have been exposed. Yet these must not
deter Muslims from absorbing its many services to scholarship. Louis
Massignon is seen as the paragon of these in both spirit and technique.
Dia cites European contributions to philology, the study of Arabic as a
language, to literature and art in Islam, and to historical criticism with
its stimulus to a true *Ijtihād*. He wants a breaking away from purely
defensive apologetics. Massignon inspires him to welcome a spiritual
sense of the Qur'ān, a hermeneutic of the heart, whereby the
ecumenical potential of the Qur'ān may be released into religious
dialogue. He holds that theology in Islam has always had an instinct for
philosophy and that philosophy is surest and truest when it dwells
meditatively in the soul. He has strictures later for some forms of
aberrant Sufism and he deplores its social passivity. But he insists that
Islam and the Qur'ān clearly combine an exoteric religion of law and
an esoteric religion of 'penetration' into mystery, and these – *Al-Ẓāhir
wa-l-Bāṭin*, 'the outward and the inward' – must not be divorced.

But European orientalism has also helped to elucidate the sociology
of Islam and to present the Qur'ān as a faith whereby social justice was
made concrete in a setting of gross economic evil, the Quraishī
Jāhiliyyah. Sociology has served to demonstrate the revolutionary
character of the Prophet and so to educate his emulation today.

Dia's recognition of the positive potential of Western scholarship,
however, is by no means uncritical. He sees it as lacking in imaginative
participation, merely phenomenological, and so impervious to deeper
meanings. Its concern with the phenomena of religion conceals from it
the ultimate significances. The same is true of exegesis when, as with
Western practitioners,[20] it concentrates on grammar, syntax and
incident, and misses the symbolic, the divine wisdom. Sociology tends
to relativise all else. The prophetic is, thus, itself de-sacralised. The
true Islam will always be a stranger to the kind of secularised *schema* to
which sociological determinism is minded to reduce it.

European Islamicists need also to immerse themselves in the totality
of Islam, beyond Arab confines, and to realise its ecumenical quality, in
order to transcend their own subjective temptations. These Dia finds
intriguingly documented in J. D. J. Waardenburg's *L'Islam dans le
Miroir de l'Occident*.[21] Agreed, any search for a 'pure' objectivity is futile.

For no one, whether historian or theologian, can escape his sub-jectivity. But the aim must be a true intersubjectivity, in which one's 'approach' is not imposed abstractly, still less proudly, but related in humility and alert to the future and the inter-human.

VI

From this assessment of European Islamic study, Mamadou Dia turns to expound his fundamental concept of the *Ḥaqīqah* of the Qur'ān. All meaning, for Muslims, is a discerning, a decoding, an unveiling, of the sign quality of the Qur'ān, through meditation on its multiple symbolism, by a sustained and personal effort which excludes all magisterial dogmatism purporting to act on behalf of the inalienable self. It is thus non-authoritarian. Tolerance and humility are indispensable to its pursuit. Religious certitude is not an adherence given but a constant effort of interior belief. This deeply esoteric, personalist spirituality of the soul is balanced by the juridical, outward *Sharī'ah* which sets the rules of life. The latter ensures historical continuity, inserts Islam in the stream of the real world, enables the *Ummah* to bring the divine order to pass. Inevitably there are tensions between the two in the dual structure, to be monitored by their bipolarity.

Muhammad, 'hôte d'honneur de Dieu', held the balance duly, between history and meta-history, between *Sharī'ah* and *Ḥaqīqah*, between the temporal and the spiritual. Because the two are thus conjoined there is no cause, says Dia, for that 'laïcisation' (secularis-ation?) which, outside Islam, demands the separation of the one from the other. Neither has any true autonomy: they interdepend. For that very reason roles *can* be specified in either realm. But such roles are subject to the mutuality. The juridical and practical cannot degenerate into a tyranny of rigorism, nor the spiritual, like Al-Hallaj, lose itself in escapism. The spirit is the essence which vivifies the faith, while the *Sharī'ah* propels Muslim society day by day. Dia sees this com-plementarity as also resolving the issue between the Sunnī and the Shī'ah, between *Tafsīr* of the Qur'ān and *Ta'wīl*, reading for guidance and reading for knowledge. Sunnis, broadly, have cared for the law and society, the Shī'ah for the symbol and wisdom.

In Dia's view, however, this dual account of a truly Quranic Islam leaves room for reason, for personality and for the order of history. It is in expounding this confidence that his debt to de Chardin is clear. The Islamic sense of the transcendent excludes the magical. The prophetic is transparent to the intelligence and indeed requires to mobilise it in the apprehension of what it signifies. Dia sees the wisdom of the

Qur'ān 'descending' to the human level, integrating history. It does not, in his opinion, present itself as something dictated, as bare injunction, as sheer decree, an absolute imperative. On the contrary, it seeks to explain and convince, to teach and discourse.[22] This, he believes, is evident within Muhammad's role, his engagement of mind, his dialogical relation to his deliverances. The Qur'ān reader, too, is called into rationality, to reflection, to self-education via the text. Islamic theology Dia sees as proceeding, from this Quranic 'pedagogy', by a similar appeal to reason, logic and mind. Law likewise, witness *Ijtihād* and *Qiyās*, or arguable analogy, in the definition and enlargement of law.

This, it must be noted, is not a materialist rationalism. The reality of God is a 'given', beyond proof or the necessity of proof. *Al-Ghaib*, as the Qur'ān calls it, cannot be the theme of rational demonstration: it can only be directly confessed. This, Dia says, is the point behind Al-Ashari's famous dictum about 'without asking how' (*bilā kaif*).[23] The way, then, to mediate between reason and faith is simply to move within the dualism of Islam, i.e. the exoteric law and the esoteric meaning of revelation.

Islam et Humanisme then turns to ask whether the absolute transcendence of God in Islam does not involve a negation of human autonomy, and of a free personhood. God and man are, indeed, in the relation of master and slave, in that revelation is directive and God the Ordainer (*Al-Mudabbir*) (e.g. 10.3, 13.2). Nevertheless, man is the privileged custodian, the executant, the viceregent. Witness itself is free. Man, in this sense, is co-present with God. Personhood is realised and possessed in relation with God and with one's fellows. As we accept and operate within the sensible world, we are in a dialogical relation with God, the source and sustainer of our authority. Here Dia quotes Surah 21.105: 'We have written in the Psalms, after the remembrance, "the earth shall be the heritage of My pure servants"' – a verse paralleled in Psalm 37.9.[24] From this *khilāfah* of man over nature under God, Dia deduces the socialism which he expounds in the *Essais* earlier noted.

His view of man the Promethean creature takes Dia into his account of Islam and history. Islam is the religion of triumph, of success and power and accomplishment. It faces time and the future with assurance, in active, positive grasping of occasion and situation. This dynamism has generated its culture and its vitality, in that prophecy was joined with history and mystical wisdom with the drive of a conqueror. The Muslim today has to make good that same quality in a new integration of his dual vision of society and the transcendent.

VII

In his final section on the contemporary calling of the Muslim, Mamadou Dia turns explicitly to de Chardin with his sense of the open future, his planetary vision, his quest for a 'religion of humanity and of the earth'. The real problem is not atheism, but an insufficient theism. No faith historically appeared within the cosmic totality into which all faiths now have to mature. Our very image of God must move from the vertical to the horizontal, in the sense that the static 'decree' concept of biology and the physical order must give way to a dynamic awareness of the ongoing extrapolation of these into a gathering cosmic purpose of which God is the goal as well as the origin.

This must necessarily disavow the remoteness often popularly attributed to the God of Islam. It is here that the perceptive reader finds the most telling and refreshing feature of Dia's version of Islam. 'Creative Islam', he writes,

> bases itself, not on a God cut off from the world and from man, dictating His Law from outside, instituting His justice from without, but, on the contrary, on a living God, present in heaven and on earth. Islam is a gift of God, a guide, a light for the intention of man. It is God coming towards His creature, responding to his anguish. . . . To witness to God in such a world is to restore to Him his living reality, it is to rediscover the sense of divine engagement, the awareness of the divine presence among us.

The degree to which these sentiments are close to those of Christian faith is made explicit. Dia pleads for leave to

> comprehend, without heresy, how God could reveal Himself as a Person with whom a relation of knowledge and of love became possible . . . Contemporary Islam must have a place, an option, for the study of contemporary Christianity, to become more informed of its doctrines, including that of the Incarnation.[25]

He sees in recent Christian Biblical and liberation theology an active 'theology of the divinisation of man', which Islam needs to emulate, in likewise abandoning an immobile theology tied to scholasticism.

His criticism of Islamic modernism is sharp. The paradox, he says, of Muslim modernism is that it totally ignores the modern problems. Exegesis which discovers the origin of scientific discoveries in the Qur'ān is pointless and naïve. Here he shares the view of Kamil Husain. Muslim reformers set fidelity to its institutions above fidelity to the faith. Hence its 'modernism' is no more than a facade laying modern ideas on archaic forms. This can be seen in its preoccupation over opening the gate of *Ijtihād*, about which, in any modern temper, there ought to be no debate. Reform needs a total reorientation away from what is 'fixed and written' to what Dia calls 'the living word of God'.

Religion is in need of radical autocriticism, in order to grasp the truth that God is not merely the 'efficient' Creator of a once-for-all *Kun* (*fiat*) but the animating Creator within a cosmic dynamism. He is no evasive Deity, outside of events. The truth of His perpetual creativity is the only authentic counter to contemporary atheism. For, in the several forms which Dia analyses, this atheism does not so much deny God as ignore Him. He has gone, as it were, into redundancy, while man presides and disposes. Scientism excludes God by its closed circuit of material causation, its confinement of experience to the empirical and the observable. Marxist atheism excludes God by an inclusive thesis of politico-economic humanism, in which the goal of a classless society is held to come by human praxis. Or there is a sort of neo-Stoic atheism, a pessimist humanism, which insists on man's aloneness and posits 'the death of God' by its need to give the lie to comforting faith.

The only true retort to these false humanisms is the truly religious humanism which only transpires by the renewed awareness of God as the ever-active source and goal of the cosmos and man and their mutual future. Fidelity to Islam, as Dia sees it, means above all fidelity to 'the living word of God', the word which has to be attested by the institutions and rules of life that conform to its directive. This means that by manifesting it spiritually and in things temporal on the earth 'Islam cannot be other than the creation of Muslims, responding at one and the same time to God, to their own problems and to the problems of the world'.[26] Such fidelity is the meaning of *Al-Ṣirāṭ al-Mustaqīm*, 'the straight path' of the opening Surah, *Al-Fātiḥah*. Through it, an authentic humanism fulfils a theology for which God's absolute claim is *within* man, not *to* him, involving a steady 'liaison with God' in the forward thrust of His ends in history and the soul. Such a theology is vastly more important for Islam today than things juridical about law.

Mamadou Dia concludes on a high note of eloquent and ardent appeal. Muslims must no longer allow themselves to hide like the Seven Sleepers of Surah 18, secreted in their purity from the real world. Dynamism, resolution and the joy of being must banish resignation and the pariah state. Not with the wand of Moses, nor with the sword of Ali, but with 'the modern grace of God which is contemporary techniques', they must possess the sanctuary of contemporary secrets and, while becoming Promethean, still render thanks to God. A

socialism of the community legitimises profit deriving from develop-
mental projects which repudiate private gain and serve the corporate
human present. The *Ummah* factor makes possible, and licit, what
would be impossible, and illicit, on the private, individual level.
Islamic culture, art and literature all have their vocation, within a true
sense of the existential mystery of human experience 'in the ground of
being'. The challenge which Islam must face today is

> to make of 'the abode of peace' [*Dār al-Salām*] one vast people,
> and one vast workshop, a temple in which each servant of the act of
> worship is also a creator, a promethean hero; to make a world where
> things objective are taken in hand and there is adoration at the same
> time, an earth of 'to have and to be,' where every act of production is
> one that improves upon itself in fulfilling a dialectic of creativity and
> the transcendent.[27]

VIII

There is a refreshing vigour in all that Mamadou Dia writes and a
disarming enthusiasm. His steady insistence on Islam taking its place
with other cultures and traditions in facing the modern age is in welcome
contrast to the theological and spiritual isolationism in which some
other writers secure their psyche and privatise the world. He makes
good his ecumenical sense by the range and frequency of his quotations
from non-Muslim sources. Indeed, there are times when he lets
another's pen set down what the reader might crave to find specifically
documented from the Qur'ān by his own. It is notable that his
confident formulations of what Islam truly is, and requires of the
Muslim, leave a strong impression of a commitment of mind brought to
his exegesis, rather than textually learned.

The extreme paucity of direct citation may be taken as sustaining this
impression. His references to the text, especially in the light of the old
tradition of learning by heart, and of his own insistence on the Islamic
primacy of Arabic,[28] seem inordinately rare. While the direction of his
thinking may win a grateful admiration, there are points at which it
arguably carries him to expressions hardly reconcilable with the 'feel' of
the Qur'ān as normally registered both by Muslims and outsiders.
Thus, for example, he writes of 'restoring to God His living reality',
and of 'the living One, whose colour is that of the time'.[29] To be sure,
as he says, 'the Eternal' is 'neither an anachronism, nor an archaism'.
But as it stands the comment has not safeguarded Him from being a
fashion.

Such a lively, risk-taking, style of writing some would absolve, for the merit of its drive and integrity. But it signifies deeper issues also. Is Mamadou Dia's temper altogether too sanguine? Has his eager sponsorship of the dynamic, in man and religion, quite failed to reckon with the perverse? Kamil Husain, as we will see, could hardly approve of Dia's ready trust in the *Ummah*, in a socialist collective, to ensure honesty and the common good, nor in his belief that to collectivise is to immunise from the evils that afflict the private sphere, because 'community is infallible'.[30]

This sanguine quality is one that puts a large mark of wistful interrogation, for the perceptive reader, around some of the ideas of Dia's mentors and they must stand or fall together. The range, subtlety and aspiration of de Chardin's mind must not be allowed to obscure the deep considerations in the human scene, and story, which give us pause. The merging of the exoteric/legal and the esoteric/ spiritual, which Dia asserts, is not so readily feasible in the actual world. On his own showing, the faith in an absolute imperative, enshrined in an authoritative Scripture, is liable to generate rigidity and arrogance or exclusivist self-esteem. These may truly need the corrective of inner wisdom and humility, such as esoteric knowledge may nourish. Yet these, in turn, often maintain themselves, as Dia concedes, only in abstraction and neglect of the actual world. A cynic may say that Dia's reconciliation of the two is more hortatory than operative. There is no echo in his writing of *zulm* and *ḍalāl* and *fasād*, those dark evils that the Qur'ān acknowledges so strongly in the human story. Nor, correspondingly, does he dwell in its themes of *istighfār* and forgiveness, its call to *taʿwīdh* and refuge from the evil that lurks *fī-ṣudūri-l-nās*, 'in the bosoms of men'.

Nevertheless, Mamadou Dia is finely responsive to the dimensions which Islam must reach in both intellectual penetration and active response *vis-à-vis* the contemporary situation in which the human spirit toils and hopes. In particular, his sense of the divine engagement with man, of God's participatory presence, opens out vistas of hope, not least for Christian relationship to Muslims, which are often quite forbidden in the bleak quality of commanding divine transcendence commonly drawn, by both Muslims and others, from the Qur'ān. Divine 'sending' and divine 'coming' need not be seen as exclusive of each other – the *Tanzīl* that mediates revelation into Scripture and the *Tanāzul* which makes revelation present in the Christ-event.[31] The two have a common context in the unity of God, the mystery of creation, and the vocation of man. With his keen sense of these, Mamadou Dia provides a frank, incisive measure of the ecumenical duty of Islamic – and, therefore, of all other – theology today.

NOTES: CHAPTER 3

1 Though the term and the theme of *négritude* – the glad affirmation of 'negro' being – are linked essentially with Senghor, the term was first popularised by the Caribbean poet, Aimé Césaire, in *Cahier d'un Retour au Pays Natal* (Paris, 1947). On Senghor see, e.g., his *L'Orphée Noire* (Paris, 1948) and *Senghor: Prose and Poetry*, edit. and trans. by John Reed and Clive Wake (Oxford, 1965).

2 See note 9 in Chapter 4, on Ali Shariati.

3 Senghor signalled his bicultural experience by always linking his local name, Sedar, with his French name, Léopold. His fluency in French poetry earned the warm admiration of French *littérateurs*, yet its themes were so often the whispers of Africa. See *Chants d'Ombre* (Paris, 1945) and *Hosties Noires* (Paris, 1948).

4 On the general subject see, J. S. Trimingham, *Islam in West Africa* (Oxford, 1959). There is a remarkable evocation of traditional Islamic piety in Senegal and its contemporary stresses in the autobiographical novel of Hamidou Kane, *L'Aventure Ambiguë*, trans. into English by K. Woods (London, 1972).

5 Dakar and Abidjan, 1977.

6 *Written by a Father in Prison to His Son* (Oxford, 1965). The author, who himself translated these twenty-four letters from the original Arabic, was twice Iraqi Prime Minister. His imprisonment, under sentence of death, lasted three years, from 1958 to 1961. He was later Professor of the Philosophy of Education at the University of Tunis. His letters to his son cover a wide range of Islamic topics, personal and social.

7 Muhammad Ali, of *My Life, a Fragment* (Lahore, 1942), was a leader in Indian Islam, brother of Shaukat Ali, with whom he co-operated in the Khilafatist Movement, seeking to rehabilitate the Ottoman Khalifate in the early twenties. His autobiography was meant to be part of much larger *confessio fidei* (hence its title). He bears eloquent witness to the power of the Qur'ān within the meditative occasions of political confinement. (He should not be confused with Muhammad Ali, of the Ahmadiyyah Movement, and a translator of the Qur'ān.)

8 Teilhard de Chardin, *Le Milieu Divin, An Essay on the Interior Life*, trans. from the French (London, 1960). The paper here summarised will be found in *Cahiers Pierre Teilhard de Chardin* (Paris, 1962), 3, pp. 13–65.

9 *Cahiers*, p. 56.

10 ibid., pp. 52 and 62. He reasons that as there are 'Protestant Teilhardians' so there may also be Muslim ones, without staying to ponder the differing alignments, or lack of them, with de Chardin's Roman Catholicism, which, in any event, was long involved in tension with authority – witness the long delay in the publication of his thinking.

11 There was, however, a close friendship between Kamil Husain and Muhammad Lahbabi, of Morocco, who periodically visited Husain in Egypt and was the author of *Le Personnalisme Musulman* (Paris, 1964), in which he developed concepts broadly akin to some of de Chardin's emphases.

12 *Cahiers*, p. 65.

13 *Essais sur L'Islam*, vol. 2, *Socio-Anthropologie de L'Islam* (Dakar, 1979), pp. 9–10.

14 ibid., pp. 13–20.

15 ibid., p. 31.

16 ibid., p. 56. These, of course, were strong points in de Chardin's thought.

17 ibid., pp. 58–9.

18 ibid., pp. 124–5. *Fitnah* is a frequent term in the Qur'ān. It denotes any situation, e.g. persecution, danger, sedition, which might divert the faithful from their duty and so constitute a 'test' of their quality.

19 ibid., pp. 157–9. He cites Israel here in this context as exemplifying a splendid technological expertise directed, however, to an exclusive, not a regional, concern.

20 With exceptions like Henry Corbin and Louis Massignon. cf. *Essais sur L'Islam*, vol. 1, *Islam et Humanisme*, Dakar, 1977, p. 37.

21   The Hague, 1961.
22   *Essais*, vol. 1, pp. 60–1.
23   ibid., p. 65. The famous formula, *bilā kaif*, explained that the Names of God must
     be used 'without asking how' they signify. Being human descriptives they cannot
     apply to God. To make them so apply would be a form of *Shirk*. But, since they are
     all that language affords and language is crucial to worship and to theology, use them
     we must, but with this reservation of 'non-comparability'. Dia gives a mystical turn
     to this highly scholastic theological device.
24   ibid., p. 77.
25   ibid., pp. 116–19.
26   ibid., p. 116.
27   ibid., p. 142.
28   ibid., pp. 138–9.
29   ibid., pp. 124 and 122.
30   ibid., p. 128.
31   *Tanzīl* means the sending down of the Qur'ān. *Tanāzul*, a further form from the
     same verbal root, denotes a bringing of oneself down, a condescension, reciprocal to
     need and expressive of love. It does not occur in the Qur'ān but it expresses what
     Dia urges here about a divine presence in and with mankind for due purposes of
     grace.

4

Sayyid Qutb of the Egyptian Muslim Brotherhood

I

On trial in Cairo in 1965 on a capital charge of plotting against the state, Sayyid Qutb, a leader of the Muslim Brotherhood, courageously acknowledged the charge. He insisted that resistance to a regime he deemed to be un-Islamic was the legitimate duty of the true Muslim. He set loyalty to the *Ummah* of Islam over obedience to the *Watan* of Egyptian nationalism, the whole 'nation' of Muslims everywhere above the citizenship of an individual state. The State Prosecutor, sensing the danger in his defence, countered with the accusation that it was not 'Islam' that Qutb belonged to but the Muslim Brotherhood. To which the prisoner replied that in his opinion it was the Muslim Brotherhood which expressed and enshrined Islam. The scene in court dramatically captured the crucial issue 'What and Where is Islam?' and did so in the context, always vital to Muslims, of political allegiance. Was the jurisdiction of the court itself a betrayal of a true Islam, its 'nationalism' a perversion of the holy *Sharī'ah*, a virtual return to the *Jāhiliyyah* which obtained before Muhammad and, therefore, fit only to be repudiated by a right Muslim? Was the 'traitor', in fact, the guardian of a true Islam?

Sayyid Qutb, on every score of biography and books, demands to be included in any company representing pen and faith in recent Islam. His presence helps to balance the sharply contrasted thinkers we have included. He stands with costly passion for a verdict about Islam which must be heeded. He has close mentors and associates elsewhere in the Islamic world, like Abu-l-Ala al-Maududi and Abu-l-Hasan Ali Nadwi, protagonists of a strongly conservative Islam in Lahore and Lucknow. With them he shared a deep discipleship to the medieval champion of the doctrine that *Jihād* may have to be pursued against ostensibly Muslim rulers who behave untruly, the redoubtable Ibn Taimiyyah of the seventh Muslim century. With them he represents a vision and a venture within Islam today that call into question in radical ways the response to modernity and the West made by writers to whom it might well be more congenial for us to listen. But our listening to them will be both the wiser and the more alert for our steady attention to the themes and positions of Sayyid Qutb.

II

This is the more so because he was no crude *muqallid*, a pundit incapable of relating to modernity. On the contrary, he was a thinker who expressly rejected a West he had come to know. Born a villager, he had graduated in Cairo University and had begun his career in the 1930s as a literary critic. In that capacity he had spent a period at the end of the forties in the United States on a research fellowship. It was after his return to Cairo in the early fifties that he cast in his lot wholeheartedly with the Muslim Brotherhood and their interpretation of a pure Islam. His devotion to this cause was such that, after some years under the regime of Abd al-Nasir in unavailing ideological campaign for his style of Islam, he passed into active political agitation and resistance. In this, of course, he was very close to the logic of Muhammad himself, namely that if a strenuous effort to persuade and to preach seems to be permanently fruitless of results then loyalty requires that objectives be politically, and if need be violently, pursued.

This was a development which emerged in the mid-fifties, partly in disillusionment about the new regime (*Al-'Ahd al-Jadīd*, as it was called)[1] inaugurated by the army officers, with Muhammad Naguib as the frontman, in July 1952. They had ousted the corrupt King Farouk and some of their ideals of unity and justice were in close parallel with those of the Brotherhood. But the Muslim Brothers soon became disenchanted with the new regime, for its emphasis on Egyptian nationalism rather than Islamic unity,[2] and for its pragmatic approach to Egypt's problems. Though the cells and popular discipline of the Brotherhood had seemed potentially useful to the Revolution, the army officers were suspicious both of the theories and of the ambitions of the Brotherhood and of the threat they posed to the leadership. It was this disappointment and frustration which led the Muslim Brothers to conclude that the only effective political translation of their aims into fact must be their own. Worsening relations with the new regime aroused within it the suspicion – in this way self-fulfilling – that the Brotherhood was becoming conspiratorial. In late 1954, Abd al-Nasir's government moved strongly against the Brotherhood and Sayyid Qutb, along with many others, suffered long imprisonment, during which he completed his major work, a long commentary on the Qur'ān, *Fī Ẓilāl al-Qur'ān*, 'In the Shade of the Qur'ān', and became the 'shaikh' of numbers of humbler Brothers incarcerated with him. His release in 1964 was followed by the publication of his polemical work *Ma'ālim 'ala-l-Ṭarīq*, 'Signposts on the Way', the contents of which decided the Government on his arrest and trial. He was executed in 1966. With Ali Shariati, he is the only martyr among our chosen eight. On every count he demands to be understood.

III

One of the student's first tasks in reckoning with Sayyid Qutb's presentation of all things Islamic is to appreciate his declaration of independence from all other systems, religious and political. While he sustains the familiar confidence that Islam is the quintessence of all that religion should be, the final and perfected form of the faith that properly goes with human nature, he nevertheless insists that its patterns for human society and the political order are *sui generis*. He rebukes those who, for their own reassurance or in the will to associate beyond their confines, acknowledge affinities between what is Islamic and what is Western or other. Islam, in its finality, does not need these kinships and, properly sifted, they do not exist.

> Islam presents to mankind a perfectly integrated exemplary system the like of which the earth has not known either prior to Islam or since. Islam does not seek, and has never sought, to copy any system whatsoever or to concede any sort of link or similarity between itself and others. It has chosen its own singular path uniquely. It has offered to humanity a wholly integrated treatment of all human issues.[3]

It is, he believes, only a suspicion of inferiority which causes Muslims to discern likenesses with others. But, by the same token, his position might be queried on the opposite ground of denying them so sharply. The assertiveness is more in the psyche than in the facts. It contrasts strongly with that sense of the need for openness which we find later in Kamil Husain and Hasan Askari and have already noted in Mamadou Dia.

Sayyid Qutb's stance means that his expositions of Islam and society, Islam and theology, Islam and the state, are made from within a given dogma. They are declarative, not apologetical. This does not mean, however, that he can rightly be identified with the *taqlīd* of the fundamentalists of the popular kind. His intellectual calibre was too vigorous for such rigidity. There are fascinating ways in which his

earlier 'liberal' orientation persisted within his firm adherence to the
position of the *Ikhwān al-Muslimīn*, ways which, had their logic been
extended, might have called in question the conservatism in which he
accommodated them. Two interesting examples may be noted.

In his discussion of the *Ḥajj* ritual he disowned the traditionalist view
that Islamic pilgrimage was totally unrelated to the practices of the
Jāhiliyyah, immune in its God-given detail from all such contamination. On the contrary, he said, pagan antecedents were
undoubtedly present, their traces so evident that it would be foolish to
deny them. But in that assertion he is not merely rebuking obscurantism. He is illustrating, as he believes, how Islam in fact cleansed and
refined what it inherited. What it thought fit to retain it quite
transformed, so demonstrating its ripe wisdom and spiritual perception.[4] The question arises whether a similar capacity for discernment would not, arguably, have been right in respect of the modern
'paganism' which Sayyid Qutb so strongly identified as in fact a new
Jāhiliyyah. For it was very much part of his logic to insist that
decadent, Western-infected, 'liberal' Muslims were virtually reproduc-
ing the situation before Islam, in fresh wilful 'days of ignorance'. Might
there, then, not be something potentially redeemable by contemporary
reproducers of the Prophet's original purity, some way of doing for,
and with, their misguidedness what pristine Islam did with pagan rites?
Or do we conclude that Qutb's cast of mind was unable to recognise in
'modern' vagaries any latent wistfulness, any genuine lostness, any
retrievable asset, indeed any aspect other than damnable?

A second intriguing area of his writing relates to the literary
cherishing of the Qur'ān. This deep emotion is, of course, utterly
authentic and, as we must see later, played a great part in his exegesis.
But his early interest in literary analysis and criticism (*Al-Naqd
al-Adabī: Uṣūluhu wa Manāhijuhu*, 'Literary Criticism: Its Sources
and Methods')[5] prompted him to a more technical awareness of the
Qur'ān's literary virtues than the ordinary believer could attach to the
fundamental doctrine of its *I'jāz*, or matchlessness. Such sophisticated
appreciation of Quranic qualities, however, raised issues about the
consciousness of authorship and the actual role of the Prophet in its
language. These had become a sensitive point of controversy in
academic circles and one thesis in particular on 'The narrative art in the
stories of the Qur'ān' had been the occasion of sharp controversy both
in Cairo university circles and in the political arena.[6]

What was at stake here was simply that the more one spoke of artistry
and purposive literary acumen in the Qur'ān the more one implied an
active human factor, namely Muhammad himself, and that human
factor in terms of skill, discernment, artistry and, ultimately, genius.

Such implications necessarily collided with the concept of a totally illiterate prophet and of a celestially dictated Scripture. It would, of course, be possible to attribute these qualities of the Qur'ān exclusively to divine *waḥy*, or inspiration. But the awareness of their presence inevitably tended to an appreciation of the Book for which there was at least a latent tension between its divine status and its human stature as literature. With his firm orthodoxy and his alert discernment of literary values, Sayyid Qutb was able on the one hand to 'appreciate' as a *littérateur*, and on the other to exclude any human artifice in what he was appreciating. The tension can be felt, for example, in his comments on the striking style and form of Surah 78.

> Another aspect of the style of this part is its artistic use of fine expressions, images, rhythm, meter and rhyme to touch upon areas of exceptional beauty in the human soul and in the universe at large . . . Allegory is often employed and an unusual derivation is sometimes preferred in order to obtain the intended musical effect. All this shows the artistry which so entirely pervades this part of the Qur'ān.[7]

Words like 'artistic use', 'preferred', and 'intended', may, no doubt, be comprehended within a totally illiterate prophethood and credited to arbitrary *waḥy*. But they more credibly suggest a *waḥy* with a human partnership. Were such a partnership of the divine Spirit and the human self to be conceded in respect of artistry, a like partnership in respect of content could hardly be excluded. But, in the case of Sayyid Qutb, we have to leave this lively question within the ambiguity that his orthodoxy imposed.

It was, of course, his political preoccupations which determined Qutb's doctrinal position though, equally, it was his doctrinal position which demanded the political form. It was their interplay which made him so formidable a figure. It was as if, after his conversion to inclusive politicisation, questionings of intellectual or spiritual vintage became luxuries he could not afford. Yet, for lack of them, his politics also was overtaken in tragedy. His story is thus an epitome of the underlying dilemma of all things Islamic. He read his cause as requiring, indeed imposing, a pattern of action which disallowed the very reservations which might have redeemed it. The philosophy of power left no room for reservations of spirit within which alone other vital factors in religious struggle can survive and effectuate what power of itself can never achieve and will often frustrate.

Sayyid Qutb's was not a faith which had any room in itself for doubt of itself. He reserved no independence of mind or hesitation of will in his commitment to the authority of Islamic dogma as he believed it to be. His position was squarely within the theological norms and moral prescripts set down by Hasan al-Banna in the genesis of the *Ikhwān* in the 1920s. The inviolate truths to be asserted and applied were the unity of God, the finality of the uncreated Qur'ān, the ultimacy of Muhammad, the status of Islam as perfected religion, its divine programme of legislation and injunction as the effective pattern for human society, the obligations of Muslim discipline in the Five Pillars steadfastly fulfilled, and the exemplary integration of all areas of life under the political order of the true Islamic state. It was these, as he saw them, which he served with unswerving devotion and a heroic capacity to suffer in their name.

The shape of his career would seem to warrant a sequence of presentation here which moves, in ascending order, from his view of Islam and the state to his sense of Islam and society for the sake of which power was central, to his life with the Qur'ān as the source and sanction of all else. This will be a logic of exposition in line with his legacy. In following it we are close to the very marrow of Islam, both original and contemporary. To recover the original in the contemporary was the aim of his mission and the nerve of his purpose.

IV

What was at stake about Islam in Sayyid Qutb's doctrine of legitimate, indeed imperative, political action against a Muslim state which fails to make good the *Sharī'ah* of Islam in its laws and policies stems from a disputed exegesis of a crucial verse in Surah 5.44: 'Whoever does not judge by what God has sent down, well, they are the wrongdoers.' Surah 5.49 continues: 'Judge among them by what God has sent down and do not follow their desires', while 5.50 asks: 'Is it the rule of the *Jāhiliyyah* they are after?' This classic passage was used by Ibn Taimiyyah (1263–1328) and by Ibn Kathir (1300–72) to enjoin upon loyal Muslims the duty of resistance to rulers considered to be reverting to the *Jāhiliyyah* in their compromises or their hostility to 'loyal' Muslims – subjects who kept loyal to the true Islam and so withdrew loyalty from 'pseudo' Muslim rulers. The passage was so used against 'deviant' Mongols and on many other occasions. That precedent is at the heart of Sayyid Qutb's disqualification of the regime in Egypt in the fifties and sixties of this century. Failing to pass muster by the test of *Ḥukm bi mā anzala Allāh* (judgement according to God's revelation), that regime no longer deserved faithful Muslim obedience. Rather, obedience to Islam necessitated the repudiation of the pseudo-state.

It is, of course, assumed here that the ruler in Islam is required to obey the injunctions and observe the prohibitions of the Qur'ān. That broad principle would be generally agreed. The rub comes in determining what the Qur'ān and the *Sharī'ah* enjoin and what transgresses them. Many in Muslim history have held back from pressing criteria, agreed or otherwise, too closely or belligerently, for fear of disruption and chaos, preferring that legitimacy be a theme of the academies and not of civil strife. But others, from the seventh-century *Khawārij* onwards, have invoked strife in the name of their true Islam against the *de facto* Islam of their rulers. Sayyid Qutb became convinced that it was these who had to be emulated both in the strictness of their criteria of a true Islam and their withdrawal of allegiance when these were not met.

It is by no means sure that Surah 5.44–50 refers in context to matters political or juridical so that it might be a watchword for the disaffected. The setting is one of dispute about earlier revelations and their communities, Jews and Christians, and may well relate to matters theological. A warning to the Prophet need not be interpreted as a basis for rejection of a Muslim ruler. There is even a suggestion of distinctive codes for distinctive communities, which God – had He so willed – could have made one, and whose diversities are not to be reduced to a single authority. Judgement, too, relates to options like that instanced between permitted vengeance or blood payment in lieu. If 'the people of the Gospel' are to 'judge by the Gospel', as 5.47 enjoins, then a communal frame of decision must be meant. This still leaves us with the judgement proper to the Islamic *Ummah*. But even here 5.44 does not necessarily direct the Muslim to rebel, unless the exegete explicitly makes it do so. In line with his charge of a *Jāhiliyyah* today, Sayyid Qutb certainly did.

This resolute posture of militancy colours all that Qutb writes and certainly rides with a dimension that is undoubtedly present in the Qur'ān. He can credibly claim that he is genuinely in the spirit of Muhammad himself, renewing what the original *Hijrah* exemplified. He intends to belong with *Ḥizb Allāh*, 'the party of God', and believes that it can be surely identified and that its credential is the will to fight. He cites Surah 22.40: 'Were it not for God's repulsing people, some by means of others, cloisters, and churches, prayer halls and mosques, would certainly have suffered destruction'[8] – a passage which is echoed in 2.251. Sayyid Qutb's invocation of this right of self-defence and the obligation to use force in such defence conceals an unresolved issue about the nature of the menace to which it is responding. In 22.40 the context has to do with expulsion from homes and properties, that is to say the oppression which preceded the *Hijrah*. The contemporary situation for which he invoked the passage is not comparable, unless one is warranted in regarding an uncongenial regime as a persecuting tyranny. Can an ideological will to revolt be comprehended under self-defence, in the meaning of 22.40, especially when the regime in question claims to be reformist and Islamic?[9]

In effect, what Sayyid Qutb's position implies is that there is a monopoly of decision about what is Islamic and so worthy of allegiance – a monopoly wholly exercised by his and his group's verdict. The fact that power has a role in Islam, as in all human societies, indisputable in itself, is here made the ground of a unilateral assertion of the specific Islam for which such power should exercise its role. This, it might be argued, is inconsistent with that other, oft-quoted, Quranic principle: *Amruhum shūra bainahum* – 'They handle their affairs by mutual consultation' (42.38). Perhaps, however, that verse would still leave open an argument about 'they', about the authentic Muslims properly consulting and properly consulted.

There is, of course, no categorical end to the business of identifying 'the true' in any religious faith and faithful, and Sayyid Qutb has right to his mind on the point. But so too have those he disowns. The observer, facing that tangle, has to appreciate not only how unavoidable it is but also how real and urgent are the emotions and intentions which propel Sayyid Qutb to his categorical closure of the options – fear for the future, concern for the past, sincerity of commitment, frustration in debate, and the deep psychic factors which underlie all religious action. Even total illogicality can be eloquent in situations of defiance.

There is, further, a different problem behind the idea, so strong among the *Ikhwān*, of a new *Jāhiliyyah*. For, on one score, this ought to be impossible, and unthinkable, once Quranic revelation is in hand. In so far as *Jāhiliyyah* means a state of ignorance (which is one of its meanings), then it cannot obtain after Muhammad, the Prophet to 'seal' all prophecy, and least of all in the bosom of his community. In so far as *Jāhiliyyah* means a state of folly or wildness, which could be wilful, it *might* obtain after knowledge had come. But if there is point in this distinction it can only serve to indicate the underlying dilemma of all law and injunction and prohibition (the means on which Qutb so totally relies until force is invoked), namely the inability of these to ensure what they require. For they encounter a perversity in mankind which revelation *per se* does not overcome, indeed may even arouse. The conviction that 'to know is to do' is thoroughly disproved if 'paganism', in whatever shape, persists so stoutly after fourteen centuries of Islam. Those, like Sayyid Qutb, who wish to incriminate those who name themselves Muslims as virtually pre-Islamic in their unbelief and wrongness must surely probe more deeply into the nature of evil and the relative efficacy of exhortation and direction. For relative, on this showing – and even at times impotent – his own characterisation of the situation shows it to be.

It is here that experience outside Islam, could it be mediated to a mind as rigorist as Qutb's, might prove significant. He is liable, like so many within Islam, when assessing Christianity, to reproach it for neglect of social issues in its concentration on so called 'private' piety, for opting out of the power realism which Islam embodies, and for virtually writing off the state as separate from religion.[10] These charges need scrutiny and rebuttal. But the immediate point here is that Christian experience, in deep consensus, concludes that the state, the power structure, how it is conceived, contested and operated, are all emphatically within the responsibility of religious faith and the faithful. But it also concludes, out of its understanding of man, that what can be expected of the state, as to justice, righteousness and compassion, will – because of the power equation – always be no more, at best, than a modicum of these. That realism does not absolve us from pressing for a maximum, from holding the power structure to rigorous concepts of its responsibility under God for human well-being, sanity, and peace. But it is a realism which also knows that the ultimate and adequate conformity of man to the divine wisdom and love cannot come from the state's auspices, with their power sanction, but only from grace and regeneration. To these the Christian faith witnesses without letting such witness exonerate it from the utmost responsibility for active citizenship and concern with statehood in the sphere which these command.

The so-called 'separation' of faith and state does not mean, therefore, an abdication of social duty. It is not a renunciation of the political on behalf of the devotional, nor is it an escapism. It *is* a recognition of just that dilemma of power to which Sayyid Qutb's thought of a 'Muslim' *Jāhiliyyah* leads, namely the capacity of statehoods, after long centuries of Islam, *not* to yield the fruits of righteousness, or – conversely expressed – the capacity of revelatory knowledge *not* to ensure a due obedience. Both indicate expressly the same truth, which is the proneness of the human to be wilfully rejectionist of God. The vehemence with which Qutb sees it necessary to denounce this wilfulness, as he identifies it in unworthy Muslims, is tempted into its own religious manifestation of evil's subtleties by the fact of its pride and violence.

He gives indications in many places of his keen awareness of how perverse humankind can be.[11] His whole case – slanted on others – involves this realisation. But he does not let the sense of it deepen his own diagnosis of society or give pause to the assurance of his own religious prescripts as perhaps themselves sharing in it. For there is much in the realism of the Qur'ān which would have sustained him, notably the concept of *ẓulm*, as explored, for example, by Kamil Husain.[12] Qutb falls back resolutely on the belief that exhortation and directive *can* suffice the situation, provided only that the state is so minded and oriented and effectual. Thus his sense of sinfulness in the world (if we may so phrase it) leads him back to a reinforced determination about the political agency when it ought rather to have caused him to suspect and distrust it and, while not deserting it, to seek beyond it in a larger quest for a surer salvation.

All his instincts, however, ran the other way, and it cannot be denied that they have an authentic Islamic ring. It is striking how, with Sayyid Qutb, the pivotal term *al-Da'wah* – 'the call', 'the appeal' – becomes almost synonymous with 'the campaign', 'the battle-cry'. The call to faith is the call to conflict, since its acceptance as a message recruits militancy for its victory. So it was in the pristine days of the Prophet; so it must be today. *Fiqh al-Da'wah*, published posthumously, chosen and edited by Ahmad Hasan from Qutb's *Fi-Zilāl al-Qur'ān*, in addition to items which Qutb himself published under the title *Ma'ālim fī-l-Ṭarīq* ('Signposts on the Way'), bears out this quality in the very headings of its contents.[13] He draws lessons for the present day from his reading of the *Sīrah* of the Prophet. The Battle of Uhud, for example, was 'on the plane of the earth and on the plane of the soul', and Muslims should realise how God schools them in adversity. He brings a sharp irony into his account of 'a long campaign', in which there were many in the Muslim ranks, 'perhaps the most honourable and esteemed among them', who let private interest, fear for pilgrim traffic, or sheer timidity impede their fulfilment of the dire command to eliminate all opposition to Islam and make the peninsula of the Arabs free of all *Shirk* and *mushrikūn*.[14]

Quoting again 22.40, he writes of 'the law [*qānūn*] of the struggle' as Islam's steady augmentation of power, step by step, and its abrogation of pacts made tactically at an earlier stage. Citing 2.217 ('They will not cease to war against you till, if they can, they make you desist from your religion'), he finds the same implacable necessity today to maintain 'the steadfast principle' of holy resistance basic to Islam. While the last extract in *Fiqh al-Da'wah*, 'In God's Scales', is movingly in praise of *ṣabr*, 'patience', it is a patience geared to militancy, the shouldering of a struggle which patience, of another sort and perspective, would comprehend in quite other terms than these.[15]

V

Sayyid Qutb's basic militancy and his view of the Islam-state relation raise questions he did not handle for areas outside the Arab world and Pakistan, where Muslims have at best to share, and at worst to suffer, a nationalism they can never dominate. But the fact that these – for all their vast numbers – were not within his ken in contending for what he saw as a right Egyptian nationhood, we cannot take further here, however heavily it bears upon his idea of Islamic polity. Other writers discussed in this book have addressed themselves to the role of Islam in such circumstances. But Sayyid Qutb's thought on Islam and society may be made relevant anywhere, in so far as it is detachable from his position on statehood and revolt.

It was in the first work after his 'conversion' to the *Ikhwān* that it was most coherently set out. *Al-'Adālah al-Ijtimā'iyyah fī-l-Islām* begins with the familiar contrast, as Qutb sees it, between 'Religion and Society in Christianity and in Islam'. This serves to underscore Muslim 'non-separation' of religion and life, and to state the inclusive nature of Islamic direction, intending to bring all areas of human life and affairs under the acknowledged Lordship of God, the authority of the Qur'ān and the Sunnah, and the comprehensive system of the *Sharī'ah*, regulating the human, and ordaining the divine, will. The exposition follows familiar lines and opens with observations about creation, man as the custodian of nature, and nature as, basically, friendly to man. Social justice stands in faith about the divine cosmos and mutual responsibility between persons and communities. The foundations and procedures of social justice follow. Freedom of conscience and human equality are fundamental. Freedom belongs with 'the fear of none but God', with the creaturely capacity to pray, with an inclusive sense of the divine will which leaves no need to fear vicissitudes. It is also to be had through the non-exaltation of prophets and others to divine status, through emancipation from inordinate desire, and through the ordinance of *Zakāt*, which should banish want and the fear of want. At each point Qutb quotes freely from the Qur'ān to support his exposition. In justifying the severity of punishment for, among other things, rebellion against God and the Prophet, it is perhaps odd to find him affirming that 'there is a public consensus of opinion that dissension and unruliness [*fitnah*] are a greater crime than crimes that are individual' in the light of his own later appeal to civil revolt.[16]

Zakāt is at the centre of his discussion of the means to social justice, and with it the prohibition of hoarding and the appeal to generosity. The method of Islam is to recruit the conscience for the duties it prescribes. Usury is not simply forbidden: it is shown to be unworthy and exploitative, so that the spirit abhors it. It is likewise with all other prescripts. Law is mandatory, yet it may also be man's delight.

Even so, the political role of the state is indispensable and Sayyid Qutb devotes a chapter to it in his *'Adālah* before proceeding to expound Islamic economic theory, which he does along traditional lines. Private possession and free disposal of property are secured, but the responsibility of possession is emphasised. Work and income are religiously significant. Right and wrong methods of acquiring and disposing of wealth are presented, together with the limits of luxury and the reproach of niggardliness. There is a certain ideological naïvety about these pages, furnished as they are with Quranic quotations relating to situations and social forms from a wholly different time. Their corroboration in the long, following section on 'The Historical Reality of Social Justice in Islam' comes entirely from the early Caliphate, with the Ummayyads bringing in the tragic change which jettisoned its disciplines and left it only a shining, distant memory.

How its reproduction in our time might be concerted leads Qutb into a long discussion on Western influences, and an affirmation of confidence in Islamic resurgence, buoyed even by the alleged support of George Bernard Shaw, as well as by an analysis of why the Ummayyads and other despoilers were able to work the despoliation. He ventilates certain cursory ideas about how Muslim education should cope with Western effects in science, law, literature and the arts, in order to guide and protect Muslim youth, and then turns to a few final points of economic law. His conclusion faces the sense of current crisis with the assurance that, rightly construed and enforced, Islam has comprehensively all that modern conditions demand for the discipline and realisation of man. His source throughout is the Qur'ān and Tradition. His way with the former is our final concern.

VI

In an opening reflection on the Qur'ān in *Fiqh al-Da'wah*, Sayyid Qutb stresses its active significance in the immediacy of the situation into which it was divinely brought. To miss this inherent dynamism and to reduce the Scripture to a pious item of devotion is quite to mistake its meaning. Its whole ethos has to do with the actuality of the era into which it effectuated Islam and the reader must mentally re-occupy that time and place and participate in the actual enterprise against *Shirk* and on behalf of *Tauḥīd*. It is the Qur'ān's response to all that the Quraish are understood to embody, of what is heinous and disorderly and foul, which study must repossess.

This mental posture of ardent identification with the Qur'ān's challenge to its context is reinforced, for Sayyid Qutb as for Muslims at large, by the practice of knowing and reciting the text by heart. *Dhikr*, or rehearsing of the Book, develops a sort of mind-habituation by which the faithful think instinctively the thoughts of the Qur'ān as these are assimilated in its accents, its nuances, its sequences and its rhythm. This dimension of Muslim experience is well known and has its counterpart, in some measure, in soul experience in other scriptures. To Qutb it is all important. The outsider can hardly appreciate it in Muslim terms, still less so if he inclines to suspect that it serves soul-devotion at the expense of intellectual scrutiny. Qutb had no such fear. On the contrary, he took the Qur'ān to be the absolute and sufficient measure of all meaning. Writing of twenty-five years of Qur'ān study, he said:

> I have not ever once found myself in need, in my encounter with these fundamental [Quranic] themes, for a single source outside it – apart from the sayings of God's messenger (the blessing and peace of God upon him) which anyway bear the impress of this Qur'ān. Rather, any other sayings, even though true, seem quite feeble alongside what the student finds in this amazing Book.[17]

In his emphasis on the Qur'ān's dynamism in the Arabian context, Qutb speaks of its 'leadership' in the day-to-day affairs and issues of that society. 'We see', he writes, 'how the Qur'ān took it by the hand, step by step, as it stumbled and got up again, strayed and was righted, faltered and resisted, suffered and endured.'[18]

This pre-eminence of the Book, its definitive and decisive role in the story, is bound up, as he sees it, with the fact that the Qur'ān disallows any adulation of prophets and messengers. The ordinariness of the agents of revelation, which elsewhere is enveloped in 'divinisation' of their personality, means in Islam that the text alone mediates the divine will. The believer's participation in the divine is strictly 'textual', via reading, recital and memory. Clearly, this does not preclude the utmost esteeming of Muhammad, instrumentally: indeed it may be said to require it. But, for Qutb, as for all conservative Muslims, the status of the Qur'ān disallows the kind of celebration of Muhammad that inspires popular *Maulids* and Sufi mysticism. The title of Sayyid Qutb's many volumed commentary is *Fī-Ẓilāl al-Qur'ān*, 'In the Shade of the Qur'ān', not 'In the Shade of Muhammad'. The latter's significance is his role as obedient executant of what Qutb understands as *Qiyādat al-Qur'ān*, the Book's active and concrete task in the world. The mission is primarily the Book's and only derivatively Muhammad's.

Qutb disavows those ideas of the Qur'ān which make it a repository of current scientific knowledge and discovery. The work and works of science flow from the divine authority to man to possess the earth and develop it. His technology fulfils this vocation and privilege. What the Qur'ān deals with is truth, the rule of God, the spiritual nature of

man, and the divine ordering of society. To try to 'establish' the
Qur'ān by appeal to some 'prescience' about things scientific is to
invert the real order of knowledge. It would be a sorry misconception to
relate the truth of the Qur'ān with the empirical 'truths' of science and
research. While the former is eternal and constant, the latter change,
progress, become obsolete, give way to new ones. The two realms are to
be radically distinguished. This does not mean, however, that we
should not welcome, utilise, and harness the discoveries and techniques
of science. The Qur'ān calls upon us to do so within the given
imperium of man. If, for example, Surah 21.30 reads 'The heavens and
the earth were tied into one and We separated them', it is not for
modern geological theory to come along and say, 'Here the Qur'ān
anticipates the way the earth once spinned out of the sun.'[19] No, says
Sayyid Qutb, 'this is not what the Quranic verse means', though, for
some, the example he gives might be thought more apposite than many
other, more far-fetched, examples of this approach. Qutb's main case
against such ingenuity of exegesis is that the notion being read into the
Qur'ān, being itself subject to revision, cannot ride with the Qur'an's
absolute quality of truth. Both the fact and the logic of his rejection of
such pseudo-interpretation are significant. Here at least, on this one
point, he is one with Kamil Husain.

Writing on the style of the Qur'ān, he observes that the text does
not follow events in order to relate like a chronicle or expound as
history. It draws from events what arrests, enlightens and directs the
inner heart and soul. It is not concerned to be a record, but an
education, not a narrative but a nurture of souls. It uses occasions as
tutorials. It begins a story, broaches something else, then returns to it,
repeats itself constantly, all in its educative purpose in the heart. 'The
Qur'ān comprehends the abiding realities from within the passing
happenings, and absolute principles in the wake of isolated events . . .
and this enduring yield is stored up in the text of the Qur'ān for every
heart opened to faith, whatever the time or place.'[20]

Qutb's commentary makes frequent use of material from Tradition
in exploring the context of incident or situation allegedly involved in
particular passages. In this he follows a long habit in Islamic exegesis
and his conformity to it is closely in line with his sustained insistence
that the text belongs with a sharp and prolonged campaign which must
dominate the reader's mind and kindle his will. Such kindling might be
missed in overpreoccupation with verbal or grammatical minutiae. But
he is careful, too, to dismiss traditional material used even by what he
calls 'authentic sources' if he feels that it reflects adversely on the
Prophet's character or practice.

As might be expected when its writing proceeded in solitary

confinement and much personal hardship in prison, the commentary breathes a keen awareness of suffering and illustrates strongly the nature of Islamic *ṣabr*, or patience. Moving as this is, there is also about it an instinct to stop short of the deeper dimensions of the mystery and to brace the spirit by the Qur'ān's own strong accent on 'the believers' being finally 'the upper ones', and the evil-doers in desolate damnation. Thus, in commentary on the phrase of Surah 90.4 'Truly We created man in trouble' (*fī kabad*), he dwells more on the physical content of the word – in which he follows Al-Baiḍāwī very closely – rather than on the interior stresses of the spirit. He ponders the struggles of the embryo in the womb, the trauma of birth for the infant as well as the mother, and the sundry adversities the natural order presents to growth and health. He concludes, without broaching the finer issues of tragedy and redemption, with the words:

> One strives but achieves no more than Hell and another strives for Paradise. Everyone is carrying his own burden and climbing his own hills to arrive finally at the meeting place appointed by Allāh, where the wretched shall endure their worst suffering while the blessed enjoy their endless happiness.[21]

His comment on the dire wretchedness of the last endless state of the damned is quite factual. He does not venture into academic concern as to the source or significance of apocalyptic detail in such passages as Surah 84 about the rending of the heavens, concentrating, rather, on the moral and the warning.

Occasionally he indulges his first love, Arab literature, by citing, for example in Surah 84, the tenth-century poet Al-Mutanabbi, a celebrated paragon of Arabic verse if also a Muslim of dubious orthodoxy.[22]

> Suffice it a malady that you should think death a cure. It says much that doom should be desired.

Qutb understands 'calling upon destruction' (84.8) as the doomed sinner desiring, or pleading, to escape his doom by asking for extermination. But such citations of the poets are very infrequent.

Another occasional name he cites in discussion is that of the great Grand Mufti, doyen of Islamic 'renewal', Muhammad Abduh (1849–1905), to whom, however, he has an ambivalent attitude. Thus, for example, he quotes from him in comment on the Surah of the Elephant (105) and the meaning of the birds who 'bombed' Abraha's army in the expedition against Mecca at the time of Muhammad's birth. He agrees that the rational mentality behind Abduh's desire to attribute the phenomenon referred to in Surah 105 to natural causes, like plague or infestation, is 'the Islamic mentality' too. He approves the desire to prefer the rational to the 'supernatural' and the need to avoid credulity and resulting superstition. At the same time, however, he suspects this instinct as somehow diminishing the mind's readiness for the actuality of divine power and intervention in whatever way, albeit seemingly fantastic, God may inscrutably choose to effectuate it. Qutb's total reliance on the text of what the Qur'ān says, and his refusal, as it were, to read between its lines with 'modern' eyes (for, after all, what are they?) makes him ill at ease with anything that seems to be slanted at making the Qur'ān more 'credible' or congenial to our way of thinking. For 'ways of thinking' have no writ to judge what the Qur'ān contains and the true believer finds it no 'easier' to believe God's word when modern thought proposes ways of 'easing' his credence than when it does not.

This stance sheds interesting light on Qutb's commitment to a complete and willing 'literalism', while still approving rationality and deploring 'superstition'. Thus, from Surah 105 he deduces a general principle:

> . . . a safe rule for approaching the Quranic texts . . . We must approach the Quranic statements in order to derive our concepts and formulate our ideas from them. What the Qur'ān says is final *as it is* . . . The Qur'ān comes from Allāh, the Absolute. Hence it is binding on us in the sense that whatever it states is the basis of our very 'rational' concepts . . . Human reason is not the arbiter of what the Qur'ān says.[23]

In other words, the Qur'ān must be understood not merely as seeking but also as conditioning the mental verdict which accepts it.

This is a position difficult indeed to sustain, or even to align with the Qur'ān's own reiterated appeal *La'allakum ta'qilūn*, 'perhaps you will use your intelligence', and similar pleas to a *qaumin yatafakkarūn*, 'a people who reflect'. The confidence that 'the Qur'ān is final in what it says' will not absolve from the task of deciding rightly what it does 'say', via metaphor, analogy, statement, and how, in all these, 'as it is' can be taken. But the whole principle, here carefully stated, concealing issues in its very finality, intimates very clearly the mind of Sayyid Qutb, his will to be inclusively submissive and to avoid whatever might, in fact or appearance, imply some independence of decision. Whether it is either feasible, or within the Qur'ān's – and revelation's – own prescripts, thus to disengage all that a readership normally involves of active perception and discernment must surely be doubted.

Language and literature, however truly sacrosanct and revelatory, communicate only in communicability which turns inescapably on deliberation and decision.

VII

Sayyid Qutb's mind about his Qur'ān and his life story belong together. They represent within Islam a deep and constant religious phenomenon which recurs throughout the world of faiths, namely the life and mind which require certainty and demand to assert it. For them God must be indubitable and faith unquestioning. The absolute cannot be other than imperatively so. Truth must be affirmed without diffidence or query, as if there were no patience in God. Witness can only rightly be categorical.

Whatever its context in history or creed it is difficult not to respect this phenomenon for the tenacity it possesses and not to deplore it for its lack of resilience. It is difficult also to know how to woo it from its inviolate fortress and win it for a different, more wondering, sense of truth, or to bring it to the realisation that there are no guaranteed certainties in the life of religious faith, but only open ones. The criticism might be most harshly put if one were to say that Sayyid Qutb, with those in Islam who share his mind and have shared it down the centuries, claim, and believe firmly, that their faith 'meets the whole of life', in a total comprehensive system leaving nothing out and fully fitted to the *fiṭrah* or 'nature' of man of which Surah 30.30 speaks. Yet it has not met one of the most persistent facts in human experience and society, namely the problems that make doubt, and the doubt that makes problems. Its instinct about these is to dogmatise them into submission or to will them not to exist. Must we not see that we can only bring these within our acknowledgement of God if we do not foreclose them – foreclose them as though we had no confidence in His ability to meet them or faith's ability to contain them?

This whole issue of unquestionable dogma, as Qutb exemplifies it, takes us into the meaning of the familiar passage in Surah 2.2: *Dhālika Kitābun lā raiba fīhi* (cf. 10.37, 32.2). Should it be understood as meaning 'That is the Book in which there is no doubt', that is, nothing dubious, indicating a total absolute inerrancy, as Sayyid Qutb would assume? Or does it mean that, as a 'guidance for the people whose will is towards God' (the following phrase, *hudan li-l-muttaqīn*), it is truly trustworthy? There could be a quite significant difference between the two readings.[24]

Sayyid Qutb's conclusion that political action was crucial, and militant methods within it necessary, which – as we saw – had the character of a decisive conversion, was the corollary of his theology. An absolutist faith meant an absolutist cause and campaign. The one strengthened what the other proposed. Both required to be untroubled by the thought that they might be mistaken. And the sort of militancy which he believed necessary affected profoundly the temper of the martyrdom which he gave to both the faith and the campaign. This, in turn, conditioned the role and nature of the suffering he courageously accepted. For the *shahīd*, the martyr, in any cause, may be so in the context of employing force or in the context of renouncing it. He may be either with the Maccabees or with Al-Hallaj. If the former there may be victory or – as with Sayyid Qutb – present failure, but in either case compromise and impermanence. With the latter only apparent failure but an unambiguous witness which endures.

If Sayyid Qutb's life and story give point movingly to these perennial issues in faith and for religion, he stands squarely thereby in the central theme of Islam, that of truth and power. His whole biography can be seen as a reading of the Qur'ān, a commentary given in a personality.

NOTES: CHAPTER 4

1 '*Ahd* is the word used in Christian Arabic for 'Testament'. Thus the name given to itself by the post-1952 order in Egypt coincided with the title of the Christian Scripture.

2 One of its early slogans was 'We are all Egyptians' – in an effort to reduce tension and divisiveness between Muslim and Copt. This countered the implicit assumption of many Muslims that authentic Arabness presupposes being Muslim, so that Christian Arabs are, somehow, less authentically Arab. The slogan, of course, was based on an Egyptian need for unity and compromised, at least by implication, the claim that 'All Muslims are one', and that 'All Arabs are Muslim'.

It is interesting to note how Jamal Abd al-Nasir's *Falsafat al-Thawrah* ('The Philosophy of the Revolution') (Cairo, 1953), trans. as *Egypt's Liberation* (Washington, 1955), deplored how various factions clamoured to promote themselves and their cause via the revolution.

3 *Al-'Adālah al-Ijtimā'iyyah fī-l-Islām* (Cairo, 1954), p. 91.

4 See *Fī-Zilāl al-Qur'ān* (Cairo, 1964), vol. 1, pp. 129–30. It is intriguing to recall that Augustine of Canterbury in the sixth century received comparable advice on tactics from Pope Gregory. On inquiring about how to regard the pagan temples in a newly Christian Kent, he was advised to cleanse them in a clear 'discontinuity' and then establish Christian worship in them so that the inhabitants would link the familiar with the new but without compromise.

5 Beirut and Cairo, n.d.

6 The writer was Dr Muhammad Khalafallah and his tutor Dr Amin al-Khuli. The latter, being a government appointee, was the butt of bitter attack from orthodox sources and the issue of academic freedom was involved.

7 *In the Shade of the Qur'ān*, trans. of vol. 30 of *Fī Zilāl al-Qur'ān* by M. A. Salabi and A. A. Shamis (London, 1979), pp. 7–8.

8 *Al-'Adālah*, pp. 15–16. The same words come in Surah 2.251.

9 The 'New Regime' in 1952 and following years certainly claimed to be Islamic and reformist and many of its ideas about discipline, work, and honesty, came from, or were congenial to, the *Ikhwān*.

10 See *Al-'Adālah*, pp. 5–21, and *Fiqh al-Da'wah* (Beirut, 1970), pp. 255–79.

11 For example in *Al-'Adālah*, pp. 43f, where the bondage of conscience goes beyond pagan instincts and material things and is prey to inner wrongs. A sense of the range and reach of evil in man is implicit in the many strictures Qutb makes on unworthy Muslims and misguided Christians. But it is fair to say that his theology does not really penetrate the depth of wrongfulness, not least the wrongfulness which can belong with religious 'righteousness' itself. 'Islam', he writes, 'is the immortal mildness [*ḥilm*] of humanity embodied in a reality alive on the earth' (*Al-'Adālah*, p. 30).

12 In 'The meaning of Ẓulm in the Qur'ān', *The Muslim World*, vol. 44, no. 3 (July 1959), pp. 196–212.

13 *Ma'ālim fī-l-Ṭarīq* (Beirut, n.d.).

14 *Fiqh al-Da'wah* (Beirut, 1970), pp. 105–12 and 237–9.

15 ibid., pp. 235 and 305–9.

16 *Al-'Adālah*, p. 72. But such civil revolt on the part of the *Ikhwān* would not, on their premises, be *fitnah*.

17 *Fiqh.*, p. 26.

18 ibid., p. 17.

19 ibid., pp. 37–8. It is interesting that Muhammad Asad, in his *The Message of the Qur'ān* (Gibraltar, 1980), p. 491, commenting on this passage agrees that 'it is, as a rule, futile, to make an explanation of the Qur'ān dependent on "scientific findings" which may appear true today, but may equally well be disproved tomorrow.' After thus approving Qutb's case, however, he adds: 'Nevertheless the above unmistakable reference to the unitary origin of the universe . . . strikingly anticipates the view of almost all modern astrophysicists. . . .'

20 ibid., pp. 131–2.

21 *In the Shade of the Qur'ān*, p. 174.

22 ibid., p. 106. Al-Mutanabbī (915–65), a celebrated poet whose name 'Pretender to Prophethood' captures his dubious standing. He aired prophetic pretensions which landed him in prison in Damascus. For all his wide popularity, lasting till the present, as the paragon of Arabic poetics, he seems a hardly fitting associate for Qutb's rigorous orthodoxy.

23 ibid., p. 302.

24 The root verb *rāba*, to cause disquiet in someone, to arouse suspicion, to make for distrust, would seem to sustain the second reading, against the frequent translation which would assert that the Qur'ān is literally 'inerrant'. 'Trustworthiness' (for moral and spiritual guidance) would be one thing, 'indubitability' (i.e. absolute factual and/or literal exactitude) another. The sense of a religious trustworthiness would be closer to Sayyid Qutb's argument that the Qur'ān is meant for the faithful, rather than for the curious, is to be read for faith and not science. Nevertheless, the thought of religious certitude, distinguishable from literal certainties, is largely uncongenial to Muslims, and 'a Book in which there is nothing dubious' is, for the most part, the preferred translation of 2.1. and parallel passages. But Yusuf Ali has: 'This is the Book: in it is guidance, sure, without doubt, to those who fear God.' Syed Abdul Latif, however, separates the two parts and translates: 'This is the Scripture wherein there is nothing to doubt. It is a guidance for those who care to live aright.'

5

Ali Shariati of Tehran

I

'I will end by purifying my pen with this verse from the Qur'ān: "The Hour draws nigh and the moon is rent asunder"' (Surah 54.1).[1] The writer is Jalal Al-e-Ahmad, his pen perhaps the most abrasive and passionate in contemporary Persian literature, his voice a sort of Voltairean 'Écrasez l'infame', only that his 'l'Infame' is the iniquitous and intrusive West, the curse and disease of the Iranian world. His *Gharbzadegi*, written in 1961, which concludes with this Quranic citation, is a highly popular and influential manifesto against alien factors within the Shah's Iran. His theme and title are of a nation 'west-smitten', 'struck' or 'mesmerised and undone' by a destructive invasion from without, afflicted and wellnigh prostrated by un-Islamic forces imported by fellow conspirators within.[2] With its passion and its urgency, *Plagued by the West* is a useful measure of the psychic and social situation which Ali Shariati – our major figure in this chapter – set himself to cure with analyses and intellectual treatment far more competent and considered than those of Jalāl Al-e-Ahmad whom we use to introduce him. For the two belong together as a single index to recent Iranian history and to the internal struggle for self-understanding within Shī'ah Islam.

For the moment we stay with *Gharbzadegi* and its author. This concluding quotation of Surah 54.1 is in fact the only time he cites his Qur'ān. But we have noted elsewhere that frequency of quotation, or facility with proof-texts, are by no means the only or necessarily the best measure of a writer's loyalty to the Qur'ān. What precisely Al-e-Ahmad intends by 'purifying' his pen his reader must guess. It cannot mean that he has some departing regret for the vehemence of his language. For his wit, sarcasm and demagoguery are all within a deep and deliberate indignation. His allusion is probably to a sense of the contagion of the unholy germs and cultural bacteria he has been handling. The Qur'ān, anyway, is always a hallowing and cleansing reality which, indeed, 'none but the purified' should appropriately touch (Surah 56.79). To write or utter it makes for sanctity in him who uses it. Just as it draws out the skill of the calligrapher, the careful reverential diction of the reciter, so it makes wholesome the conclusions of the essayist, the more so when he has been dealing with the plague on behalf of those beset with fever in a wretched epidemic.

But the choice of citation is intriguing. There is in the opening of Surah 54 an apocalyptic note well suited to Jalal Al-e-Ahmad's acute reading of disaster in events. His repudiation of Westernised man brings him in conclusion to those Western prophets of absurdity and futility such as Albert Camus, Eugène Ionesco and Ingmar Bergman, whom he recognises, in their very despair, as 'apostles of resurrection', and he continues:

> I understand all these fictional destinies to be omens, foreboding the Hour of Judgement, warning that the machine-demon, if not harnessed and put back into the bottle, will place a hydrogen bomb at the end of the road for mankind. Therefore I will end by purifying my pen with this verse from the Qur'ān . . .[3]

The supreme – and supremely destructive – achievement of technology becomes for him, as for Western social analysts too, the fiery symbol of nemesis on a society which is enemy to itself. Jalal Al-e-Ahmad has at least this much in common with Western absurdists, seeking a way out.

What is the way out to be? *Gharbzadegi* is content to end in apocalyptic doom. Its whole thrust is accusation of outsiders as a ready substitute for interior self-examination. It is the latter which we come upon in Ali Shariati, equipped with a philosophical and religious acumen not evident in *Plagued by the West*. Shariati is minded to probe into the issues implicit in Al-e-Ahmad's tirade and does so with an alert awareness of Western experience and the need to go beyond angry rejectionism into the social and spiritual predicament of contemporary man, whether Persian or European or American.

II

It is this perception which admits of our linking him in some sense with those religious concerns which are sometimes known in the West as 'liberation theology'. Not that any discernible affinity is in any way conscious. But it has for some time been a fascinating question to inquire whether, and if so how far, Islam generates in any of its exponents the sort of religious motivation in the facing of contemporary problems, both as to diagnosis and solution, which belongs to Christian doctrine and action in, for example, Latin America. Ali Shariati will best represent the answer. For there was about him a comparable concern that religious faith should be committed to revolutionary change in society, honest and incisive in the criticism of what it sees, and bold and decisive in its will to transformation.

There are, obviously, quite radical differences between the postures, resources and criteria of the two faiths in their perception of the contemporary world and its disorder. But there has always been about Islam that sense of divine imperative which plays so large a part in the dynamism of 'liberation theology' in the Church. One only has to read such a work as José P. Miranda's *Marxism and the Bible* to appreciate the 'Muslim' quality of his insistence that the being of God is to command and the being of man is to be commanded. What direction from the one and obedience by the other presuppose is, of course, subtly different. But there is no mistaking that theology means a right society, that to acknowledge God is to require a conformed humanity. Miranda's sense of the divine claim registered in Mexico has features close to Shariati's sociological implications of *Tauḥīd*, or divine unity, interpreted as opposition to all usurping powers and forces as these degrade and deprive one's fellow man. Thus Miranda writes:

> The God of the Bible stops being God the moment his injunction ceases. And man has many resources at his disposal to cause this command to come to an end. He need only objectify God in some way. At that moment God is no longer God. Man has made him into an idol: God no longer commands man. . . . If in any way he neutralises his being commanded, it is no longer God whom he worships. . . . God, perceived essentially as a demand for justice, ceases to be God at the moment in which he is objectified into any representation and thus ceases to command.[4]

Such sentiments are eminently 'Islamic' in their equation between ignoring God and denying Him, between disobedience and *Shirk*, or 'alienation' from God of what is God's. And what is God's has so much to do with what is man's as justice, dignity and freedom from oppression. Miranda even goes on to jeopardise all those other Christian 'dimensions' of divine reality in nature and grace when he insists unilaterally on the theme of obedience:

> God . . . clearly specifies that he is knowable *exclusively* in the cry of the poor and the weak who seek justice. Transcendence does not mean only an unimaginable and inconceivable God, but a God who is accessible *only* in the act of justice . . . Beyond all metaphysical

questions . . . the God of the Bible is known in the implacable moral imperative of justice.[5]

Shariati is one with Miranda at least in this conviction that to believe God 'One' is to be militant against what thwarts His Lordship in society and not to bring, in cultus, a mere conforming piety. He wrote:

> *Tauḥīd* may be said to descend from the heavens to the earth and . . . enters the affairs of society. It poses the various questions involved in the social relationships, class relations, the orientation of individuals, the social superstructure, the family, politics, culture, economy, ownership, social ethics and the rest.[6]

There is here the same impatience with abstract theology, the same accent of passion and protest, the same demand that worship, in an unjust context, must mean its correction in God's Name if it is not to become a hollow form and a virtual idolatry. Religion in both cases is hypocrisy if it is not a social imperative received as divine. *Shirk* has to be negated on the human plane and not in idly proclaiming *that* 'God is One'. In the ultimate analysis the only idolatry is in the conduct not in the concept. It is in this basic interpretation of ruling Quranic terms like *Tauḥīd* and *Shirk* that Shariati employs his Scripture. In his characteristic Shī'ah Islamic way, he is a liberationist.

Born in 1933, Ali Shariati, like Jalal Al-e-Ahmad, had a devout upbringing, being the son of a leading *'ālim*, and studying in Mashhad, the symbol of Shī'ah traditionalism. His later strictures on inept and obscurantist imams and shaikhs should not be read as unqualified anticlericalism. On the contrary, his sense of the secular world made him avid for a dynamic quality of religious custodians. The temper of his adolescence is well captured in Al-e-Ahmad's *Gharbzadegi*. Shariati was himself imprisoned for his expression of comparable sentiments. 'We are like self-sown weeds,' he wrote of Iranian university students, 'a people alienated from ourselves we try to find solutions to every problem like pseudo-westerners.' Victims of Pepsicolonisation, 'we became caretakers of graveyards . . . beggars at the door of the innocence of martyrs'.[7]

Shariati's maturing passion saw no reason to spare either Shī'ah martyrology, or Safavid reputation, or modern secularity. The first relied on superstition and lavished all its emotion on a receded past whose tradition of lamentation for innocence atrophied the nerve to rebel. The second was really a pseudo-Islam since it lacked the true charisma of the Shī'ah Alids perpetuating the true genius of Muhammad. The third was hopelessly lost in rootlessness and irreligion. Nor was Sufism any use. For it wrapped its devotees in a cocoon of apathetic piety quite incapable of vigorous action or even of recognising social ills. The 'virtues' of sanctity or fortitude which it sometimes nourished were pointless in a society of the oppressed and the humiliated. Even 'His Majesty, the Lord of the Age, whose advent we pray God to hasten', namely the twelfth Imam, would need to be allied with the forces of indignant change.[8]

Stirred by these activist emotions, Shariati travelled to the University of Paris where he developed a more penetrating awareness of the West than Al-e-Ahmad attained. He studied there between 1959 and 1964, taking a degree in sociology. He was much impressed with the thinking of Franz Fanon, author of *The Wretched of the Earth* and other works of revolutionary fervour, and chief mentor of the Algerian Revolution. While Fanon's philosophy of violence and psychic decolonialisation was sharply secular, Shariati was grounded in a personal Islam in which 'submission to the absolute rule of God . . . summoned him to rebellion against all forms of compulsion, dissolving his transient individuality in the eternal identity of the human race'.[9] Fanon had argued precisely this abnegation of the private self in the cause of corporate liberation. Even the misgivings of private conscience must be surrendered to the all-demanding claims of the revolution.

Despite the wholly contrasted view of Muhammad Kamil Husain, whose pacific Islam concerns us in a later chapter, there *is* something strongly 'Muslim' in this instinct for necessary struggle in which absolute right overrides what might otherwise be scruple. It belongs with the Qur'ān's accent on *Jihād*, or contention on behalf of God, and its dictum that '*fitnah* [civil and religious sedition or violation of Islam] is a worse evil than killing' (2.191). Shariati liked to associate the case for militancy with the Quranic theme of *Hijrah*, that 'going out' from the unworthy *status quo* which had taken the Prophet and his *Muhājirūn*, or emigrants, from Mecca and their kin, to Medina and solidarity outside their kin, in the decisive act that originates the Islamic calendar. 'Life', he affirmed, 'is conviction and struggle and nothing more.' 'Look at the companions of the Prophet: they were all men of the sword, concerned with improving their society, men of justice.'[10] Only such militancy effectively countered the evils which Shariati saw as '*Shirk* on the human plane'.

He returned from Paris to teaching posts in Iran. His lectures at the Husainiyyah-yi-Irshad in Tehran made him a household name and his books became the cherished pride of like-minded activists, who borrowed them avidly from lending sources in clandestine clubs or risked imprisonment by owning them. He was himself imprisoned, though later released. He died in England under mysterious circumstances in 1977 and it is assumed that he was a victim of Savak, the Shah's secret police. He was buried in Damascus.

III

The career of this meteoric and tragic figure in recent Iranian history presents the serious student of Islam with a vital question not easily resolved. It has to do with the Qur'ān in his hands. Is it the Scripture which truly inspires and determines his mind? Or is it that mind, shaped independently, which recruits the Book to approve, clothe, and commend the themes originated elsewhere? The alternative is a real one, even though it should not be harshly pressed. It occurs, of course, in every situation of exegesis, whatever the Scripture, and it belongs with all the Muslims studied here. What gives it special point in the case of Shariati is the radical reach of his ideas and the peculiarly difficult climate of Shī'ah Islam. If there is an ambivalence about his view of Muhammad – as we shall see – it stems, in part, from the need for prudence *vis-à-vis* religious authority and the complexity of fusing that authority with the role of the masses to which Shariati was wholly committed.

To elucidate his problem it is necessary to explore, if only in the broadest terms, the contrast between Sunnī and Shī'ah Islam in respect of politicisation. The former, as developed under the Ummayyads, is a more straightforward situation, with scriptural authority finalised in the text of the Qur'ān, entrusted to exegetical scholarship and passing down into a Quranic scholasticism in such stable figures as Al-Ashari – a scholasticism which Shariati deeply distrusted and despised as being incapable of radical action.

Shī'ah Islam, by contrast, possesses the Qur'ān in different terms. Whereas for the Sunnis only Muhammad's rulership, his political role, is perpetuated in the Caliphate – his prophethood having once for all mediated into time and history an authoritative text – Shi'ah Islam requires a continuing mystique of revelation, not in any way superseding the prophetic Muhammad yet also not possessing him unilaterally by text and scholarship upon it. Rather something in the charisma and status of the Prophet within the once-for-all Qur'ān still demands to be mediated via the Imams, who came to be called by the time of Muhammad al-Baqir, the fifth Imam, *al-Qur'ān al-nāṭiq*, 'the speaking Qur'ān'. That Imamate was held to perpetuate the *walāyah*, or guardianship, of Ali and the hereditary charisma it possessed was understood by the Shī'ah as alone sufficient to achieve and sustain the ideal Islamic society.

One recent Shī'ah writer in Malaysia, in this context, even reverses

the familiar view that Islam was originally 'religious' by virtue of
Muhammad's preaching and then became 'political' at the time of the
Hijrah when obduracy in Mecca against his preaching of divine unity
and judgement required his appeal to the arbitrament of force, issuing in
the Medinan state. For Abdulaziz Abdulhussein Sachedina 'Islam as a
religious phenomenon was subsequent to Islam as a political reality'.
He means that the Imamate, which emerged through the Alid cause
and the rise of the Shī'ah, was '*the* religious phenomenon', inasmuch
as only thereby was a genuine *religious* possession of the Qur'ān and its
guidance possible. By contrast the sheer politicisation of the
Ummayyad Caliphate was served only by a growing scholasticism,
developing over following centuries into an 'orthodoxy' which lacked the
authenticity only Shī'ah mystique afforded.[11]

Below we shall find Shariati in a similar quandary about the
'religious' and the 'political' in the career of Muhammad and in the
subsequent institutions of Islam. For the question weighed heavily on
his theory of 'the masses' in the structure and programme of Islamic
ideology. But before documenting this it will be well to appreciate how
far Shī'ah approaches to the Qur'ān in general conditioned his
thinking. If the power, not to say the right, to interpret the Qur'ān
without corrupting or distorting its meaning belongs only to the Imam
and if only the Imam is endowed with the divine knowledge that, via
Muhammad, mediated the Qur'ān, and if the Qur'ān is not otherwise
possessed within the institutions of Islam, then a radical ideology like
Shariati's can only be 'Quranic' by operating within the Shī'ah system
of authenticity. But, by the same token, that system, as personified in
the Ayatollah Khomeini, presents any reformer with the sharp dilemma
of having to concede it as master, to woo it as ally and to surmount it as
obstacle.

The sense in which the Shī'ah ethos could be revolution's ally was
dramatically evident two years after Shariati's death in the triumphant
return of the Ayotallah to Iran and the collapse of the Pahlavi regime.
Its doctrine of *taqiyyah*, or dissimulation, could work both ways.
When, under long adversity, the Shī'ah 'dissembled' allegiance to a
wrong regime, for the sake of prudence and survival, they merely
followed a tactic of quiescence making no inward surrender. The tactic,
of course, might become a habit. But the doctrine required that when
regimes became insufferable, defiance should move out into the open.
To maintain *taqiyyah* then was to betray its very meaning. This was
Khomeini's weapon against the timid. He disowned the 'ulamā' who
continued to plead *taqiyyah* as traitors, the Shah's rule having reached a
degree of oppressive iniquity quite inconceivably admitting of
simulated docility by Muslims. Here, plainly, was a powerful force

making for the confrontation which Shariati strove to join and educate, an ally in resistance of a calibre well proven in Khomeini's long years of symbolic defiance and exile.

But the factor of authority with the Qur'ān remained a daunting one. Even the Ayatollah himself, with all his political prestige and spiritual status, insisted in his lectures on the *Fātiḥah* to students in Qum that Quranic interpretation was only 'possible' never 'certain'.

> The Qur'ān is not a book that someone can interpret comprehensively and exhaustively. For its sciences are unique and ultimately beyond our understanding. We can understand only a given aspect or dimension of the Qur'ān. Interpretations of the rest depend upon the *ahl-i-'iṣmah* who received instruction from the Messenger of God.

He went on to disown those who, lacking all qualification, tried to impose their own ideas on the Scripture. Such people were trying to beguile Muslims into falsehood on the pretext that it was Quranic. It is, he said, forbidden in Islam to use personal opinion in exegesis of the Qur'ān or to try and make it conform to one's own ideas and interests. He reiterated that even his exegesis remained tentative. The *Ahl-i-'iṣmah*, the immaculate ones, the family of Ali, the Twelve Imams, alone possessed the secret of the meaning, and could not convey their witnessing to men.

> The Qur'ān has seven or seventy levels of meaning, and the lowest of those levels is the one where it addresses us. . . . The Qur'ān descended from level to level, from degree to degree, until finally it assumed verbal form. The Qur'ān is not verbal in substance. It does not pertain to the audio-visual realm. It does not belong to the category of accidents. It was, however, 'brought down' so that we, the dumb and the blind, might benefit from it to the extent of our ability. But as for those who can benefit more fully, their understanding of the Qur'ān is different and their orientation to the principle from which the Qur'ān was descended is different . . . When we wish to study the Qur'ān and its interpretation, we have recourse to the commentaries currently in use that contain indications likely to be of use to deaf and blind persons like ourselves. The Qur'ān contains everything but only he who was addressed by it fully understands it.[12]

The enigmatic dimension here is, of course, in strange contrast to the Qur'ān's own insistence on its Arabic form as being for the purpose of clear understanding leading to intelligent obedience (cf. 12.2, 13.37, 20.113, 41.3, 42.7 and 43.3). But the general aura of mystery and elusiveness it conveys could certainly be used, as Khomeini emphatically used it, to deter and disown all deviant and venturesome exegesis. Yet the utter centrality of the Qur'ān to Muslim life and experience made it an indispensable recourse for any would-be reformer, revolutionary, or pioneer of social change. It may well be that this situation explains Shariati's care to avoid complex textual tangles and to base himself squarely on ruling Quranic concepts which could be borrowed and explored, in his own idiom, without unduly inviting censure or incurring argument over minutiae.

IV

Those inaccessible *Ahl-i-'ismah* might have their own incommunicable insight, giving pause to all simple perusers of the text. Shariati called for 'an Islam of the aware' in a different sense. He meant 'the aware' who registered injustice and alienation, who had shed the blinkers of idle piety or scholastic complacence, and were alive to the crisis of contemporary man, chronically misread and exported by the West. But awareness meant a philosophy of action in the given situation, a tactic in pursuit of social righteousness. Here Shariati's problem seems to have been how best to recruit the potential of religion and especially the aura of the religious leadership, and at the same time neutralise their propensity to obstruct or divert objectives which, in any other context, might be described as 'lay'. Shi'ah Islam needed, as it were, to be saved by itself from itself, transformed from itself through itself. In this subtle and exacting task, Shariati saw a crucial role for 'the masses', the people. His inspiration here may have been partly Marxist. But it was also a deeply Islamic instinct deriving from the (Sunni) confidence that Muhammad's community would 'never converge on what was error or wrong' – the principle of *ijmā'*, or consensus, taught by *ijtihād*, or enterprise. Whatever quarrel there might be around 'the gate of *ijtihād*', a painful familiarity like his with the toils of Western sociology and the questionings of Western literature surely qualified him to bring such 'enterprise', while his lively imagination and strong moral impulse spurred him to do so.

Ventures of change, then, must move with and from the masses. It was here that he was most at issue with the philosophy of Khomeini for whom the masses were a political lever for religious leadership to operate, but not, in their own right, the protagonists. It was to make the masses central in his vision that Shariati developed a novel thesis about Muhammad himself, whom he saw as essentially a *religious* figure whose message addressed autonomous man as a person and allowed 'the people' to respond with *their* own effective 'movement' of change. This was the *Hijrah*. When, subsequently to this essentially 'popular' *démarche*, Muhammad emerged as a political leader and ruler, this was due to his stature and eminence as the Prophet of God whose *religious* mission, in non-political form, had released the people-movement which fulfilled his goals but only by *their* free initiative and *ijmā'*.

It was certainly a novel reading of the historical Muhammad with which few mere historians would concur. But it had obvious relevance to the strategy of change in a context likely to be dominated by 'clergy', a clergy liable to claim a monopoly of authority. It could readily be sustained by appeal to those frequent pre-*Hijrah* passages in the Qur'ān which enjoin upon Muhammad the sole obligation of *al-balāgh*, or the giving of the word. Thus, for example, Surah 5.99 says: 'The apostle's one duty is to give the word' (cf. 16.35, 24.54, 29.18, 64.12, etc.). Reckoning belongs to God. Shariati argues from these passages that Muhammad left to the people the onus of response. It is hard to square this with the post-*Hijrah* engagement with force through which submissions came steadily into his cause stimulated by his increasingly evident sanctions of political and military success. Nevertheless, focusing on the Meccan situation prior to 622, Shariati writes:

> The mission and characteristics of the Prophet are clearly set forth in the Qur'ān and they consist of conveying a message. He is responsible for conveying a message. He is a warner and a bearer of glad tidings. And when the Prophet is disturbed by the fact that people do not respond and he cannot guide them as he would wish, God repeatedly explains to him that his mission consists only of conveying the message, of inspiring fear in men, of giving them glad tidings, of showing the path. He is not in any way responsible for their decline or their advancement. For it is the people themselves who are responsible. In the Qur'ān the Prophet is not recognised as the active cause of fundamental change and development in human history. His mission being completed, men are then free to choose.[13]

The stress, surely, in the penultimate sentence, must be on the word 'active'. For it is the pride of Muslims that fundamental change *did* result from the mission of the Prophet. One of the most frequent themes in contemporary apologetics has to do with the concreteness and active achievement of Muhammad, often contrasted with the case of Jesus, a teacher who was not involved in the world of affairs.[14] Shariati can hardly be countering this view. His point is to claim that

Islam always invokes the people and sees issues turning on *their* role. People are the norm of God's law, rather than 'personalities', however charismatic.

This view is argued by reference to the familiar words of the final Surah (114) where God is named 'the Lord of men, the King of men, the God of men' – the word being *al-nās*, in each case. For Shariati 'the masses' would be the proper translation. God is 'the God of the masses'.[15] 'The Qur'ān', he wrote, 'begins in the Name of God and ends in the name of the people.' It was, in the event, the masses, that is to say the people believing, who were the vindication of Muhammad's mission. Surah 94,1–4 is cited in this sense – with its 'lifting of Muhammad's burden from his back' and 'the lifting high of his repute' (lit. 'mention'), that is, his coming in to his own through the people's espousal of his message.

Thus even the exalted 'personality' of the Prophet is in league with 'the masses' and does not contravene the dictum that 'personality is not in itself a creative factor in Islam'. Muhammad, in any event, is exceptional. Shariati sets him in splendid isolation. The Arabian peninsula and Mecca within it were far from the contagions and cultures of this world.

> The peculiar geographical location . . . decreed that just as none of the vapours that arose over the oceans ever reached the peninsula, so too no trace of the surrounding civilisations ever penetrated there.[16]

This extraordinary verdict is surely meant to be symbolic. For it is not factual. Shariati sees Muhammad free of all external influence, immunised by Arabia's apartness, and 'unlettered' so that no mould of schooling should shape him. Even his father and mother were taken from him, the one before birth, the other in early boyhood. Detached in this way he is more manifestly universal. 'Destined to destroy all racial, national and regional forms and moulds, he should not himself be subject to the influence of any such form.'[17]

For all his strong realism, Shariati was clearly capable of hyperbole. Or was this the Persian factor detaching from the Arab/Arabic particularity necessary to the incidence of the Qur'ān? Or was it his way of deflating the cultural factor given that Western culture was so proudly dominant? Or was his ideology getting the better of his sociology, the ardent cause repressing the academic discipline?

V

It is time to assess Shariati's way with the Qur'ān in his handling of the feature of Western culture which most occupied him and with which, as we saw, Jalal Al-e-Ahmad prefaced his quotation from Surah 54.1, namely existentialism. He had a certain sympathy for its heightening of personal awareness and approved its actual, or implicit, repudiation of machine-dominated, bureaucratic materialism. It had recovered a sense of human primacy, of the intimate, inescapable fact, and burden, of selfhood. It had concentrated experience on the inner reality of the being of man and so radically challenged complacent, servile or convention-ridden patterns of life. In all these ways it could merit a certain Islamic acknowledgement. There were situations and traditions which very much needed to be confronted by such an assertion of human autonomy, the demands and stresses of freedom.

But only to assert autonomy was to lack a goal. Alienation *from* the order of society was bound to languish in purposelessness and absurdity unless, and until, it was integrated into that sense of human meaning and destiny which the Qur'ān proclaimed. Here Shariati quoted familiar pivotal passages. God had not created the world 'in jest' (21.16), nor 'in vain' (38.27). There was a primordial human nature, God's design in man (30.30) which was not to be thwarted by human perversity or delusion. 'Everything indeed was perishing', as the existentialists discovered, if not 'oriented towards God' (as Shariati read Surah 28.88: 'Everything is perishing except His countenance'). But so oriented it could and should be. Sartre and his kind were sad negative evidence of the human void when the human is desperately misread as in their philosophy. Man, Shariati wrote, 'is a theomorphic being in exile, the combination of two opposites, a dialectical phenomenon composed of the opposition "God-Satan" or "spirit-clay".'[18]

So existentialist 'choice' was authentic. But 'choice' had to be 'struggle', social and spiritual struggle, migration inwardly and outwardly from wrong to right, from false to true. Shariati deplored the way in which the existentialists were non-programmatic, exiles brooding on exile and not obeying any vision of liberation. Man in Quranic terms was the responsible 'caliph' of God, His viceregent, always and everywhere 'on behalf of God'. Existentialists were in danger of making autonomy vacuous, a mere indulging in intellectualism enervating the will. It was sounder to espouse a programme than to ponder a prison. Otherwise

my freedom might turn into vagrancy, in which case it would no longer be clear that I was well served in being set free. If freedom has no purpose and touchstone, it is vagrancy. Next it will turn into futility, and after that it will take the form of . . . looking for hashish in Nepal or the Khyber Pass.[19]

Programmatic Islam, Shariati believed, had found the way to unify the intellectual and the activist, the sophisticated and the simple, in the

community. Noticing that Latin American revolutionaries had done
the same, and Franz Fanon too, he saluted this equality in action
between vision and programme in ideology.

> Among the companions of the Prophet and the *mujāhidīn* in the
> early days of Islam, who is the intellectual, who the activist, who the
> cleric? Absolutely no such classifications exist. Everyone pro-
> mulgates Islam, fights, and also farms, cultivates dates, or herds
> camels. Each person is simultaneously worker, warrior and
> intellectual.[20]

In this context, he took occasion to observe that in every case official
religion has opposed such movements because of the vested interests
that clerical castes acquire and out of which they 'narcotise the people'.
This returns him to his view that 'the people' are the real 'family of God
and of the Prophet'. 'The people were a single nation' (2.213).

If existentialists truly wanted autonomy and choice they should come
out into struggle. So also should the dogmatists sheltering in their
credal certainties and the mystics aspiring in their *zāwiyas*. Writing of
his tactic among students in his Husainiyyah-yi-Irshād, Shariati
wrote:

> I wanted to create a struggle in their intellects, so I did not give an
> answer . . . I said: 'Dear Sir, I have come to disturb the comfortable.
> Did you imagine I was heroin or opium to make everyone feel easy? I
> am not one of those who have all the answers written out.' If someone
> really wants to perform a service . . . he should plant contradiction
> and conflict in stagnant people. By God, it would be a thousand times
> over a greater service to sow doubt among some of these people . . .
> We seven hundred million Muslims have a certainty that is not worth
> two bits. What comes into existence after doubt, anxiety, and
> agitation has value: 'Belief after unbelief.' . . . The prophets came
> essentially to produce controversy. Otherwise the people would have
> gone on grazing peacefully in their folly.[21]

It may be questioned whether Shariati here – shock tactics apart – is
doing justice to Islam and the Qur'ān, 'a Book in which there is
nothing dubious' (2.2), about *al-Fauz al-mubīn*, 'the evident victory',
pointing to *Al-Yaqīn*, 'the utterly certain'. But it is also a question – by
the same token – whether he is doing justice to the existentialists. For it
is precisely their fundamental questioning which he does not answer
except out of the splendid assurance of the Quranic view of man (which
is also the Biblical view of man). Was it not just such confidence which

Sartre and his kind willed to put in doubt? Are they to be reproached for lacking a will and a programme when these are the very comforting illusions activists cherish? Should not believers, Islamic or otherwise, be implanted with contradiction and have doubt sown among their Scriptural warrants? To urge lack of drive and purpose against existentialists might be likened to deploring the Buddhist's refusal to fuel the fire of appetite. The charge is missing the whole point of the position it accuses, which is that religious confidence is within the meaninglessness of life and can, therefore, afford no rescue from it. Such a fundamental scepticism is not fully measured by a response which speaks out of a conviction, Quranic or Biblical or other, that does not allow itself to be questioned, but relies upon a 'divine' status sanctioned by doctrine, culture and tradition.

It may well be that there is, in fact, no viable or agreed criterion for religious faith outside its own givenness, whether reason, experience, intuition or consensus – all of these being adjudicators which are themselves on trial. Perhaps it has to be, at the end of the day, a faith in faith and that, in the case of Islam, the givens of Muhammad's prophethood, the Qur'ān's descent, the *Sharī'ah*, are the decisive facts which do not admit of being 'established' by other than their own authority. But if thinkers of the quality and passion of Shariati are to react comprehensively to the temper of the world that confronts them from outside – whether in existential doubt, or Marxist materialism, or the perspectives seen through the lens of sociology – they must be open to these ultimate questions of why their Islam deserves and possesses the allegiance they bring to it. This is not to say the allegiance is either not sincere or not appropriate. On the contrary. But it *is* to say that being conscious of its total liabilities and obligations must be part of its sincerity.

Meanwhile, it is evident that Shariati faced with courage and high intelligence, immediate problems of thought and action which left little opportunity for these more ultimate questions. His handling of the Qur'ān wisely centred on the deep and positive truths of *Tauḥīd* and *Shirk*. Whereas the Sufis, whom he partly admired and partly castigated,[22] interpreted *Tauḥīd*, or unity, as the absorption of personhood in the undifferentiated 'One', by the *fanā*' or 'passing away' of the empirical self through the discipline of *dhikr*, Shariati saw it as the strife to bring all things within the rule of God. Divine unity was not a mathematical dogma about transcendence. It was the assertion of the 'unrivalledness' of God against all that flouted His will and sovereignty. What flouted these was social wrong, political tyranny, injustice, oppression, materialism and – not to be forgotten – religious obscurantism and lethargy.

Shirk, or the alienation from God of what belongs with God – that is, the antithesis of *Tauḥīd* – was, therefore, much more than crude idolatry, the worship of literal idols, or pagan superstition. The Qur'ān should be read as the dethroning of all that denied the divine Lordship. Such denials were at their most subtle and their most heinous in the chronic self-deifying of human institutions and powers. Marx, for example, was right in identifying an alienation of man in the patterns of the productive system and the exploitative instincts of capitalism. But he compounded that alienation by erecting the pseudo-deity of economic order in a classless society. His dialectic of material forces took no account of divine authority, indeed excluded belief in such authority as no more than an outgrowth of a doomed order which had basely generated it. Thus his doctrine of goals and means in history was essentially idolatrous. The true Muslim would have to see him as a *mushrik*.

VI

Shariati's thought, developing *Tauḥīd*, *Shirk* and *Hijrah* in these ways, was a most apt and eloquent reading of the Qur'ān, and free of those jejune naiveties sometimes offered by text-quoters countering 'the enemies of Islam'. In circumstances of great tension under the Shah, and treading a difficult path in relation to the clergy, he brought a vigour and a focus to Islamic liberation and to a Shī'ah interpretation of man and society, the state and reform. He gave contemporary form to the long Shī'ah tradition of resistance and aspiration, while countering in modern terms its long proneness to acquiescence and inertia. Against what he saw as bankrupt and materialist humanism, whether capitalist or Marxist, he wanted to re-affirm the spiritual nature of man and marry that spiritual nature to an effective programme of social action. Brooding on the failure of Western civilisation, he wrote:

> Over this dark and dispirited world, humanity will set a holy lamp like a new sun. By its light, man alienated from himself, will perceive anew his primordial nature, rediscover himself and see clearly the path of salvation.[23]

Islam had a vital role in this renewal. Its *Tauḥīd* was a total spiritual view of the universe and within it man's unity in Adam was a single, noble essence to master earthly reality in heaven-given wisdom. Surah 5.32 declared the inclusiveness of humanity, both for good and for ill. A private piety, nourished by personal devotion and *dhikr*, might produce deeply reverent personality, but if, in pursuit of its intimate Paradise, it repudiated the world, then it could well conspire with tyranny and oppression.

Alternatively, the avid socialist who sacrificed his whole being to that one idea ignored whole dimensions of the human meaning and blighted even his own ends for lack of a spiritual vision. The existentialists did stand for a total self-awareness and so were delivered from illusion and pretension, but only at the price of atrophy of will. Shariati wanted to find 'a return to man', to authentic humanity, by surmounting the negative factors in religious devotion, socialist action, and existentialist inaction, believing that the positives in each would then be released in unison. The mystic would save the socialist from thinking only of economics and politics. The socialist would save the mystic from evading real responsibility. Both would give the existentialist drive and purpose, while he would give them the true measure of their freedom.

Islam, he thought, truly understood, exemplified the harmony of spirit, action and freedom which these three, mutually related, could attain. It set man under God within a spiritual universe. It summoned him to social justice and communal responsibility. For did it not hate the usurer even more than the *mushrik*? It confronted man with his essential selfhood, unconfused by enervating illusions whether from religion or from ideology. Deploring what he called 'the inherited religious sensibility in both Shī'ah and Sunnī Islam', Shariati continued:

> To the extent that the man of *Tauḥīd* perceives his poverty, he perceives his wealth: to the extent that he feels humility, he feels a pride, a glory within himself: to the extent that he has surrendered to the service of God, he rises against whatever other powers, systems and relations exist. Thus, in Islam, there actually exists a paradoxical relation between man and God – a simultaneous denial and affirmation, a becoming nothing and all, essentially an effacement and a transformation into a divine being during natural, material life.[24]

This remarkable passage in *Marxism and Other Western Fallacies* may be thought to bring Shariati, no doubt unawares, to a close approximation to the Christian understanding of the paradox of baptism, of a self that dies in order that a self may live. Paradox is deep in the Christian faith but usually finds little acceptance with Muslims. Some repudiate it altogether. But Shariati sees clearly that the claims of social righteousness are costly to fulfil and require an end to the kind of insulation that unworthy religion buys, and also disallow the kind of impatient, merely activist, response which socialism is ready to bring.

The question which arises is whether the paradox demanded of the self may not be taken truly and reverently into our understanding of God. 'Shall the creature outdo the Creator?' Browning asked.[25] The world in which self-giving is alone the true realism in being rightly 'on behalf of God as One' in the human situation is, surely, so constituted within the divine intention. When man, in a true *islām*, must find 'transformation' only through 'effacement' it is so because God has made His will to turn upon the human readiness – a readiness which means this radical experience within the self. Since the readiness and the experience, as Shariati shows, are crucial to the realisation of *Tauḥīd*, they are, therefore, bound up with the very nature of God, recognised by man. In that sense *Tauḥīd* means human regeneration, since it will not be operatively acknowledged in the world, such human, personal transformation apart.

May we not ask, then, whether there is not in God and through Him some initiative of grace and love which might undertake the cost of just that human remaking which His being all-in-all, His *Tauḥīd*, makes requisite? If so, may it not mean a divine counterpart to that glory through self-giving which Shariati identifies with a creaturehood truly and realistically doing the Creator's will? May not such a divine counterpart be found to participate, to exemplify the role, to give us the earnest of its fulfilment and so to inaugurate a human community to which its reproduction can be hopefully entrusted? If so, are we not close to what the New Testament understands by the reality of Christ and the society of His church?

Whether that sequence of thought is acceptable or not, we are left firmly by Shariati's thought with the truth that *Tauḥīd*, the real Oneness, of God cannot be a bare assertion. It has to be an enterprise. It is not a concept of number but an issue of sovereignty. It is an active subduing of 'whatever powers, systems and relations' deny or defy it, and such subduing does not happen, so Shariati strenuously insists, without that active commitment to inward righteousness and self-transforming love which Christians call grace and which they understand only to be feasible in this human world by virtue of that same divine *Tauḥīd* undertaking and enabling their human cost.

To urge that this is to take paradox into our thought of God will not avail against it. For the paradox is already there in what He has willed of man and yet given into his freedom, as the crux of His true worship in a right society.

We can only guess what Ali Shariati's genius might have given to Quranic relevance in the contemporary world had his life not been tragically cut off in his prime.

NOTES: CHAPTER 5

1 The translation uses the present tense though the Arabic has past tenses, often used to express immediate intensity. Purists might disapprove. A. J. Arberry has: 'The Hour has drawn nigh: the moon is split.'

2 Jalal Al-e-Ahmad, *Gharbzadegi*, trans. by Paul Sprachman as *Plagued by the West*, Modern Persian Literature Series, no. 4 (New York, 1982). On a malady analogy he suggests 'Westitis' (cf. neuritis, arthritis) as a rendering, or 'West-struck' or 'Westoxination'.

3 ibid., p. 111.

4 José P. Miranda, *Marx and the Bible, A Critique of the Philosophy of Oppression*, trans. from the Spanish by John Eagleson (London, 1977), pp. 40–1.

5 ibid., pp. 48 and 60. Italics mine. 'Implacable' is a word used, of Islam, by Gai Eaton in his *King of the Castle* (London, 1977), p. 20: 'an implacable religion rooted in the transcendent'.

6 Ali Shariati, *On the Sociology of Islam*, trans. from the Persian by Hamid Algar (Berkeley, Calif., 1979), p. 32.

7 ibid., pp. 87, 33, and 22.

8 ibid., pp. 49f.

9 ibid., p. 122. Thus Franz Fanon in *The Wretched of the Earth*, trans. from the French by C. Farrington, New York, 1963, p. 73. 'Violence is in action all inclusive . . . At the level of individuals, violence is a cleansing force. It frees the native from his inferiority complex and from his despair and inaction.' And again, 'Political education means opening their minds, awakening them, and allowing the birth of their intelligence . . . there is no such thing as a demiurge . . . the demiurge is the people themselves and the magic hands are finally only the hands of the people.' (pp. 157–8).

10 ibid., p. 81.

11 Abdulaziz Abdulhussein Sachedina, *Islamic Messianism: The Idea of the Mahdi in Twelver Shi'ism* (Kuala Lumpur, 1981), p. 4. His view is that the continuity of the Quranic revelation is not in the fact of the Book and the strictly *political* rule of the Caliphate (as Sunnis believe) but in a charismatic polity which both rules and possesses the secret within the revelation and interprets it through a hereditary gift resident in the Prophet's 'family'. Only such a succession to Muhammad could accomplish the ideal Islamic society.

12 Ayatollah Khomeini, *Islam and Revolution: Writings and Declarations*, trans. from the Persian and annotated by Hamid Algar (Berkeley, Calif., 1981), pp. 365–6, 391, and 393–4.

13 *On the Sociology of Islam*, p. 48.

14 Thus, for example, Fazlur Rahman, *Islam and Modernity, Transformation of an Intellectual Tradition* (Chicago, 1982), p. 2: 'The Quranic revelation and the prophetic career of Muhammad lasted for just over twenty-two years, during which period all kinds of decision on policy in peace and war, on legal and moral issues in private and public life were made in the face of actual situations. Thus the Qur'ān had from the time of its revelation a practical and political application. It was not a mere devotional or personal pietistic text.' (See Chapter 6.)

15 *On the Sociology of Islam*, p. 117.

16 ibid., p. 54.

17 ibid., p. 58.

18 ibid., p. 95.

19 Ali Shariati, *Marxism and Other Western Fallacies, An Islamic Critique*, trans. from the Persian by R. Campbell (Berkeley, Calif., 1980), p. 118.

20 ibid., p. 105.

21 ibid., p. 113.

22   He expresses a profound admiration for such great Persian poet mystics as Shams-e-Tabrizi and Jalal al-Din-Rumi, yet observes that their presence made no difference to the Islamic society of their day and place.
23   *Marxism and Other Western Fallacies*, p. 95.
24   ibid., p. 120.
25   Robert Browning, 'Saul', *Collected Works* (Oxford, 1905):

> Do I find love so full in my nature, God's ultimate gift,
> That I doubt His own love can compete with it?
> Here the parts shift?
> Here, the creature surpass the Creator, the end, what began?

6

Fazlur Rahman of Karachi and Chicago

I

'Muhammad never returned to Mount Ḥirā' and the Cave.'[1] An unproven matter of fact often goes with an overriding intention of thought. So it is here, in this strangely confident opinion of Dr Fazlur Rahman. It belongs with his insistent view of the Qur'ān as wholly 'functional', a Book which has to do, not with personal devotion and the inner life of the human spirit, but with a concrete programme for a socio-political order in human society. This constant emphasis, which must be explored more fully below, requires that the Muhammad beloved of the Sufis, 'wrapped in the mantle' (Surahs 73.1 and 74.1), must give way to the Prophet who inaugurated a new society through a revelation essentially geared to action. His true followers today will be neither mystics nor scholastics, all of whom have mishandled the Islamic Scripture. Muhammad's significance lies not in inaugurating ecstasy but in definitive public action and institutional achievement. Neither speculation nor private sanctity are the goals of the Qur'ān, but *Hudā*, guidance, into the public rule of God.

Dr Fazlur Rahman brings a distinguished academic experience to his exposition of the duties of contemporary Muslim exegesis and theology. After graduate studies in the universities of the Punjab and Oxford, and teaching activity in the universities of Durham and McGill, he worked in the Central Institute of Islamic Research in Karachi (since relocated in Islamabad), whose Director he was from 1962 to 1968. He has known personally the tensions involved in Quranic studies, especially in respect of how the role of the Prophet should be understood in the incidence of *Tanzīl*, and *Waḥy* – the interplay (if any) between the mind and spirit of Muhammad in recipience and the action of the mediating agency. There is intelligibility in the language medium, when revealed. How is that intelligibility related to the intelligence of the Prophet in its receiving? Fazlur Rahman was both sound and courageous in insisting that the answer given here has vital consequences for the whole approach, not to say the decisions, of *Tafsīr*, or commentary.

After emigrating to the United States, he became Professor in Islamic Studies at the University of Chicago and in that chair has become an esteemed elder statesman in his field, enjoying an authority which allows him to present a firm and bold position in a contemporary Muslim self-understanding. His textbook *Islam* (2nd edn. 1979) is an outstanding work. His two publications which mainly concern us here are *Major Themes of the Qur'ān* (1980) and *Islam and Modernity: the Transformation of an Intellectual Tradition* (1982).

The second of these belongs to an area which must always be of crucial concern to faiths and their custodians, namely the sequence of belief within the sequel of the generations. Education must always be a central preoccupation of theology. For it has in trust the vital question of continuity and poses it in the most searching way, not in the often closed circuit of traditional dogma, but in the open world of other disciplines, at once hostile, indifferent, or bewildering, to faith. As an eminent educationist, Fazlur Rahman has been deeply committed to what must be seen as the faith obligation in the overlap of generations – an overlap which has never been more critical.

'Thy truth endures from generation to generation,' the psalmist said, in his praise of God (Psalm 100.5). He put it wisely. Not 'from century to century', for centuries do not overlap. But can we be so sure today? New educational fields, avidly possessed by Muslim youth in the race to absorb technology, or thrust upon them by the attendant and intrusive 'social sciences', especially sociology and psychology with their disquieting assessments of what 'truth' may be, together create sharp issues for the commendation of time-honoured Scripture and heaven-given Word. Those issues, as Fazlur Rahman believes, are all the more exacting if official custodians, in their 'fundamentalism' or their 'modernism' (for both are culpable), have given wrong and distracting answers. One might almost cry in an education 'out of joint': 'O cursed spite, that ever I was born to set it right.'[2]

Taha Husain as early as the twenties had sensed this problem and dedicated his *'Alā Hāmish al-Sīrah*, 'In the Margin of the Prophet's Story', to the task of retrieving Islamic history from misconception and of transmitting it credibly to Muslim youth.[3] We see the same preoccupation in all the writings of Kamil Husain.[4] Fazlur Rahman, comparably, sets it as the primary task of Islamic thinking and it informs all his work. He knows that the theologian or the exegete who only reflects traditionally on his heritage may well consign both it and himself to the museum.

All Fazlur Rahman's impulse in Quranic scholarship derives from this urgency. He is aware of the deep dichotomy in Muslim education between traditional studies as in Al-Azhar and Deoband and the modern sciences, with their practical bearing and their instinctive empiricism and man-centred view. He finds that 'all efforts after a genuine integration' between these patterns 'have so far been largely unfruitful'.[5] He wants to Islamise all the fields of education, especially the higher levels, where the main damage is done, either by the neutralising effects of the physical sciences or by the subjectivism of the social sciences. Experiments like Aligarh have quite failed in this task. Any hope in it requires a clear obedience to the Qur'ān, investing factual knowledge with sure Islamic values. He scouts the 'feverish activity', as he calls it, of Saudi Arabian-sponsored university conferences dealing with the Islamisation of education, though he seems unaware of their publications.[6] It is the scope and tension of this aspect of modernity which imbue his whole handling of the Qur'ān.

II

It is necessary to begin with the insistent view, already noted, that the Qur'ān is 'the Command of God for man'. It is 'a document squarely aimed at man'.

> The Qur'ān is no treatise about God and His nature: His existence, for the Qur'ān, is strictly functional. He is Creator and Sustainer of the universe and man . . . the giver of guidance for man . . . who judges man, individually and collectively, and metes out to him a merciful justice. . . . The aim of the Qur'ān is man, and his behavior, not God.[7]

There is a strange ambivalence about this position. On the one hand, Fazlur Rahman reproaches Islamic intellectualism as enshrined, for example, in Al-Ashari and the *Kalām*, and calls for a synthetic view of the Scriptures which must necessarily be rational and intelligent. Yet he affirms this absolute 'Command of God' status without any effort to explore its ground. His is a kind of positivism for which the Qur'ān is 'a unique repository of answers . . . true answers to virtually all situations'.[8] This ambivalence is implicit in his use of the significant verse in Surah 50.37: 'Therein is a reminder for whoever has a heart in him or who listens with a ready mind.' Such a passage, and the verses calling for *tadabbur*, or deep pondering, would seem to imply more than access to a 'repository of answers'. Indeed, as we shall see, in his radical discussion of contextuality in the Qur'ān Fazlur Rahman does engage with the Qur'ān in richer, deeper terms than simply being 'commanded' by it.

But, more importantly, what would seem quite desolating about his sense of God, as well as the Qur'ān, as strictly 'functional' is its total neglect of the implications of the divine Names (mentioned as these are) and such concepts as a human 'desiring of the face of God'. There may be legitimate scholarly reasons for Fazlur Rahman's scant appreciation of Sufism and Sufis, and Ibn Arabi, for example, has doubtless wrought much ill. But can a true theism survive in this bleakly imperative mood? If God is only functional to us, can we be more than functional to God? Students of Islam have long been familiar with its concern for law and obedience, rather than theology and communion, in respect of God and man. But can there be a divine will dissociated from divine nature? Or a right conformism shorn of loving aspiration? Does not the will of God become sincerely answerable by man in being in measure answerable to man? Perhaps we should leave to Najib Mahfuz, or better still to Job, the burden of reckoning with a God whose being is only to command us. Bare functionality would seem a very attenuated account of omnipotence. Nor does it do justice to all the rich fund of imagination, tending to worship and gratitude, present in the sacramental principle in the 'signs' of the Qur'ān and the impetus it has always given to the art of praise – praise that has no place in 'function'.

Dr Fazlur Rahman, happily, is better than his own severity in this theme. He proceeds to develop his understanding of the Qur'ān's imperatives to man, in a clear stress on its setting in seventh-century Mecca and Medina.

> The Qur'ān is the divine response, through the Prophet's mind, to the moral and social situation of the Prophet's Arabia, particularly to the problems of the commercial Meccan society of his day.[9]

That situation was the 'burden breaking Muhammad's back', (as 94.3 has it), requiring for its guiding and correcting 'the word of weight' used to denote the revelatory *Hudā* in 73.5. As the document of his experiences under *Waḥy*, the Book is 'absolutely normative', 'inspiring that irreducible attitude of mind called faith'. This is so because the Qur'ān is, quite literally, 'God's response, through Muhammad's mind, to that historic situation', chosen by God for just that incidence of celestial direction.[10]

This view of the role of the Prophet we must explore later. Fazlur Rahman's immediate point is to require that all exegesis must study the time locale and understand how tenets and directives respond to the specific situations. From those specific directives, or divine answers, further significance must be distilled by translating them faithfully into the idiom of the time situations which we now confront. We must do this with an eye for the inner unity and not by random citation. It is just here, he says, that traditional commentary has so far failed. A right veneration for the text engendered a habit of adherence to set patterns and imposed an excessive concern with minutiae of grammar and with literal meanings.

In the search for the coherent unity as the clue to interpretation, the history of commentary has only a limited relevance. The task belongs creatively to every generation. Fazlur Rahman sees a sense in which getting into the original specifics and distilling the present relevance in fact assist each other. An interpretation yielding views which could not now apply means either a failure to comprehend the Qur'ān or a misreading of present situations. One must either identify correctly the application of the Qur'ān or else change the present situation so as to make it conform to the Quranic one. Doing either or both constitutes one's intellectual *Jihād*. Its success vindicates the fact that the Book is truly a socio-political, ethical charter for all time.

One's sense of Quranic coherence must be truly derived from it, and not imposed upon it. The latter was the sad error of esotericists like Ibn Arabi, or rationalists like the Asharites. They may have found a unity. But it was in fact a false one. Modernisers, like Mustafa Mahmud, have fastened on extrinsic notions and read them into isolated verses.[11] Even Iqbal, for all his dynamism, allowed a passing fashion for Bergsonian vitalism to misguide him. Yet neither had the old traditionalists done wisely. Indeed they had 'buried a vibrant and revolutionary religious document . . . under the debris of grammar and rhetoric'. Furthermore, a right sense of the unity of the Qur'ān *in* its actual time situation did not mean the minutiae of its chronology preoccupying such studies as those of Richard Bell. The *asbāb al-nuzūl*, or 'occasions of revelation', must be read cohesively, not in isolation.[12]

All in all, an outsider might be tempted to wonder whether Fazlur Rahman's confident invocation of the cohesive Qur'ān *and* his generous disavowal of major forms of exegesis does not suggest the liberating, but perplexing, conclusion offered, for example, by Wilfred Cantwell Smith, namely that the Qur'ān means what Muslims take it to mean.

Meaning exists only inside the consciousness of living persons . . . The Qur'ān has meant whatever it has meant to those who have used it, or heard it, or appropriated it to themselves. The Qur'ān as

Scripture has meant whatever it has meant to those Muslims for whom it has been Scripture. . . . We leave out nothing that Muslims have seen in it. The *Ummah* is as integral as Muhammad in constituting the Qur'ān as Scripture.[13]

But the dictum with which Smith concludes could hardly commend itself to Fazlur Rahman, to the effect that 'the meaning of the Qur'ān as Scripture lies not in the text but in the minds and hearts of Muslims'. For that is to legitimise those many Muslim hearts and minds Fazlur Rahman is at pains to exclude or correct, whether liberal or traditionalist, theosophic or myopic, whom he believes to be mishandling the Scripture or blurring its unitary repository of answers. It is also to impugn the controlling authority of the text in the terms in which it has been steadfastly received within Islam, as the absolute and final documentation of the divine Command. Further, it would reduce to entire subjectivism the right readership which he is labouring to identify and guide.

Yet it is difficult to see how Fazlur Rahman's aim for present translation, here and now, of the Quran's chartering of humanity, there and then, can achieve itself, given the several disavowals of various Qur'ān-possession, past and present. His plea may well be right and sound. But are not his criteria of how the vital Qur'ān-clue is to be read a personal decision, and their acceptance by others a matter for persuasion, or dissuasion, again on grounds which must remain themselves at issue?

All Scriptural structures of authority are, of course, subject to this problem. An outsider may wonder whether there does not need to be some overall institutional 'court' of reference, some 'sanhedrin' or 'council' which could guide and inform men's private readership, without enslaving it. It is to be noted that there is no doctrine of the Holy Spirit, no formulated sense of a continuing divine stake or aid in the apprehension of the divine 'writtenness'. Given the vicissitudes inherent in human reception of a sacred text, might not such a continuing divine operation be proper, seeing that 'Scripture will have future meanings'?

There is, also, here intriguingly, a question whether the right reading, or indeed any reading, of the Qur'ān must be confined to Muslims. As 'a mercy to the worlds', the Qur'ān certainly addresses all mankind. How and why, then, is its meaning only in 'the hearts and minds of Muslims'? These, to be sure, must have the last word. But must it be the only word? May the interpretative application from the seventh century to the twentieth, via a realisation of the unitary meaning, engage those concerned outside Islam, to whom that twentieth century also belongs?

III

Despite his confidence that Muhammad never returned to Mount Ḥirā' and the cave of vision, Fazlur Rahman lays great emphasis on the Qur'ān as 'God's response' in the Prophet's situation, 'through the Prophet's mind'. So doing, he strongly rejects the traditional view of Muhammad as a wholly passive recipient. This courageous initiative – for such it is in the Muslim context – is a most significant feature of his scholarship. And it is one for which he clearly has the Qur'ān on his side. The strange popular credence in the utter passivity of the Prophet in the state of *Waḥy* has always been at odds with the evident quality, content and impact of the Qur'ān. It stems, no doubt, from a desire to maximise the miraculous in the divine ways, or rather to assume that the more a phenomenon is held to be divine, the less it can be human. It belongs, too, with a mistaken view of Muhammad's being *al-Rasūl al-Nabī al-ummī*, 'the Prophet Messenger unlettered' (Surah 7.157 and 158).[14]

Fazlur Rahman gives extensive discussion in Chapter 5 of *Major Themes of the Qur'ān* to the phenomenon of the Qur'ān. He stresses that Muhammad in no way *sought* to be a Prophet and that the calumnies against his preaching which dismissed or scorned him as a mere 'poet' or a *kāhin* were false. There is no question *whether* his message was divinely given. The only question is *how*. That revelation is wholly God's does not mean, does not need to mean, that prophets, as its instruments, are not superlatively endowed minds and spirits, recruited, not neutralised, in the revelatory employ.[15]

There is much that is inherently impenetrable in formulating this faith in 'the total "otherness" of the agent of revelation from the conscious personality of Muhammad in the act of revelation'.

> But it is equally clear that the words heard were mental and not acoustic, since the Spirit and the Voice were internal to him, and there is no doubt that whereas on the one hand the Revelation emanated from God, on the other it was also intimately connected with his deeper personality . . . The spirit of Revelation in terms of potentially total Revelation . . . made its contact with the Prophet's mind.[16]

The active role of Muhammad, so understood, in no way jeopardises Muslim faith in the reality of *Tanzīl*, as a divine initiative. It fits far more congruently than the passivity view the actuality of Quranic situations, the place of 'occasions' in *Tanzīl*, the cumulative character of the Scripture, and what may be called an intelligible account of

I'jāz, or matchlessness. It also, of course, goes far to enable and undergird that plea for an exegesis alive to context, for which Fazlur Rahman has called throughout. Nevertheless, there are still great numbers of scholarly exegetes and simple believers who cling to the old view for which Muhammad was the mouthpiece of celestial dictation. Rightly he insists that orthodox faith is not in danger by leaving behind, once and for all, a view that so sadly diminishes the stature of Muhammad, the concept of *Tanzīl* and the liveliness of Muslims.

IV

In another particular, however, Fazlur Rahman is less refreshingly aware of a spiritual issue central to prophethood. He does not share those misgivings about the role of power and the collective in society and religion which we find so tellingly in Kamil Husain. On the contrary, he is insistent on the power equation and the necessity of success. This follows, of course, from his strong emphasis on activism in Muhammad's mission. Given that God's revelation is a socio-political programme for execution at all costs and over all resistance, the Prophet who speaks it can hardly fail to be the ruler who effectuates it. On this reckoning, failure to achieve, on his part, would be a sort of hidden treachery, disqualifying the word he brings. Implementation of the message, being so dire a necessity, must ensue upon its verbal delivery. To think otherwise, he implies, would turn *al-balāgh*, the communicating word, into 'conventional speech-making'. Failure here, on the Prophet's part, would mean that God, too, had failed. The questions as to the criteria of 'failure', the compromises of 'success', the time-scale of the reckoning are left to silence.

This success criterion is linked here with the doctrine of the finality of Islam by the claim that there has been no *successful* claimant to prophethood since Muhammad. He achieved the implementation of a society based on ethical values upholding God's sovereignty. 'The basic élan of the inevitable success of God's cause and vindication of the Truth' carried Muhammad through all the tribulations he faced in combating the vested interests of the Meccan pagans and in attaining the *Hijrah* as the crux of 'manifest victory'.

In reading the prophetic task this way Fazlur Rahman is, of course, in line with the familiar and instinctive stance of Islam. There are two deeply religious issues which arise and which are left unresolved or unrecognised. One is the fact that, given the time context, emphasis on which is so central to his view, success – even assuming that it is the right criterion rightly attained – will happen within the *Sīrah*, or career of Muhammad. Its relevance after his death can only be that of a paradigm, or model, of how the programmatic Qur'ān might be given 'successful' expression in later times. No 'success' is automatically perpetual. This is the central problem of Islamic history and lies at the heart of its most radical schism. There *may* be a finality in the exemplification of what 'success' means and achieves. There can be no finality in the achieving, given the flux of history.

The other issue has to do with the cost of a success which turns on the invocation of force and political power. Power-based 'success' endangers the quality of its mission, deprives it of necessary witness against itself, and attracts allegiance, not for what it is but for the fact that it succeeds or that it threatens in its thrust to succeed. The Qur'ān itself indicates these dangers in the menace of the *munāfiqūn*, the hypocritical 'recruits'. But it sees the dangers as both inescapable and containable. It does not believe that a faith is only safe in a force-free temper. But then it does not see that unheeded preaching may be much more than 'conventional speech-making', and may, by its very fidelity in adversity, and its patience, more fully discharge the trust of truth. It could mean much for Quranic study to keep company with Jeremiah.

One possible mediating clue here might be the sense of burden which Muhammad had in his mission, and to which the Qur'ān refers. Fazlur Rahman writes very freely about the human travail, even reading the controversial passage in Surah 53 about Muhammad and the three Meccan goddesses as an instance of the pressures to compromise and the inner dialectic in which he was engaged. Orthodoxy sharply rejects the implication that Muhammad was in any way liable to even temporary 'parleying' with adversaries in the struggle the witness entailed.[17] If, with Fazlur Rahman, we can penetrate in some measure into the existential experience of being instrumental to God, as the Qur'ān presents it in respect of Muhammad, we may be able to put this success preoccupation, which so dominates Islam, into a different perspective.

Does it not return us to that exclusively imperative view of what revelation is and intends? If 'God exists', as Fazlur Rahman has it, 'in the mind of the believer to regulate his behaviour . . . and that which has to be regulated is the essence of the matter',[18] then inevitably 'success' in this objective is paramount. Results, outwardly measurable and feasible, will be the ruling obligation. The sense of law will be central, and law cannot well contain failure or comprehend tragedy.

If, however, we think of God and revelation as regulative of human meaning, to be sure, and meant for obedience, yet with and beyond these intending also love and fellowship, then a longer patience may belong to them and even the possibility of 'failure' within the persistence of grace. These, of course, are Christian conjectures in the

Muslim context, and in the Christian context not conjectures but convictions. Muslims will not be minded to go along. But there is point for reflection in noting, in this way, the intimate link between the Quranic urge to 'manifest victory' in political terms and the sense that God's existence is strictly functional to human accountability. We can best proceed by noting how, in his overall exposition of theology, Fazlur Rahman is adamant about belief in God as 'functional' to human conduct, and yet, in his sense of nature and of mercy, better than his own logic.

V

He writes in *Islam and Modernity*, rather quixotically, that 'the Qur'ān appears to be theocentric'.[19] Why 'appears'? It would seem to be insistently and indubitably so. What he has in mind would seem to be a denial that its evidently central affirmation of God is to be read as encouraging human relationship with God 'as an end in Himself'. Since God is regulative of life, public and private, it is mistaken to make Him primarily an object of experience. To have done so was the error of Sufism, and it is one for which Fazlur Rahman reproaches Christianity. He assumes that to be concerned with knowledge of God and with worship for its own sake is to be diverted from the moral obedience within the social order. That this is by no means necessarily the case is fully clear from the dynamic social quality of authentic love to God. Indeed some would say that only the pure sincerity of adoration Godward can truly generate and sustain authentic social conscience manward. There is, to be sure, a form of theological curiosity and of devotional practice which neglects, or perhaps disowns, strenuous liability in and with the day-to-day world. But should a right vigilance for such religious 'opiate' warrant an entire exclusion of theocentric meanings, these being a reverent duty of the mind and a true experience of the heart?

It is not that Fazlur Rahman, in this stance, is pressing for a 'liberation theology' like that of Ali Shariati or José Miranda. It is simply that he is characterising Islamic God-consciousness as the exclusive correlate of ethical socio-political action in the world. For him to be 'under God' means that 'moral values cannot be made or unmade by man at his whim or convenience and should not be misused or abused for the sake of expediency'.[20] There are many secularists who would agree with that position, though Fazlur Rahman, on his logic, is bound to see them all as 'atheists'. 'Whim or convenience' is one thing: travail and complexity quite another. The latter surely take us back, speculatively if need be, but certainly critically, into what it can mean that 'God is God'. Fazlur Rahman's own conviction, that we must translate the Qur'ān's guidance responsibly, from its own time to ours, itself demands that 'theocentricity' must mean more than imperatives to obey and fulfil. For, as we learn from Najib Mahfuz among many others, a most urgent aspect of *our* time is precisely whether such imperatives have either ground in eternity or satisfaction on earth. We do not know our own time if we imagine that theism has no intellectual tasks or that effective obedience to God can be conceptually sanguine or emotionally dormant. It is a time when theology, as Hazlitt said of literature, 'cannot long forget, without forfeiting all dignity, that it serves a burdened and perplexed creature, a human animal struggling to persuade the universal Sphinx to propose a more intelligible riddle'.

Fazlur Rahman is less than fair to secularists and less than comprehensive with his Qur'ān. To harness our experience of God with social action and to want that action effective is excellent in warning the pietists and the pundits. It misses its own dimensions if it dismisses the saints and the theologians, the lovers of the Lord with soul and with mind. If our knowledge of God is only functional to our behaviour how will that behaviour praise Him? And what will have become of *Tauḥīd*, thus confined to ethics and society? And will the outcome be *islām*?

VI

Fazlur Rahman's strong accent on the functionality of revelation is corrobated in his discussion of nature in the Qur'ān. For his stress is on the amenability of physical nature to man's moral and economic ordering so that nature becomes the managerial sphere of the human fulfilment of the divine mandate. But the anchorage of this truth in the theme of *āyāt*, 'signs' in the natural order, admits of a softening of its strictness by the quality of those 'signs' as kindling wonder, poetry and delight, as well as making possible control. He notes that within nature's utility to man there are these other elements of mystery and mercy which kindle gratitude and joy. He makes the point familiar to many contemporary writers that nature itself is *muslim* in that, by what we call its laws and structures, it fulfils the 'measure', or *qadr*, which God has assigned to everything within it. Albeit non-volitional (and so contrasted with human *islām*), the causalities by which nature submits are, on one level, physical, on another divine. Divine causation means that the whole is constantly miraculous. The order of the universe is the primordial act of divine mercy. As Fazlur Rahman observes, there is intriguing significance in the fact that the same word, *āyāt*, is used of natural phenomena arresting human attention *and* the verses of the

Scripture, *āyāt* in the latter case being sometimes intensified by the apposition *bayyināt*, or 'clear indices'.

It may perhaps be asked whether this analogy between God's disclosure of His will and mercies to man in nature and His disclosure of both in the Book does not suggest a much closer tie than Fazlur Rahman allows between experience and theology. Worship, of course, must always go beyond phenomena to God the Creator. The paganism that failed to do so was vulgar *Shirk*. But may a right worship not go *through* the tokens in nature, recruit them for sound and sense, harness them in the arts, and ponder them, not only as the occasion of the creature's mandate to utilise but also as his invitation to celebrate? Then the *āyāt* will serve and gladden the imagination so that, in turn, the imagination may comprehend the Creator God at least in 'the edges of His ways'.

VII

It is to be expected that Fazlur Rahman's strong emphasis on the programmatic character of the Qur'ān and the life regulation which God-consciousness concerns will determine his thought about man. And so it proves. Here the definitive term is *taqwā*, 'the most important single term in the Qur'ān'. He understands it to be that quality of awareness of the divine prescripts by which man is preserved from, cautioned against, and inspired to resist all that contravenes his true being under God. The root sense of preservation, of being guarded, is gathered into the Quranic shaping of a human authenticity through 'the limits of God'. 'Conscience', then, might translate *taqwā* so long as we understand the liability of 'conscience' as being to guidance fully acknowledged as coming from God, and not to notions of good and evil based on reason, or utility, or merely human obligation. *Taqwā* has something of the idea of 'security' present in the Greek notion of *sophrosyne*, of 'a mind whose thoughts are safe', only that the 'security' derives not from some moderation or balance, rationally construed, but from the very order of God.

Taqwā means this moral responsibility 'squarely anchored within the . . . "limits of God"', of the 'Lord who is on the *mirsād*, the watch tower', as 89.14 has it. Linked with the Day of Judgement, so vital in the Qur'ān, *taqwā* can mean, as Fazlur Rahman explains it, a sort of personal 'X-raying of one's state of mind', anticipating the 'hereafter', the essence of which, he avers, 'consists in "the ends of life" [*Al-Ākhirah*]'.[21]

Such is the clear relation of the theology about God and the morality for man, the reciprocal fact of revelation as guidance, 'commanding the good and forbidding the evil', and man in conscientious conformity. In this vocation, there is no room for 'saviourship', or indeed for 'salvation' in the normal sense of that word. There is only either the *falāḥ* to which the call to prayer invites, 'success' through *taqwā*, or *khusrān*, 'failure', through obduracy and *fitnah*, or recalcitrance against the law of God. In this understanding of man under God, law and eschatology are one. 'The last Day' simply fixes eternally, records irrevocably, what life has decided. The determining choices have been cumulatively made and are climactically sealed.

Within history this brings us back to our *jihād*, our task, as enjoined by the task-shaping sovereignty divinely over us. The Qur'ān must be read and pondered as a living campaign for a just and ethical socio-political order on earth, a campaign intelligently reproduced in every generation by its light. What it aimed to 'establish' then (the word Fazlur Rahman uses)[22] we must now take as defining and exemplifying the continuing work. It meant for Muhammad a strenuous encounter with ugly vested interests. It required him to denounce the cult of wealth among the Quraish, to champion the rights of the poor, and to resist all the conspiratorial designs of the perverse and the pagan rich. When, for example, in 59.7, the booty was to be effectively shared with the poor emigrants as well as with the rich Medinans, the rule may be adduced that wealth should nowhere be allowed to circulate only among the rich. The Quranic prohibition of usury, however, must not be thoughtlessly applied to contemporary economic conditions as literalism has been prone to do. For Mecca was not then 'a development economy'. But the principle, discernible in the veto proper then, must be obeyed now. *Zakāt* is, of course, the central norm and guarantor of an active social conscience. A great area of the responsibility which *taqwā* undertakes is that liability *with* wealth, and *for*, or *to*, the needy.

The programme of revelatory ethics plainly means the political arm. 'Obey God' can hardly be separated from 'and obey the Prophet'. This means the normal duty of co-operative citizenship. But, given the primacy of *taqwā* operating always within divine parameters, there may be times when repudiation of unworthy regimes becomes mandatory. The loyal Muslim will recognise what the Qur'ān calls *fasād*, 'corruption in the earth', and combine to disown both it and its agents.

Fazlur Rahman draws out what the Qur'ān stresses as to the nemesis which history is always meting out to the 'corrupters in the world'. Its retrospect of patriarchal times, and its register of wayside ruins and departed powers, underlines the fate of the ungodly and the moral factors which ensure it. Whereas *Al-Ākhirah*, 'the last Day', is for the reward and requital of persons, history in the Qur'ān's perspective is steadily and condignly judgemental against evil communities and corroborates that sense of 'God upon the watch-tower' which breathes through all revelation. The time locale of the Qur'ān means that this sense of historical nemesis has only retrospective examples prior to Islam. One aspect of the necessary time translation which Fazlur Rahman emphasises arises here, when elapsing centuries bring Muslim histories, too, within this scrutiny of God. For it is clear, on his showing, that possession of the definitive revelation does not of itself ensure the realisation of its goals. *Taqwā* is nothing if not, in modern language, existential.

This quality of *taqwā* as being always vital, an achievement not a state, is implicit in Fazlur Rahman's insistence that the legists and *fuqahā'* were seriously wrong in treating the Qur'ān as in itself a lawbook, that is to say a literal textbook. It is *'the religious source of the law'* (his italics). Its being a 'repository of answers', as he called it, assumes *taqwā*. Thus it does not merely – or at all – decree injunctions and prohibitions in naked arbitrariness. It decrees them within this inclusive dimension of human *taqwā*, this reverent cognisance of their origin, this inner register of the fact that their claim is not their own but God's. They are not placing pawns, nor moving pieces, but constraining persons.[23]

VIII

No perceptive reader could fail to recognise the deep potential of this sincere and moving exposition of the human vocation 'anchored' (a verb of which Fazlur Rahman is fond) in norms received from God, to be sought on behalf of God and practised by the self within society. All things are to be understood *fī sabīl-Illāh*, 'in the way of God'. It will not be captious, but truly within these perceptions, to ask – as a Christian must – whether they do not point towards a less exclusivist, more expectant, stance towards others outside Islam. Fazlur Rahman rightly remarks on the interaction of cultures and how contamination is always an insidious possibility in the life of *taqwā*. The Qur'ān is alive, he says, to evil legacies of some on others, to the contagion of 'evil companionships corrupting good morals' (as Paul has it, in 1 Cor. 15:33, quoting Menander and becoming proverbial). May there not be the possibility, the necessity, the other way? Need Muslims think that in the goal of *taqwā* they have to go it alone? And just as any sense of things transcendent may aid it, so *every* religious structure may impede by its vested interests and its pride – menaces by no means confined to the Quraish.

From this angle, one notes that most of Fazlur Rahman's references to other faiths (in so far as there are any) in the two major writings here studied are derogatory. 'Christianity', he alleges, 'never envisioned any social order.' It is not clear what is meant by 'the liquidity of Christianity'. There is much disparagement and little care for insight in the characterisation of the '*savior ex machina*', as expressing Paul's theology.[24] Do we not all have need to penetrate more carefully and fairly into each other's heritage of faith rather than dismiss them roundly on the basis of travesties of what they are? To enter intelligently into the New Testament's sense of participation in grace through Christ and the Cross is to be as far as could be from *ex machina* contrivances of 'salvation'.

Such pleas for honesty in relationship must be reciprocal. The relating we have tried to attain here is one of salute for a lively venture in Quranic loyalty, for a vigorous effort to understand Muhammad cogently as the Qur'ān requires, and for a deep commitment to its revelation as programmatic for man under God in the real world. Fazlur Rahman has firmly identified the task of translating from then to now, which must belong with the Qur'ān's community. Against the diehards, this in no way means or implies that past incidence is present irrelevance. Quite the contrary. Only in being historical can revelation be also contemporary. Against the modernisers, it in no way means that present relevance is facile or ingenious. It must be cohesive, unitary and intelligent. Only such studies will allow the Quranic world view to constrain society and prevail.

But they will not cause it to constrain and prevail simply as studies, vital as studies are. Everything turns on the *taqwā* which is duly responsive to God as the Author, through revelation, of those moral and spiritual norms and limits which it is man's wisdom and preservation to acknowledge and obey. This central religious reality, crucial to everything in Fazlur Rahman's thought, conduces – perhaps necessarily – to a certain sanguine feeling about its viability. For all his Quranic realism about history's gravitation towards *khusrān*, and his awareness of contagion, he shares the characteristic confidence of Muslims, that, given the ritual, social, legal and political, constraints, man can 'succeed' and be among the *muflihīn*, the 'successful'. The odds against have doubtless increased, which explains why a right care of those constraints, their protection from distortion and disorientation, whether from traditionalists or liberals, neo-fundamentalists or Westerners, has become so vital. *Taqwā* must include its own capacity to survive. That cannot be *taqwā* which misreads its own nature or mistakes its present meaning.

IX

This leads both Fazlur Rahman's thought and our critique here back to education, which was their point of departure. It leaves us with the question whether a theology so exclusively given to 'Command' can suffice either to guide contemporary society or to instil – not to say merit – the vital *taqwā* of man. The Qur'ān, as he says, aims to induce such a state in man whereby he conforms, apprehends his creature-standing and his moral destiny, and so fulfils his being, thus understood as rooted in 'duty'.

But the world in which this definitive and concrete *taqwā* has to be commended, and so constrained, by education is increasingly beset by perplexities about the grounds and the claims of such obedience. Surely a wise theology must be open to these. The question is whether an essentially *mirṣād* theology can be so open. For it concerns the God who can only be served if He cannot be doubted, only – in the last analysis – obeyed and not 'desired'.

Technology tends to reduce the 'commandedness' of man because it seems to leave so much in his hands. Techniques are very liable to release him, operatively, from old constraints, and certainly from old prayers. There seems to be a permissiveness about our scientific experience – not in the familiar way that 'anything goes' but in a more subtle sense that things eventuate not by reference to obligation but by the impact of feasibility. It is almost as if we have just been 'let be', in a fashion most disconcerting to those who prize norms and standards, divine or traditional, to which techniques, generated only by and for efficiency, seem quite indifferent. Yet these techniques obtain and spawn within that very created order which we say is divinely commanded and divinely ordered. Perhaps it is that we have so sadly failed to enforce the disciplines that *taqwā* involves. Yet, when that failure deepens, may it not call in radical question whether the failing *taqwā* truly has either the clue or the capacity? If not, have we a theology of, or for, society today?

It is just here, perhaps, that Fazlur Rahman and others with him in Islam need both more perception and more compassion about secularity and secularists. It is easy to reproach it and them, to align it with 'atheism', and to associate it with '*fasād* in the earth', the corruption of the *dunyā*, or lower world, from which Islam must keep immune. But, for some at least, it is a lostness, a wistfulness, they would gladly exchange for faith, could the latter interpret to them how to make it. Will such a faith interpretation avail if it is confined to a theology of command that does not reckon with the autonomy which, without restraints except our own, we seem to possess?

The clue is certainly there in the Qur'ān. But it lies in more than 'enjoining the good and forbidding the evil'. It belongs with the art of sacrament or consecration, the celebration of nature and of life, not only as a realm of religious obligation under law but as a sphere of forgiveness and holiness under grace. These have to do with indicatives about God, relating us to Him not only in conformity, but in communion, indicatives which warrant us in seeing and receiving all things within a trust of love, as well as under an order of law.

Fazlur Rahman aptly describes his overall purpose as not that of 'saving religion from modernity, but of saving modern man through religion'.[25] In his critique of the method of Qur'ān interpretation, his insistence that revelation intends obedience not information, and his anchoring of personal and social well-being in the active consciousness of divine Lordship, he has gone far to serve that purpose. His rejection of what he sees as impeding it is trenchant and courageous. He finds neo-fundamentalism as only emotionally bracing Islam while failing it mentally. He deplores what he calls Islam's 'pitiable subjugation of religion to politics', rather than genuine Islamic values controlling politics.[26] He can understand, for example, why Ataturk was forced to opt for secularism, and why the young today, unless captured by traditionalism, are so readily at risk to the same option. All this is well taken. But the issue remains how the 'Command of God' in itself can be regulative for man, while the question of God Himself has become, in one way, so negligible and, in another, so elusive for contemporary society.

In a recent interview, the Chancellor of Al-Ain University, Abu Dhabi, Dr Izzedīn Ibrāhīm, was asked how modernisation in the Arab world had affected Islam. He replied that its affect had been considerable, that its benefits via technology were right and welcome, and added: 'At the same time . . . various evils accompanying modernisation have, as it were, crept into the crates in which technology has been packaged.'[27] One may assume that Dr Fazlur Rahman would state the matter differently. For ideas, norms, attitudes, are not the crates in which technology is shipped. Rather, technology is the packaging of ideas. The evils are not just stowaways that came in too but intrinsic to modernity itself and only to be encountered and overcome when the crates are seen for what they are.

NOTES: CHAPTER 6

1 Mount Ḥirā' is the traditional locale of Muhammad's inaugural vision. Fazlur Rahman, *Islam and Modernity: Transformation of an Intellectual Tradition* (Chicago, 1982), p. 15. He gives an account of his own experiences during the controversy, arising from his view of the role of Muhammad in the Qur'ān, in his essay 'Some Islamic issues in the Ayyub Khan era', in D. P. Little (ed.), *Essays on Islamic*

Civilisation, presented to Niyazi Berkes, (Leiden, 1976), pp. 284–302. While he held firmly to the verbal inspiration of the Qur'ān, he maintained that the Qur'ān itself required an active view of Muhammad's part in the recipience of it. This displeased the partisans of the traditional view of Muhammad's complete vacuity in receiving. They accused him of saying that 'God and Muhammad authored the Qur'ān.' Politicians hedged and a press campaign provoked a crisis atmosphere and Fazlur Rahman finally resigned his post as Director of the (government-sponsored) Central Institute of Islamic Research. The passage where the issue was broached came in his *Islam* (New York, 1962), p. 31f.

2 Shakespeare, *Hamlet*, Act I, sc. v.

3 Taha Husain, *'Alā Hāmish al-Sīrah* (Cairo, 1933), vol. 1, Introduction.

4 Kāmil Husain, *Al-Wādī al-Muqaddas* (Cairo, 1967). See within Chapter 8.

5 *Islam and Modernity*, p. 130.

6 ibid., p. 133. Publishing in 1982 he remarks: 'I have not seen any publications so far . . .' But note: G. N. Saqib, *Modernization of Islamic Education* (London, 1977); Syed Sajjad Husain and Syed Ali Ashraf, *Crisis in Muslim Education* (Jiddah, 1979); Ziauddin Sardar, *The Future of Muslim Civilization* (London, 1979); and Muhammad Wasiullah Khan, *Education and Society in the Muslim World* (Jiddah, 1981).

7 *Major Themes of the Qur'ān* (Minneapolis, 1980), pp. xi and 1–3.

8 *Islam and Modernity*, pp. 5f.

9 ibid., p. 5.

10 ibid., pp. 18, 5 and 8.

11 Mustafa Mahmud, a prolific and popular author in Cairo throughout the seventies, sees the Qur'ān as abreast of modern inventions and techniques, through ingenious text interpretation. It is this approach which is reproved and disowned by Muhammad Kamil Husain in *Mutanawwi'āt*, vol. 1 (Cairo, 1957), pp. 1–26, 'Al-Qur'ān'.

12 Richard Bell's translation (Edinburgh, 1937) made a critical rearrangement within the Surahs, though leaving them in the canonical sequence. While some have seen the non-chronological order of the Qur'ān as a token of its timelessness, others have – in Fazlur Rahman's view – pressed point and place too zealously. He prefers a contextualising of the Qur'ān in broad situations which illuminate its basic concerns.

13 See 'The true meaning of scripture: an empirical historian's non-reductionist interpretation of the Qur'ān', *International Journal of Middle Eastern Studies*, vol. 2 (1980), pp. 487–505.

14 See this writer's *The Event of the Qur'ān* (London, 1970), p. 56f.

15 See further Fazlur Rahman, *Prophecy in Islam* (London, 1958).

16 *Major Themes*, pp. 99–103.

17 *Islam and Modernity*, pp. 16–17. See Cragg, *The Event of the Qur'ān* (London, 1970), pp. 141f, 'The struggle to mean'.

18 *Islam and Modernity*, p. 14.

19 ibid., p. 15.

20 ibid., p. 15.

21 *Major Themes*, pp. 29, 120, and 108.

22 ibid., p. 37.

23 ibid., p. 47.

24 ibid., pp. 62–3 and 30.

25 *Islam and Modernity*, p. 140.

26 ibid., pp. 139–40.

27 *American Arab Affairs*, no. 4 (spring, 1983), p. 133.

7

Hasan Askari of Osmania

I

'The true greatness of a religion is only obvious when you do not regard it as a religion,' we will find Kamil Ramzi observing in Najib Mahfuz's *Marāyā*, after that author's familiar cryptic manner.[1] Whatever his immediate intention in that character sketch, it is a sentiment often encountered among interpreters anxious to reserve what they see as the deep spirituality and intellectual stature of their faiths from the toll of their institutional, dogmatic or popular expression. Such apologists are to be found in all traditions. What they identify as the essence, or reality, or ultimate intention, of their faith may be sharply at odds with its general image in history or even with its seemingly categorical expression according to its structure of received authority, whether scriptural, credal or liturgical. But a personal appeal to conscience, intuition, or spirit, avails to override, or reinterpret, these traditional constraints and the resulting issues can be entrusted, with all sincerity, to patience and the future. Verdicts of this order against 'religion' on behalf of 'religion', ventures in disavowal as deepest loyalty, tend – not unnaturally – to belong with efforts after 'inter-faith' and mutuality across religious frontiers.

Hasan Askari has for many years exemplified what such initiatives entail and achieve from within Islam. In his *Inter-Religion*, he remarks: 'For a religion to remain a religion it should be inter-religious.'[2] He has given notable impetus to Islamic exploration of what such readiness might mean *vis-à-vis* the Christian faith. His reading of the Qur'ān suggests lively possibilities of Muslim–Christian kinship and, so doing, central areas of interior questioning for both. Some may find them at once too bold and too sanguine, admirably conceived for the spiritually minded but for that reason scarcely fitted to master the prejudiced in their strongholds of institutional assurance. Such incapacity is no discredit. It belongs with the very nature of the enterprise. But, like 'time's winged chariot' warning the tardy about delay, it must always be in mind if right spiritual incentives are to keep faith with their total task – a task which must be forever aware of how perverse to 'religion' the religious constituency can be.

The content of Hasan Askari's scholarship is shaped by three evident factors. These are the Indian context, the field of sociology, and sustained activity in Muslim–Christian relations in the West. Like numerous other notable institutions of Islamic learning, Osmania University, Hyderabad, Deccan, experienced the trauma of adjustment to Indian statehood after the partition of the subcontinent and the Hinduisation of university life. The acceptance of minority status divested Indian Muslims of their traditional and instinctive reliance on the political arm. The creation of the separate state of Pakistan symbolised the forfeiture, for them, of that shape of Islamic destiny and threw them back, with aggravated finality, on Muslim–Hindu coexistence. That coexistence, the majority community reasonably argued, must mean the end of sectarian dominance of educational institutions hitherto regarded as communal symbols. The violent circumstances of Hyderabad's absorption into India were a sharp dismissal of the prestigious past. Though the state was predominantly Hindu in population, the Nizam was Muslim and ruled absolutely. Osmania was the state university, founded in 1918, and enjoying an envied reputation. Urdu was its official language of instruction. Islamic theology was required for all Muslims enrolled, and Islamic ethics for all non-Muslims. *Islamic Culture*, published there, earned, and still retains, a high reputation as a medium of Islamic research. Syed Abdel Latif, President of its Academy of Islamic Studies and translator of the Qur'ān and of part of Maulana Azad's Quranic Commentary, was one of its most distinguished sons. The university's Bureau of Translations, because of its policy in the use of Urdu, was the means to numerous translations into that language from Western sources. All in all, it could be said that Osmania underwent all the psychic and academic tensions implicit in the transition to 'secular' India. Certainly Islam, in that permanent minority role, had to analyse, and maybe discover, within itself, what due Islamic response might be to the fundamental changes in its status, prospects and resources after 1947.

Teaching there in the sixties, Hasan Askari developed his personal response, inward and professional, in the field of sociology. It has sometimes happened in the West also that penetrating and perceptive theologies have been generated within this discipline.[3] Its practitioners are disencumbered of the cautious traditionalism of the professional dogmatists, with their stock in trade of *Tafsīr*, *Kalām*, and – it may be – *Taqlīd*. These tend to obscure the deeper issues or obfuscate the mind. Custodians habitually confine their study to secure authority and safe precedent. There is the danger they may never raise the questions which take them behind their lines. Defensively, it is just that danger they instinctively ignore.

The sociologist, by contrast, is made keenly aware of religion as a phenomenon, whose workings he must study and compare, as a factor in the scene, a feature of the human landscape, a function in the social order, properly to be assessed by considerations other than, or perhaps indifferent to, its truth claims. He needs to be alert to a collective psyche, to face criteria which may well relativise, or neutralise, the elements, dear to the dogmatist, which prize finality, uniqueness and authority. He may suspect that these are moderated, if not discounted, by a sociological alignment of the workings of religion, however competitive their doctrines or contrasted their cults. Sociology focuses attention on the motives which underlie beliefs and takes the 'interests' that supply the motives to be more vital than alleged reasons or doctrines. It examines how a concern for identity and security dominates a human community and may go far to account for the strength of the religious faith by which the community is defined. It also claims to interpret the role in the community fulfilled by official custodians of faith and ritual, whether imams or shaikhs or clergy. What it finds that role to be may well differ from the suppositions of those who play it as to authority and sincerity. In all these ways, sociology is calculated to suggest radically different angles on religious beliefs and institutions from those of the theologians.

This is not to say that sociological assessments of religion are always to be trusted. Sociology can be liable to abstraction as much as some theology. But it is to say that it can prove a very salutary discipline in alerting and sifting thought about faith, when allied with the will for *ikhlāṣ*, or sincerity, which the Qur'ān repeatedly enjoins upon the Muslim.[4] For at least it uncovers areas and tests of such sincerity which, sociology apart, might never be acknowledged.

II

It is, however, his deep involvement in inter-faith endeavour which most fully explains Dr Askari's thought about religion. Since its inception in 1976 he has been closely engaged in the concepts and work of the Centre for the Study of Islam and Christian–Muslim Relations, at the Selly Oak Colleges, in Birmingham, England. Prior to its initiation, he had been active in the World Council of Churches' Unit on Dialogue and Witness, participating in its pioneer consultation at Ajaltoun in 1970.[5] His name has become a household word in circles committed to Muslim–Christian understanding in Asia, the Middle East and Europe and in the United States. He was one of seven eminent Muslim thinkers to contribute to Dr Youakim Mubarac's *Verse et controverse*, in which responses were made to the focal points at issue between the two faiths. His sustained commitments in the field of dialogue, against the background of his sociological expertise, have given him a stature of leadership as a uniquely formative thinker from within Islam. His work in the dynamics of symbolism and his familiarity with Western existentialism – especially Sören Kierkegaard – ensure that his personal voice from within Shī'ah Islam is alert, patient and compassionate.

Before exploring his main themes and emphases, it is well to reflect further on the way in which the prerequisites of inter-faith relationship tend to generate themselves in the very pursuit of it. It may well be a case of 'seek and ye shall find', and of the paradox 'to him that hath shall be given'. Certainly what is needed only comes about in the going. It cannot be had in the abstract. The will to personal relationship between 'differing' believers requires a certain 'abeyance' of assertion and denial in the credal or ritual realms, since insistence on these items of divisiveness would impede or exclude the willed relationship. That conscious 'abeyance' of things dogmatic or particularist may cause a sense of disquiet, or even compromise. This is not shelved or ignored and certainly not resolved. But it is held in creative suspense because the will to relationship has its own authentic impulse and plainly requires such suspension of what denies it. That very suspension – given that it is not disloyal and is warranted by its spiritual intent – may itself refine the loyalty that rises to it, by setting the doctrinal themes of loyalty in a new and possibly liberating light. 'What do they know of England who only England know?' is a familiar question. Perhaps we have only partly known either our Islam or our Christianity, if we have only known them in their mutual isolation. There is perspective in the view from the other side. Our exclusivisms, seen from a different angle, are obliged to question themselves, and, if appropriate, justify themselves, by criteria to which – open relationships apart – they could not and would not be susceptible.

This is no easy path. But it can be a liberating road. Muhammad al-Nuwaihy, of Cairo, certainly walked it in respect of Christian understanding of the Cross of Jesus. To him as a Muslim, he insisted, it remained inacceptable, indeed repellent. But he recognised generously that it was, for the Christian, the most compelling and magnificent focus of the mystery of transcendent power and grace. He could allow that, for the Christian, 'God was in Christ reconciling the world'. For the Christian. There, of course, was his reservation of the Islamic position. But dialogue and, even more, personal friendship had brought him to the point of realising a 'Christian's truth'. Comparable realisations have come to Christians relating, for example, to the sacramental sense of things in the Qur'ān, the God-centred habit of praise, the profound relevance of the meaning of *Tauḥīd* and *Shirk*.[6]

Such realisations may well suggest, or imply, a distinction between truth *for* and truth *of*. The New Testament will be truth *for* Christians, the Qur'ān truth *for* Muslims, irrespective – in the mutual situation – of the truth *of* either *for* the other. This is obviously not a final or an ultimately satisfying position. Indeed, the distinction could be a profoundly treacherous one. In any event, it is not one at which to stay. But it may represent an important waymark on the road away from bigotry and towards finality. It has been invoked by Jews concerned to accommodate Christianity in some way within an election that excludes Gentiles.[7] It has been affirmed by Christians eager to concede unbroken Jewish exceptionality and to understand their Christianity as being for Gentiles only.[8] Buddhists and Christians could work out equally feasible alignments of 'approval'. Yet they will all have continuing spiritual and intellectual obligations to what is at issue between the two prepositions 'for' and 'of' in respect of truth.

That, of course, is the unfinished task of dialogue. Some would insist that it is a hopeless one, that mutually complementing and mutually contradicting 'truths' are all we have and, given sociological and language predicaments, all we can expect. Those who accept that impasse will be in danger of declining into supine tolerance. Those who mean to surmount it will need the equipment of mind and soul which, albeit as a halfway house, it furnishes and yields. If we are ever to get beyond it, we must live within it. For, in present situations of national passion, of hemispheric tension and of spiritual alienation, it is the only hope we have. It is this fact which warrants a salute of gratitude to Hasan Askari as an outstanding Muslim practitioner of the art of Christian appreciation. Only by such a tribute of mind can a Christian critical appraisal of his thought properly develop and press the points of continuing question which it leaves at issue.

It will do so in the knowledge that these concern the nature of Islam as much as they belong with the self-understanding of Christians. For one of the characteristics of such dialogue – and it is notable in the case of Hasan Askari – is that it tends to idiosyncratic views of the faith out of which it speaks. Indeed, the interpretation of Islam is as much at stake here as the Islamic appraisal of Christianity. Perhaps that is proper and inevitable. But it will be important that pioneers in Islamic initiatives reaching into Christianity should not part company too radically with the Islam broadly understood as normative among Muslims. That the latter is often hard to identify with consensus is no warrant for not registering its pull as a rope whose tether must determine our range. The Qur'ān itself may be invoked for this metaphor when it refers to 'the rope of God', to which believers must cling in a solidarity which does not break up into divisions (Surah 3.103). Pioneers seeking open relationships across traditional borders may often be found affirming a strongly personal version of the faith. This is doubtless necessary to their openness. But it would be a dubious openness which lost sight of its own character. For it is just the closedness to each other of popular religions and traditional faiths that constitutes the heavy task of the open-hearted.

III

Hasan Askari's thought is rooted in the basic concern of Islam 'not to allow the Godness of God to suffer in men's beliefs about Him'.[9] That, of course, is the central point of *Tauḥīd*, divine unity, God's immunity from all false notions, whether these are plural, or superstitious, or representational. *Shirk*, which must always be anathema, is the name of these wronging, falsifying, derogations of the divine nature and reality. 'They did not esteem God as He should be esteemed,' Surahs 6.91, 22.74, and 39.67 say of *mushrikīn*. This deep passion for the true 'Godness of God' informs all that Dr Askari writes.

The phrase itself opens up a fascinating vista of thought. For it indicates that 'God' may be a doubtful, ambivalent, term, needing to be rescued, safeguarded, exempted, from all that would impugn true 'Godness'. There, of course, lies all the onus of theology. The mystery, even the struggle, about 'the Godness of God' underlies the Book of Job, which has an important part in Askari's case. What *are* the worthy thoughts, the proper praises, the authentic cognisances of God within our human competence? The question is in no way academic. For the falsehoods, the unworthy notions, if we have them, will distort not only our thinking but our worship. They will mean that we are idolaters. We shall be guilty in them not merely of improper thoughts but of existential travesty. It goes without saying that this issue is the common menace, and therefore also the unifying ground, of all religion. 'Let God be God' is never a denominational, a Muslim, a Christian, a Jewish, a Baha'i, or any particularist summons in which zeal for the authentic is unilateral. The question is the criterion to determine the authentic.

Here, Hasan Askari is one with all Muslims in relying on the final criterion of the Qur'ān. *Tauḥīd*, reinforced by the anathema on *Shirk*, means the absoluteness of God. From that absoluteness Islam is forced to exclude all that is earthly. It has to deny any divine character incompatible with the single principle of utter transcendence. What is clearly incompatible, on this reckoning, is anything 'earthly'. Askari, with qualifications to which we will come in his Christian relationships, is committed to that immunising dimension of the absolute which, from the first anti-idolatrous preoccupations of Muhammad, has consistently prepossessed the Muslim mind. However, he adds that 'in a secondary manner it need not deny that the relative is in God, for it admits the divine attributes'.[10]

The Christian, of course, would grasp this paradox much more confidently. For paradox it remains. Yet it is a paradox inseparable from creation – in which the Qur'ān altogether believes – and from revelation – which the Qur'ān believes itself to comprise – and from all theology and worship, which necessarily involve the 'absolute' 'Godness of God' in the relativity of language denoting and addressing Him.

The clue would seem to lie in tackling that characteristically Islamic instinct for the immunising of the divine from earthly, and from human, involvement. Why this reluctance, given that, necessarily, the very word 'God' is a relational term? Like the word 'friend' it has significance only in cognisance of relationship. This is not to say that the being of God is exhausted in the human relation: it *is* to say that, such relationship apart, *Tauḥīd* and *Shirk*, and, in their being at issue, the very 'Godness of God', would not exist. If we are truly saying, as Muslims are, 'Let God be God', then, clearly, in that sense, God has to be 'let be', and humanity is where it happens. And it happens, or otherwise, as the central issue of humanity itself.

If, as we must surely concede, this situation within creation and divine law is by divine design, then it would seem to follow that there is no divine reluctance to involve divine ultimacy within the human relation. God must be understood as that sort of absolute, which is only another way of saying that 'God is love'. Must we not make the paradox central, rather than accommodating it, regretfully and – in effect – inconsistently, as the proposition does which excludes all that is earthly from the divine absolute while not denying that, in a secondary manner, the relative is in God? Will that 'secondary manner' in some way reduce the divine quality of the divine 'relative'? If so, this was just the reduction which the Christian faith in the divinity of 'God in Christ', in Jesus as the divine Word, was intended to exclude. As the Islamic sense of the 'uncreatedness of the Qur'ān' is designed to ensure, we need to be certain that, when we have to do with God in those areas which are necessarily 'relative' to us, we have not been deprived of what He is in His absoluteness. For, were we to be, how would we have 'Him' at all? And what would have happened to

Tauḥīd, which forbids all disparities in God? Would we not have stood *Shirk* on its head by disallowing, for *our* theological reasons, the all-inclusive reach and competence of God? Would we not, in fact, be limiting the divine omnipotence as drastically as the idolaters? May it, therefore, be right to conclude that Islamic thought about God has stayed too long under the dominance of the necessary anti-idolatry of Islam's origins in a milieu of paganism which demanded a rigorous dissociation of God from human notions? Such proper dissociation needs to be distinguished from that divine-human association which is inseparable from transcendence itself, as theism – with creation and revelation – believes it to be. Hasan Askari's thought may yet help to this end.

We are on easier ground when we come to his focus on the theme of praise. In happy harmony with fellow theists, he sees the world as a sanctuary. It has 'a theophanic character'. This is his reading of the steady insistence of the Qur'ān on 'the signs of God' in nature, which everywhere constrain the intelligence to investigate and the soul to wonder and give thanks.[11] But tradition, too, can be invoked. 'If', he writes, 'the Prophet . . . said that he loved women, perfumes and prayer', this 'invokes an inter-related order of beauty, love and sanctity.'[12]

Moreover, such awareness of all worldly experience as a sanctuary, a 'dwelling in the house of the Lord', as Psalm 23 has it, must mean a passionate concern for social righteousness and religious integrity. Whatever its outward forms in ritual, prayer must always have this personal integrity, without which external expressions are hollow. 'The principle of all praise to God . . . is also a principle of constant vigilance over, and criticism of, one's position within one's tradition and in history.' If the world is a holy place, then worship has to be a kind of perpetual 'prophecy' against its distortion and corruption. 'By rising to pray, we contradict our age to save it.'[13]

IV

This at once takes Askari's thought into the theme of Islam and secularity. Unlike many contemporary Muslim writers, he does not shed the issue of the secular by blandly insisting that Islam, as a religion, covers all of life. He does not opt for the position expressed, for example, by Sayyid Husain Nasr, that any concern with secular ideologies, or empathy with secular attitudes, must be scouted by genuine believers in 'God's religion'.[14] He does not adopt the view that somehow secularity is 'the headache of Christianity', as the religion responsible for, and antecedent to, the Western culture it has overtaken. True theology and right worship must always be concerned for, and involved with, the search for a true and right society. *Shirk*, for Hasan Askari, must be understood to mean anything that flouts the divine will for man, since the divine order itself is bound up with man's due dignity and rights. *Shirk*, then, may be defined as 'the unequal distribution of knowledge, wealth and power'. 'The call to worship one God is also a call to transform the social order.' It is anti-monotheistic to make legitimate any inequality or to ignore any suffering. Only monotheism, as distinct from monolatry (which may be quite nationalistic) can undergird and achieve social justice. Therefore, to be a monotheist is to be a revolutionary, wherever the *status quo* is unjust or tyrannical or apathetic.[15]

In the Indian, and many another, context, this leads to the issue of Muslim minority status. For the response to secularity in moral, social terms has there to be made within the 'secular' state (in the legal sense of 'secular') dominated by a different religion. Here, Askari's thought, responding to the deep dilemmas of Indian Islam, is strongly conceived and, in measure, quite idiosyncratic. He believes that the Muslim community within India, since partition, has hardly begun to face the question of the social implications of its monotheism. Like many minorities elsewhere, its ruling concern has been for sheer survival. What should it mean to Indian Muslims that 'God is not one to let your faith go to waste', as Surah 2.143 might be rendered.[16] Muhammad was there comforted in the crisis of the change of *Qiblah* from Jerusalem to Mecca, with all the inner disquiet or perplexity it inspired among his hard-pressed followers. In the comparable disorientation, or reorientation, of secular India, with Pakistani options permanently excluded, what should Indian Muslim confidence in the divine assurance require of their faith in concrete terms? The question, he said, had hardly yet been put.

As we will note later, he holds that the religious manifold is a source of knowledge other than one's own. Coexistence should mean a recognition of diversity within the human whole and within the variety of symbolic, cultural systems of expression which ought not to be exclusified. But his most radical point is the belief that Islam had never established, or meant to establish, a political order. He writes:

The question of the relation of religion to the state is one to the solution of which Islam has least applied itself. For Muslims in the course of their history this has been at once a source of vigour and of weakness. It has sundered Islam into two major sects, Sunnis and Shī'ah. In my view this has done great harm to their spiritual and religious development. Even those Muslims who are animated by the best intentions have, on this question, been victims of illusion. In this domain, all the ambiguities that exist come from the claim that in Islam there is an indisputable unity between what is political and what is religious.

My profound conviction is that the Prophet of Islam did *not* create a state. Consequently, the controversy between Sunnī and Shī‘ah over the question of knowing who should succeed the Prophet is without foundation. It follows that the principles of the Caliphate and the Imamate are not Quranic. My belief is that Islam can survive without political power, without statehood.[17]

He adds that his statement of view is strictly personal and develops it as a plea for what he calls the eschatological dimension in Islam. Its current problems, he says, are neither economic, nor political. They have to do with its vision of history and of the last judgement, its awareness of the perennial human crisis. Contemporary technology necessitates an eschatological reach of apprehension and herein is a common religious task. 'Before repairing again to Medina, it is necessary to dwell long at Mecca.' He goes on: 'Islam ought perhaps to disappear as a historical and political institution, as a structure of community. Only then will the true Muslim be able to be manifest.'[18]

The courage and scope of this conviction are splendid and exciting. But what should they mean when they return us to the inescapable immediacies of politics and economics? Eschatology deals, by definition, with the last things in ultimacy but leaves us with intermediate things in chronology. That 'God is not such as to let faith go in vain' must needs be a present as well as an eschatological confidence, informing a present programme *within* the actual strains of majority–minority tensions and the given sectarianisms of popular religion.

V

In his focus on the human crisis *per se* behind all the exigencies of politics and programmes, Hasan Askari gives notable expression to Islamic prescripts alongside a lively sense of the Christian's relevance. He sees the issue of man in society not, essentially, as one of remaking, or of 'conversion', but rather of 'recollection' and 'recall'.

In Islam, there is no such thing, in principle, as conversion, but restoration, a returning and a remembering . . . The greatest challenge upon this earth is not so much to explore a God, as to remember that there is one.[19]

This is the meaning of that central Quranic term *Dhikr* and it explains the nature and function of revelation and prophethood. This bringing back to mind and into operation, of the human destiny and calling is not correcting any merely mortal forgetfulness. It is not that man is negligent or oblivious merely within life situations now. It has to do with 'the primeval dawn of creation', with the situation often drawn from the sense of Surah 7.172 and God's question to the seed of the children of Adam, 'Am I not your Lord?' to which they all responded: 'Yes, we so acknowledge.' This primal, original professed creaturehood of man within divine obligation is concealed by forgetfulness. The corollary of this is the 'apparent hiddenness of God', as Hasan Askari phrases it. It is to dispel this hiddenness that prophethood is sent, but only in recalling the content of that pledged obedience. In such revelation, Muhammad is uniquely instrumental. To speak of him as 'the seal of the prophets' means that in Islam human forgetfulness has been fully challenged. Thanks to the Qur'ān, man has been made the argument against himself.

It is in this context that Hasan Askari's discussion of the significance of the Cross in Christianity belongs. Yet the case he makes for that significance would seem, at least in Christian reckoning, to tell against the theme that associates revelation with 'recollection'. For it would seem that obduracy in man – to which the Qur'ān bears such strong witness – suggests something more radical, more heinous, than forgetfulness. It seems of indicate a deliberate defiance, a chronic capacity to know the right and yet to do the wrong, to be aware enough of God and His claim and yet to reject it. Much idolatry, Meccan and modern, seems of this order. Hasan Askari himself observes that, historically, Muslims have tended to externalise all crisis, shunning the interior significance of the history through which they pass. There is a feeling of self-justification, of always being in the right. Truth is with us.

Even so, he holds that meditation on the Cross should help Muslims in 'crisis perception'. He sees it as an existential symbol of how tragic the relationship of man to God can be. That tragedy lies in how wilful and selfish men are in their violation of faith. Whether this view can be associated with Kamil Husain's theme of Good Friday as epitomising 'the sin of the world', is not altogether clear. Certainly, in the Qur'ān and Islam, Jesus is 'a sign of how deeply man can deceive himself in the name of God'.[20] On a Quranic view that 'deception' might well include the faith of Christians about the divinity of Jesus. But credal faith apart, the crucifixion of Jesus supremely embodies the dialogical relation between God and men. It sets rejection over against reminder. It is the point where men choose to flout, in the sharpest terms, the sign of recollection that Jesus represents. Jesus has indeed 'become the Word'. As such, he disallows the complacence, if such it be, of the believer in the Word as Qur'ān – that is to say the Muslim who, possessing the manual of written direction, does not continue in 'perpetual openness before his Lord'.

VI

This understanding of the significance of 'the Word made flesh' in Jesus, as Christians understand, belongs with Askari's exposition in *Verse et Controverse* of the respective theologies of revelation. He prefaces this by regretting how, normally, Muslims take the Qur'ān as requiring an anti-Christian stance. Responsively to a Christian 'forthcomingness' about the Qur'ān, he wants Muslims to see Quranic criticism of Christian belief not as a repudiation of something alien but as within a complex of faith having that in common which can contain and reconcile disparity.

Elaborating this viable 'unity' across alternative Scriptures, he suggests that in the Qur'ān God addresses man. This is verbal revelation, divine speech. Scripture is there primal and definitive. *Yā ayyuhā-l-nās*, 'O ye people', *Qul*, 'say' – these are the notes of the Qur'ān, God commanding, exhorting, recalling, the human community.

Jesus, however, is 'the Word made flesh', the Word as personality. Qur'ān and Christ, as the Word, are essentially one. The New Testament, though, in Askari's view, is 'man speaking to God'. The Apostles describe, interpret, memorialise the Word in Jesus, the events of his life, his works and deeds, his words, the manner of his death and the mystery of his Resurrection. All this he calls 'the address of man to God'. He continues:

> I consider this address to be authentic, honest and true. It is just here that Christians and Muslims fail to appreciate the implications and meaning of their respective claims. When Christians call in question or put in doubt the Qur'ān, it is in fact Jesus as the Word of God whom they reject and call in question. To accept Jesus as the Word of God must imply that one accepts all revelation of God, all speech of God addressed to all men of all times. Likewise, when Muslims reject or put in doubt the authenticity of the New Testament, in fact they put in doubt and reject their due response to the God who speaks in the Qur'ān. . . . The Islam of Muslims and the Scripture of Christians are then one and the same thing. Each is response to the Word of God, symbolising man speaking to God.[21]

Both parties need to beware of an idolatry, on the one hand of the written Qur'ān, and on the other of Incarnation.

This formulation serves well to distinguish between the Qur'ān as definitive revelation *qua* Book and the New Testament as derivative from the primary revelatory fact of Jesus as the Christ. But it ignores several important issues belonging with just that dialogical relation between man and God in history which Hasan Askari has made so central to his understanding of man and evil.

The New Testament is, indeed, derivative from the primary fact of Jesus as Himself 'the Word'. But does such derivation warrant its description as 'man addressing God'? The New Testament community constitutes response to God addressing man no less than does Islam responding to Qur'ān. The New Testament is not analogous to the Book of Job, where anguish and faith cry out for light. The New Testament sees and interprets itself as 'the community of recognition', proceeding upon the received Word and translating that receiving into the idiom of daily life within a heathen Roman society.

What it is recognising and translating, in its definitive way, has to do with the events, as Askari sees, of the life, ministry and suffering of Jesus. Its confidence in the fact of revelation belongs with its sense of the significance of history. In this it follows the Biblical, Judaic, instinct to identify in pivotal event authentic experience, and therefore knowledge, of God. Jesus avails them as the divine Word by means of that situational context all the way from Galilee to Gethsemane and what lay beyond Gethsemane. It is 'Him there' as Matthew has it, so graphically, in the supreme hour (Matt. 27:36), as always.

The Qur'ān, too, is situational. The Book, as Hasan Askari rightly insists, is *qua* Book the revelation. But that direct scriptural quality (making it unlike the New Testament) does not preclude the context of time and place. On the contrary, there are the *asbāb al-nuzūl*, the occasions of revelation. There is a gathering story, a sequence of prophetic encounters, a climax of decisive action, a *Hijrah* with prophethood into power. Askari might have us stay long in Mecca rather than rejoin Medina. But there is no doubting that *Hijrah* happened and that Quranic meanings, albeit given into the text by direct mediation of divine speech, are bound up with situations and events apart from which divine address could not find us.

Does not the direct-speech quality of the Qur'ān, then, involve it in a human viability, of the same order as the New Testament, though in its actual content so sharply contrasted? The fact of a historicity is common: the shape of the history quite disparate. Must we not reckon with this before we can say that the Word of God, Qur'ān and Jesus, is 'one'? For Badr and Gethsemane have nothing in common. Have not many Muslims in fact appealed to the different context of Quranic situations to commend them as involving more total, more representative experience of life, in power, statehood, war, politics and action, than was comprised in the contrasted history of Jesus, who neither fought nor reigned, but merely ministered and suffered? It would seem there are issues here which need to be faced before equations of revelation are invoked.

Symbolism, of course, aligns with events and scriptural contexts, and, though it may be transcended, as Hasan Askari argues, in a larger unity within which it moves, it nevertheless perpetuates and enshrines the situational history from which it springs. It cannot well, then, be always read as a unifying element simply because it is a common factor. Its power through the imagination will tend to give emotional sanction to what is disparate in its historical associations and may perhaps fortify satisfaction, rather than arouse awareness, in respect of these.

VII

There are, it is suggested, perhaps two ways in which this issue of the history in which revelation is sited may be resolved. One is the general truth that all religions are a sort of metaphor and it is wise to seek beyond the fact sphere in which their overall meaning is housed. The contemporary crisis in the world ought to free us from issues of historical expression because of its urgent quality confronting us all. In the light of current problems it would be idle and false to press abstract disparities located in the far past.

The other consideration is Hasan Askari's appeal to intention, not to historicity, in identifying the religious meaning, whether of Islam or Christianity. He develops this point primarily in relation to a discussion, among Qur'ān exegetes, of the Quranic narratives and whether or not they correspond with actual history in so far as research or archaeology may be able to ascertain. This thought of intention *qua* meaning, not accuracy *qua* history, is, of course, a familiar point also in Biblical studies. It can be extended to cover not only points of feasible historical verification in detail but the overall character of a prophethood. The circumstantial details of Muhammad's career are part of a perhaps inescapable *Sitz im Leben*. One must go beyond this to the intention – the sole Lordship of God, the reality of judgement, the repudiation of idols, and the claim of social right.

In my opinion, this question [of historical accuracy] is totally inapplicable within a religious perspective. There are two sorts of authenticity, one of fact, the other of intention. The authenticity of all Scriptures falls within the category of intention, which is to arouse the sense of God in the life of persons and of nations. Authenticity of intention is there alike in the literal verses of the Qur'ān and the symbolic. Scientific demands which require to base scriptural accounts of events on factuality fail to reckon with the realm of religious intention.[22]

Whether this distinction between fact and intention can be applied overall, rather than simply in narratives of the Seven Sleepers, or *Yūnus* (Jonah), and the like, is not clear. But the principle is surely extendable and could help to redeem inter-faith controversy from tedium, and home it on to what truly matters. But where revelation is intimately bound up with situations – as it cannot fail to be if it is to reveal – central fact cannot well be excluded from the shape of intention. For events fulfil intention and so disclose what is exemplary and definitive within it. Moreover, in Tradition, events – and so to a degree their factuality – come to condition how intention is to be admired, received, confessed and reproduced. Scriptures that are rooted in contextuality cannot well serve without it. Nevertheless, a focus on the intention of religious documents would go far to deepen and sweeten the converse of their peoples.

VIII

The final area of Hasan Askari's thought is his question 'What is the religious implication of the multi-religious world?' If God, in the words of Surah 2.143, is not such as to let our faith go in vain, how is its vindication to be related to its 'competitors' (if we so see them), its coexistents, its partners, or its dissociators? Perhaps religious diversity is mystically one, though mysticism, he thinks, may evade the challenge of communal relationships between majority and minority faiths in the concrete. He sees a basic unity of revelation, culminating in Islam as *Dīn Allāh*, 'the natural religion' for which God fashioned man (Surah 30.30). But this ultimacy is capable of being consistent with diversity, and even contradiction, if these are held within the emotive cultural dimensions of faith and/or the cognitive systems by which they proceed.

Each has to recognise the vocation to interrelationship, pursuit of which must itself generate the solutions, intellectual and spiritual, which it requires. The sense of universality emerges from experience subsequent to the formulations in origins. Relating means a struggle within the self-consciousness of each. In this connection the concept of *bid'ah*, or heresy, or innovation, must be watched since it may stifle sensitivity. Nor must we plead too readily a sort of *Jāhiliyyah*, sharply exempting debts and contacts from our story, past or present.

It may be remarked here, in parenthesis, that the Qur'ān and the New Testament differ in respect of this feature about ongoing experience within the very definition of religion. The Qur'ān passes definitively into the future of Islam. It was complemented by Tradition of Muhammad and by *Qiyās* and *Ijmā'*. But, while these operated strictly within its prescripts, they were outside its contents. By contrast, the New Testament enshrines, in its Gospels and Epistles, the active assimilation by its communities of the significance of Jesus as 'the Word'. Such assimilation participates vitally in the documentation itself and, though much work in Christian faith formulation was transacted beyond it, the creative part happens within it. It follows that whereas urgent theological and moral issues arose for Islam outside the given text of the Qur'ān, the basic Christian ones are incorporated in the Scripture itself. This results, of course, from the difference on which Askari comments so perceptively, between 'the Word as Book' and 'the Word as Personality'.

This parenthesis apart, how are we to envisage the present and future interaction of Muslims and Christians? Hasan Askari believes there is an inherent mutual attraction between the two religions, indeed between all religions. 'Distance' and 'repulsion' arise from symbols rather than from essentials. Symbols can be regarded as mainly functional and not, therefore, worthy to justify or retain postures of enmity. Even antipathy over symbols may coexist with empathy and amity. We must realise that historical revelations, with their 'intention', are necessarily within cultural particularity. They employ given languages and presuppose given *mores*. Through sustained and mutual openness these can be transcended so that, while transacting meanings, they do not imprison these and so perpetuate enmity.

Few thinkers in contemporary Islam have so tellingly explored the issues of inter-religion or undertaken them as a strong vocation. Hasan Askari holds a unique position in the search for unity of heart within the discrepancies, real or unreal, of religions in society. Yet there are puzzles that persist. For him, 'the Christian answer about omnipotence and suffering resolves the paradox of Job, but at the cost of the transcendental aspect of God'. 'Did Islam, restoring the transcendental aspect, bring back the contradictions?' For, in Islam, 'God is not negated by negation, nor proven by proof, nor delighted by obedience, nor displeased by sins, nor merciful to the believer, nor disgusted with the forgetful . . . nor hostile to the arrogant. He is above all associations.'[23] How, then, is He *Al-Raḥmān*, how is He *Al-Shakūr*, how is He *Al-Quddūs*? Can we not rather be sure that what is transcendental and what is relational, in God, are indeed one? Then omnipotence is not compromised in love, and love is not foregoing omnipotence. Paradox, either way, there must needs be. The paradox of compassion is to be preferred to the paradox of exemption and aloofness. Or so it would seem, if indeed God is of such sort as to justify our faith (2.143).

NOTES: CHAPTER 7

1 See Chapter 8, note 6.
2 Hasan Askari, *Inter-Religion* (Aligarh, 1977), p. 108. The writer, born in India in 1932, was appointed to the Chair of Sociology at Osmania University at the early age of 25.
3 For example Peter Berger, *A Rumour of Angels* (London, 1969) and *The Heretical Imperative* (New York, 1979). Even more important, Werner Stark, *Sociology of Religion: A Study of Christendom* (London and New York, 1966).
4 The term *ikhlāṣ* and derivatives, like *mukhliṣūn lahu al dīn*, 'sincere before Him in religion', are frequent and central in the Qur'ān. The term is the title of the significant Surah 112, on divine Unity. What is 'sound' as to belief must be operative in what is sound in character. The antonym is *nifāq*, or dissembling, which is constantly reproached in the Qur'an.
5 See *Christians Meeting Muslims* (Geneva, WCC 1977), no. 1.3, pp. 21–31. Wider discussion in *Living Faiths and Ultimate Goals* (Geneva, 1974), in which Hasan Askari has a paper, 'Unity and alienation in Islam', pp. 45–55.
6 Muhammad al-Nuwaihi (d. 1980) in a privately published paper.
7 For example, by Franz Rosenzweig in *The Star of Redemption*, trans. from the German by W. W. Hallo (London, 1970).
8 Notably James Parkes, *The Foundations of Judaism and Christianity* (London, 1960) and *Voyages of Discoveries* (London, 1969).
9 *Inter-Religion*, p. 32.
10 ibid. In this context, Askari quotes F. Schuon, *Understanding Islam*, trans. from the French by D. M. Matheson (London, 1963), pp. 22–4.
11 See, further, the present writer's *The Mind of the Qur'ān* (London, 1973), ch. 9.
12 *Inter-Religion*, p. 51.
13 ibid., pp. 45 and 48.
14 See *Journal of Ecumenical Studies*, Philadelphia, vol. 17, no. 1 (winter, 1980), pp. 117–19.
15 *Inter-Religion*, pp. 57, 81, 82.
16 Surah 2.143: *Mā kāna Allāhu li yuḍīʿa īmānakum* – 'God is not the one to make your faith vain' or '. . . let it go to waste' or '. . . make it to prove futile'. The verb has also the sense of 'to lose sight of', and so 'to let go by default'. The change of the Muslim direction of prayer was initially a quite traumatic event for the first Muslims trained to think of Muhammad as heir to all the prophets of One God and, therefore, loyal to Jerusalem.
17 Y. Moubarac, *Verse et controverse: les musulmans* (Paris, 1971), p. 132. Trans. from the French by this writer.
18 ibid., p. 133.
19 *Inter-Religion*, p. 18.
20 ibid., pp. 40 and 67. See also *Verse et controverse*, p. 129.
21 *Verse et controverse*, pp. 130–1.
22 ibid., pp. 131–2.
23 *Inter-Religion*, pp. 77 and 74.

8

Muhammad Kamil Husain of Cairo

I

'As I walked through the wilderness of this world, I lighted on a certain place and laid me down to sleep.' So begins John Bunyan's famous story of *The Pilgrim's Progress*, the most translated of all English writings. It was written during twelve years in an English gaol when Bunyan was a prisoner of conscience. His words may suggest a different introduction to another quite contrasted theme of pilgrimage and progress.

'As I moved around in the hospital of this world, I lighted upon a certain clinic and took up my pen to charter how patients might progress towards purity and peace.' Muhammad Kamil Husain never penned just those words. But they may well serve to introduce him. He was a distinguished Egyptian surgeon and a medical practitioner. Many of his analogies were drawn from his profession. His books, he said, were 'my medical outlook on the future of religion'. He believed that the lower laws of chemistry and biology could be developed to yield sure guidance for human psychology, ethics and society. It was as a therapeutic that he was deeply interested in religion. Faith, for him, was not essentially a credal assent, but an attitude of will, a prescription for right personality. His understanding of the transcendent was psychological and he was deeply committed to a culture of science as the clue to the future. Since all his major writings can be seen as a sincere exercise in therapy, it is no loose metaphor to see him in 'the hospital of this world'. He was concerned with people, young and perplexed, old and anxious, orthodox or secular, as calling for the healing art.

All this means, of course, that he was a most unusual representative of Islam, with novel and radical views on what should be understood by the finality of the Prophet, the place of the Qur'ān, the role of power and the state, the meaning of *Tauḥīd*. Had he been a professional theologian, and not a highly respected 'lay' professional, with wide academic and literary interests, he might well have incurred bitter hostility and persecution.

He was the son of an Arabic teacher and small farmer in the village of Sabq, in Manūfiyyah Province of Egypt, who died when he was three. His mother moved to Cairo three years later. He had a devout upbringing and was much influenced by an uncle who was a keen disciple of the Grand Muftī, Muhammad Abduh (d. 1905). His early promise ripened into medical studies, first in France and then in England, where he was introduced also to the rationalism of Auguste Comte, whose theory of a human evolution through superstition, metaphysics and, finally, scientific positivism impressed him. His Islamic roots, however, enabled him to reserve a 'scientific' role for religion within the scientific confidence of Comte's rationalism. He was also affected by the political tensions in Egypt in the twenties, and by the massive futility of warfare in Europe. The problems of peace were to be with him deeply throughout his career. He contributed articles for a time to *Al-Siyāsah al-Usbūʿiyyah*, under the pen name of Ibn Sīnā, mainly on questions of society and public health. He was Professor, first of General Surgery, then of Orthopaedic Surgery, in Cairo University. He was for a brief period Rector of Ain al-Shams University, resigning in 1952, to take up private practice and his many interests in literature, archaeology, the history of medicine, and the reform of Arabic. He was a member of the prestigious Muhammad Ali Club, the Arab Academy and the Higher Committee of Al-Azhar. His writings earned him the unique distinction of state prizes for both literature and science.

During his student days in Europe, and in the forties, he kept a diary in which he recorded his response to the impact of the West and to the significance of world war.[1] He was convinced that Western experience would more and more decide both the pattern and the pace of change in every other culture. So he assured the Academy of the Arabic Language in a lecture before it in 1952,[2] a far cry indeed from *Gharbzadegi* with its anathema of all things foreign. His confidence in the future of a scientific culture was accompanied by a distaste for, if not a distrust in, the ways of politicians. There is a remarkable absence of political emotion, and certainly of comment on things political, in all his writings and in conversation he was not easily drawn into discussion. His distance from politics stemmed, as we must see below, from his commitment to personal healing and to the progress of souls. Seeing the human predicament as a hospital meant, among other things, that it was neither a chess-board nor a cockpit. Politics, he thought, stood very low in the hierarchy of human activities.

In that very un-Islamic stance, he was perhaps motivated in part by prudence, as well as by preference. He was at home characteristically in the clinic – the clinic he ran after professorial retirement in Shari'a Sabry Abu Alam in Cairo, greeting, diagnosing, treating his clients with his expertise and enlarging that practice of the healing art into a parable of his vocation to society. His imaginative writing and his philosophy are those of a diagnostician perceptively engaging with the human world according to the lights he had received from the sources he trusted, but informed always by a sense of compassion and obligation, taught by his reading of Islam. At the conclusion of his major work he wrote:

> I have talked with you at great length and expounded many things that have to do with your very soul, not presuming to ask the question: 'Who are you?' Now that I have come to the end, I feel that I have been talking to myself.[3]

Inward soliloquy, responding to outward concern, is the most honest form of religious commitment, however unorthodox in its conclusions. Unorthodox, to the point almost of incomprehension among the rigorists, Muhammad Kamil Husain certainly was. Muslims able to appreciate the implications of his position might well question his being Islamic at all. Yet his pastoral approach to people and to faith, though disconcerting to many in the political and doctrinal preoccupations of Islam around him, recovered and renewed some basic themes of Quranic vocabulary. If religious loyalty consists in probing gently and deeply into its own meaning there can be no doubt of it here, however deviant the findings may be.

It is useful to explore Muhammad Kamil Husain's thought and writing in five areas: his understanding of the nature of faith; his consequent attitude to the Qur'ān as revelation; his estimate of institutional religion; the position he took in respect of inter-faith relations; and his concern with pacificism and the issues of peace and war. In every particular we find him a kind of Socratic Muslim, eager for debate, starting from lively assumptions, testing them in the stimulus of encounter, and liable to provoke in order to persuade.

II

The analogy of a Copernican revolution has often been suggested in recent discussion of religion, to do with faith what Copernicus did with astronomy. Kamil Husain had very much this idea. The *taqwā* which Fazlur Rahman understands as a human awe before the face of God, a responsive awareness of an inescapable obligation, Husain interprets in precisely the reverse direction. It remains real and insistent, but it is no longer an order from God: it is a longing from man to God. 'God' in this new understanding is no longer the transcendent 'Other', the objective counterpart to man's 'commandedness', 'the Lord of the worlds'. Rather 'it' is the 'pole' of the good to which man is inwardly and cosmically 'attracted', within what might be likened to a magnetic field of awareness. Religion is response within the human psyche to this cosmic awareness and all morality, righteousness and truth derive from this reality understood as implicit in our human nature. Husain's confidence in this interpretation springs from his commitment to scientific rationalism and his intuition that the laws governing the physical universe indicate a comparable structure of reality in the spiritual order, so that principles found operative in the one can be confidently extrapolated to the other.

This, he believes, is a very Islamic conception. For, as the historian Ranke liked to observe, 'all men are equidistant from God' – a saying Husain took to mean that to be human is to have this psychic *taqwā* which makes us liable to, and answerable for, cosmic conformities of right and wrong. The force that aligns the needle to its pole similarly orients the mind and spirit of man to absolute claims requiring to be fulfilled within the human situation. Husain's commitment to scientific criteria meant that religious truth could not be grounded in other than psychic law seen as constitutive of the human soul. Given his empirical view, truth – in areas such as those of faith, where proof via the senses was impossible – could not be located other than in belief about it. Truth and faith would have to be a sort of continuum, the one validating the other. Religious meaning could not be separated from religious believing and religious believing could only be grounded in human nature.

It is clear that much of the impetus to Kamil Husain's thought sprang from his sense of religious indifferentism and the increasing scepticism among the educated. He was concerned that many were tempted by the sophistication of the secular mood to dismiss the significance of faith in near contempt for its dogmas. He had a lively mind for the pressures on the young in coping with the confusions of the day and in surviving both the blandishments of the worldly and the tyrannies of the dogmatic. Nevertheless, it would be mistaken to think that his writing was merely a tactical response to the problems of education. It was the fruit of his positive reflection on the nature of *homo religiosus*. However, an ironist might say that his positivism was as much open to question as the dogmatisms from which it was meant to rescue a right faith. For, as Rudolf Otto had to concede in his *The Idea of the Holy*, he had no answer for those minded to dispute his basic premise that man *was* religious in the sense required.[4]

Kamil Husain had ingenious medical metaphors to sustain his case. Did not the heart, in the body, possess inhibitory mechanisms to signal danger and suggest caution when its functioning was being over-charged? Could not conscience be so understood? Did not the individual need to be slowed down, to be checked and brought to desist, when overstretching himself into cupidity or false ambition, or – in their pursuit – some false reckoning with truth, some flouting of ethical value and social responsibility? The physical check to what was destructive or harmful to the heart, by the heart, had its parallel in the moral personality. Conscience was its name. Such precious built-in precautions in nature should not be jeopardised by rejection. Similarly the precious 'governor', faith, vital as it was to soul well-being, should not be burdened or clogged by doctrinal minutiae, its facility risked by extraneous arguments. It was its operability that mattered within an ideally self-regulating system.

Or – to change the medical analogy – was there not a common physical misfortune, known as 'deprivation' or deficiency in some vital chemical element, the lack of which, though easily corrected, could have dire consequences for general health? Could religion, then, be the thyroid extract to cure the world of myxoedemia?[5] Might there not be 'psychotonics' like biotonics, hormones and vitamins for the soul? Was there arguably a religious counterpart to iodine? At all events, there were plenty of failed alternative 'medicines' offered to sufferers from deficiency. Permissiveness was one. But, as a cure for boredom or life disease, it was totally unsatisfactory, indeed counterproductive. It generated only satiety and futility and left the sufferer even more chronically ill. Moderation was surely the clue to happiness, and how were moderation, modesty, contentment and serenity – those hallmarks of soul health – more likely to be attained than by understanding them to be the very psychic secret of the soul's own 'mechanisms' to be wisely elucidated and put to work by the discerning therapist? Was not this the true orbit of 'theology'?

The analogy suggested to Husain a further important consideration. The remedial psychotonic must be properly dosed. Enough was enough. Faith, in these terms, need not, should not, be excessive. Fanaticism overreached itself. Medicinal faith should be strictly confined to medicinal functions. Bigotry was not one of these. Rather it was excess of religion, whether in dominating authority or exclusivist pride, that had brought it into disrepute and contributed to the world's malaise. Such excess was closely linked to what Husain saw as the outmoded concepts of the divine. These he sought to replace. They would be avoided if we could see ethical and religious attitudes as a law of our own physiology.

Just as we had to understand rightly what we meant by the divine as the correlative of our psychic make-up, so we must truly appreciate our responsive behaviour. This meant that 'sin' should no longer be items in a catalogue of 'specifics' which were necessarily absolute for all persons at all times, or even for the same person at different times. Too much had been made in classical ethics of 'thou shalts' and 'thou shalt nots' when the enjoining or inhibiting within these ought rather to be inward and flexible. This was to avoid that arbitrary diktat of the rule and the veto, which disallowed the proper responsiveness of the individual soul to its own awareness of the magnetic field of good and the right. That same arbitrariness also contributed to a blunting of the very faculties on which it avoided to rely. It was right to sense and cultivate a direct and personal relation to the transcendental.

III

It might seem that in this radical reordering of religion and of faith little room would remain for the Qur'ān, at least in terms of the traditional understanding of *Waḥy* and *Tafsīr*. The 'Copernican revolution' would appear to counter belief in guidance sent from above by its version of obligation deriving from within. The pole of an attraction is different from the word of the Lord. Yet there are several senses in which Kamil Husain may feel himself still within the Quranic field, though it is true that he does not widely quote its texts.

In the first place he recognises the actuality of faith in the Qur'ān in the Muslim context. In the case of believers untroubled by doubts or secular pressures, he acknowledges that their confidence in the Qur'ān, on the traditional basis of a divine gift, may avail them as the way they register their sense of truth and value. If such faith operates effectively for them, he has no wish to turn them into doubters or to disturb their assurance. Its 'truth' will be its efficacy in *their* case. This in no ways suits the book of orthodox Islam and certainly represents an unwarranted 'pragmatism' in evaluating the Islamic Scripture.

There is a further sense in which he validates revelation on his own terms and, so doing, dismays the pundits. It is in allowing that prophethood may be seen as, so to speak, a superlative form of the 'polarity' lesser mortals experience more dimly and erratically. *Waḥy* then emerges as what happens when there is a response to the transcendental on the part of human psyches uniquely sensitive thereto. Scripture makes this response comprehensible by less endowed members of the human family. It helps people to express faith. Its prophetic figures exemplify that purity of heart which is the goal of the religious quest. This psychic relevance of Scripture makes the notion of an infallible status or an inerrant text superfluous, unless those items of credence about it in fact contribute to the attainment of inner peace by this or that believer. Such 'success', however, in those cases in no way warrants the demand that it should be universally or categorically assumed to operate.

It was on this and other counts that Kamil Husain was sharply opposed to all attempts to give the Qur'ān a pseudo-scientific reading as if it were abreast of the findings of modern technology. He devoted a strongly worded essay on this theme in his *Miscellany (Mutanawwi'āt)*, Vol. 2, under the title: *Al-Tafsīr al-'Ilmī lī-l-Qur'ān Bid'ah Hamqā'*, 'Scientific Exegesis of the Qur'ān – a Stupid Heresy'. He suspected that the habit arose from a sense of the prestige of science and a desire to let the Qur'ān bask in it. But to defend *Tanzīl* in this way was perverse and futile. The Qur'ān's innocence of scientific knowledge was in no way to its discredit. It was a religious Book. Facile claims to scientific lore within it, anticipating time's inventions, would not impress genuine scientists and could only bring the exegetes into disrepute and ridicule. After instancing several far-fetched examples of their ingenuity over radar, relativity, democracy, atom-splitting, and the like, he expressed the hope that he had banished the folly of it for good and all.[6]

This robust rejection of what he believed to be misguided in the veneration of the Qur'ān enabled him to celebrate more freely those aspects of it which coincided with his sense of its religious efficacy within its Islamic community. This he did, for example, in a long essay in *Miscellany*, Vol. 1, headed by the words from 12.2, 20.113 (cf. 42.7, 43.3): 'We have sent it down an Arabic Qur'ān.' He hailed its linguistic quality as possessing an incommunicable beauty. Initially it was 'a thing heard', not a thing read or perused. Its literary excellence had to be appreciated by the ear. He rejoiced in the descriptive power of the Qur'ān in Surahs like *Al-Qamr* (54) and *Al-Raḥmān* (55) or verses like 11.44 – 'O earth swallow thy waters, and O heaven desist!' – in the narrative of Noah. The surpassing beauties of the Qur'ān belonged eloquently with the Arabs of the desert. Its essentially verbal character was of an utterly different order from the decorative art of Christendom with angels around the Virgin's throne. He concluded:

It seems to me that if those who discusss the Qur'ān who are non-Muslims would study it in all sincerity from this angle they would surely find no word to describe its secret authentically than to say that it was divine revelation.[7]

But by the same token he knew that the impact of the Qur'ān, for a time and a temper so different from that of the seventh-century Arabian desert-dwellers, would have to be its content. Others would never be reciters 'to the manner born'. Here his instinct was to move and plead from certain salient terms in its vocabulary from which he could draw the meanings which coincided with his overall philosophy of faith as a human phenomenon. Some of these like *ẓulm* and *fitnah* belong below in the discussion of his position in respect of the politics of religion. Those which concern us in this section, relating to inner faith, may be illustrated from three examples, namely *dhikr*, *ṭahārah*, and *iṭmi'nān* – 'reminder', 'purity', and 'serenity'.

Husain devoted a whole study to the first, in *Al-Dhikr al-Ḥakīm*,[8] or 'The Wise Mentor'. The term is one of the titles of the Qur'ān itself as well as the name of the familiar 'liturgy' of Sufi devotion used in quest of the mystical experience of absorption into God. Kamil Husain grafted the term into his pattern of *islām* as a realised personal responsiveness to the divine 'pull' of transcendent obligation, in free alignment with which human nature is truly fulfilled. The association of thought is not hard to seek. 'Reminding' implies something innate in the soul to which appeal can be made. This is the sensitivity on which he placed such reliance, provided it was not 'deprived', or numbed or discounted. But that which addresses and recruits it is of its own order. As in an echo, the call and response are reciprocal. This explains why the Qur'ān can be called *Al-Dhikr*, both in its source as God's voice and in its recital by the believer who, in recital, acknowledges his human meaning. 'So remember Me: I remember you,' says Surah 2.152.

The term is very frequent throughout the Qur'ān and is closely linked with the phenomenon of prophethood itself. 'He remembered the Name of his Lord and prayed' (87.15). 'O you who believe, remember God intensely and worship Him by dawn and by evening' (33.42). 'Remember the Name of your Lord and be His unreservedly', in 73.8, comes in the immediate context of Muhammad's early vocation. The Arabic of 'Be His unreservedly' occurs uniquely in this verse and calls for just that uncomplicated quality of integrity which Husain prized as the index of right religion and truth of soul.[9]

It was here he focused on his favourite theme of 'purity'. In fact the root *ṭahara*, with its noun *ṭahārah*, are relatively rare in the Qur'ān, though *Ṭahārat al-Qulūb*, 'Purity of Hearts', is one of the most celebrated manuals of personal religion in Islam.[10] But 'cleansing', sometimes in the sense of 'vindication', is notable in reference to the prophets (cf. 3.42 of Mary, 3.55 of Jesus, 22.26 of Abraham summoned to purify God's house at Mecca as a true sanctuary, 74.4 of Muhammad told to 'purify his robes' as the symbol of his calling, and 33.33, the verse central to Shī'ah Islam concerning 'the purified' of Muhammad's family, the first Imams). Surah 5.41 refers to 'those whose hearts God did not desire to purify'. *Zakāt*, too, the vital duty of alms-giving, is closely associated with the purifying of possessions and of possessors, a legitimisation of property by the fact of responsibility. In Surah 9.103 purification is achieved by the eliciting of alms.

There is thus no doubt of the centrality of the concept of purity in the Qur'ān and Kamil Husain made it the crucial theme in his *Al-Wādī al-Muqaddas*, 'The Hallowed Valley', which might well be character-ised as a Muslim study on Kierkegaard's familiar saying: 'Purity of heart is to will one thing.'[11] Where Moses was commanded, 'Take off thy shoes: for thou art in the sacred valley' (20.12), Husain places the summons to man to awareness of his whole being, 'situate' in the 'field' of transcendental obligation with its call to self-realisation via spiritual response.

> The hallowed valley is the place on earth, the point in time, the state of mind, where you reach upward beyond the form of external things, beyond your own nature and the necessities of life, and even beyond the bounds of intellect. . . . It is where your hopes are altogether good and your dreams worthy, having no springs of evil willed by you or willed against you . . . In the hallowed valley you hear the voice of conscience, clear and plain, enjoining upon you unconfusedly the obligations of the good, and leading you undeviatingly towards the truth – conscience as the very voice of God.[12]

Two twin Quranic ideas are implicit in such *Ṭahārah* of the self. They are the supersession of doubt and the correction of deviation. *Raibah* and *dalāl*, dubiety and wandering, are very common topics in the Qur'ān, which at the outset in Surah 2.2 declares itself 'a Book in which there is nothing dubious'. But, whereas that *Yaqīn*, or certainty, is normally understood in terms of inerrancy of text and finality of truth, in Husain it denotes that identifying mark of a pure conscience, namely that it possesses an inner, confirmatory peace. Likewise, *dalāl* – a major chapter heading in *The Hallowed Valley* – is not meant in the usual sense of pagan misguidedness, the error of the polytheists, and the like. There can even be a Muslim 'misguidedness', too, as the fanatics demonstrate. It means, rather, the waywardness, the boredom, the deceptive satiety, or the oscillation of soul, when the needle of the human spirit is not yet fixed on its true 'north'.

Religion, in the proper sense, is the necessary context and condition of this 'purity of heart'. When religion does not achieve it or actively disserves it, such religion, however prestigious in its claims, is false and unworthy. The only tests of its 'truth' are its attainments in souls. Teleology, in the intellectual sense of finding rational 'ends' in the scheme of things and so reaching 'proofs' of God, must be disallowed. The only purpose, or purposefulness, which we can allow in the world is this of soul welfare. This is what Kamil Husain means by the banishment of metaphysics, in order that religious 'truth' may be limited to its proper domain in the soul. It may be asked whether a due cognisance of the circumambient world of nature and the sciences, and so of metaphysics formulating such cognisance, is not integral to the interests of the soul – not to say implicit in the Quranic doctrine of the *āyāt*, or 'signs'. But such is Husain's concentration on his therapy-faith, or his faith-therapy, that he does not admit such widening perspective.

> The making of your own self is the most definitive thing in your life. Everything that goes with this shaping of yourself is to be considered sure and decisive in your case, while all that is contrary to it is not for you to be guided by.[13]

Intellectualism cannot add to that psychic crux of things, nor detract from it once attained. Nor is the love of beauty a final criterion and certainly not doctrinal authority, unless these happen to serve the end. Turning to the *Fātiḥah*, Husain observes:

> There is nothing in this prayer: ('Guide us in the straight path etc.') to prevent our seeing the source of the guidance in the believer's own soul, with God as its focal point. 'The straight path' would then be the road that links God and the soul of the believer undeviatingly. There is nothing to preclude our understanding the wrath of God ('not the path of those on whom Thy anger rests') as some lack in the nature of man, preventing him from being guided effectively by the divine authority.[14]

IV

Ṭahārah, or purity of heart, so attained, means a state of *iṭmi'nān*, a Quranic term ready to hand to denote this state of cleansed and healed and settled benediction. The root word indicates being at rest, calm and quiet, free from stress and anxiety. Surah 13.28 asks: 'Is it not in the mention of God [*dhikr Illāhi*] that hearts are at rest?' (cf. Surahs 3.126, 5.113, 8.10). Muhammad is addressed in 89.27 as 'soul at rest', and that quality of inward peace is contrasted with 'the soul prone to evil' in the story of Yūsuf (Joseph and his temptation in 12.53) and 'the soul in self-reproach' of Surah 75.2. These three states of the soul have often been cited by the Sufis as stages on the way from sin, through repentance, to rest and peace. The last is *iṭmi'nān*. Kamil Husain identifies this Quranic theme with the blessedness which flows from the harmony of the soul with the purpose of God, a quality of personal being no longer distracted by vain desire or deceived by false ideas. *Iṭmi'nān* is the goal of divine therapy.

He assures his readers that it is within their reach, given their will to heed the errors which impede its attainment and to follow the claims it requires. This is his interior version of the familiar 'enjoining the good and forbidding the evil' which Muslim moralists have drawn from the Qur'ān. For Husain, however, it is not an external injunction implying a sort of subservience that can only submit. Nor is it an absolute that speaks the language of institutional authority. It belongs with an inner awareness suited to response, as the flower opens to the sun or the tides to the pull of the moon. Its norms may vary from person to person, according to their psychic nature. So they cannot be arbitrarily imposed via dogma or tradition. These may serve to foster it, if the individual finds them congenial. But, if not, he should not worry, or reproach himself for being sceptical in respect of them. He should look, in that case, for those factors which suit his mentality. 'The good things outweigh the evil things', in the words of one of his direct quotations (Surah 11.114) when 'all things are bathed in the light of faith'.[15]

Our response to the pole of the divine and the good makes for *iṭmi'nān* also in loosening us from the fear that besets our mortality and our precarious life. It also makes good the incompetence of reason, limited as that faculty is – in Husain's view – to the perceptible world and, therefore, unable to serve our confusions and perplexities about areas outside our sense experience. It is also a refuge against the social and economic inequalities of the world. It equips us to transcend what would otherwise be the ennui or disquiet stemming from that old puzzlement of the psalmist, namely the apparent prosperity of evil men. It also preserves us from deceptive desires and teaches us to avoid petulant excuses. It occupies us in that quality of reaction in which true dignity is found. Invoking the *Qiblah*, or direction of prayer in Islam as a parable, Kamil Husain sees purity and inner peace as the reward of the human soul on 'the axis of attraction', oriented towards God.[16]

V

Though there are significant differences between Husain's version of *islām* and the patterns of Buddhism, they have certain resemblances, not least a comparable preoccupation with the personal self and the soul life of the individual. Given the analogy of the patient and the hospital with which we began, it could hardly be otherwise. But Kamil Husain is realist enough about personal *ṭahārah* and *iṭmi'nān* not to ignore the problematics of society and of human collectives. In this area of his thinking, too, he is intriguingly exceptional as a Muslim writer. For Islam, broadly speaking, has a very hopeful view of the power structure, a vital role for the state, and a strong instinct for the collective – on condition that all these are properly Islamic. From its origins it has married the religious and the political in a confident match.

Kamil Husain, by contrast, has a lively suspicion of collectives and communities. Conscience is never collective. Institutions acquire vested interests and have a way of multiplying by compound interest the selfishnesses of private persons, unchecked by any restraints of conscience once they have passed into the public domain. In *The Hallowed Valley*, he wrote:

The effect of individual purity on the refining of the relations between man and the community is less than its influence within the person himself. As for its impact on the inter-relationship of communities – that is a frail thing and hardly to be depended on.[17]

Ten years earlier he had turned his attention to the problem of institutional religion in the most striking of his works, *Qaryah Ẓālimah*, or *City of Wrong*.[18] Once again he based himself on a familiar Quranic concept, that of *ẓulm*, or wrongdoing, and applied a reference in the Qur'ān to 'a wrongdoing community' (lit. 'village') in Surah 21.11 to the city of Jerusalem on the day of the crucifixion of Jesus. Here, at the heart of a people priding themselves on the most lofty religion and of an empire preening itself on justice, was perpetrated nevertheless a deed of iniquitous *ẓulm*, an act of rejection of the good, fit to be described as 'the darkest day in human history'. He used his power of imaginative narrative to develop a profound indictment of human society and its collective ways, with clear, if tangential, references to Islam and *its* implication in its own sphere. *City of Wrong* is thus a remarkable document of Muslim self-criticism in a context from the New Testament.

The idea of linking the theme of *ẓulm*, on which he had long reflected,[19] with the central event of the New Testament came to him during a train journey on the way to Venice. He might have used the story of Socrates, rather than that of Jesus, to depict the human perversity of 'establishments'. He felt that the event of the Cross generated a much deeper feeling and this, more than any strong theological reason, decided his choice. But, having made it, he found himself closely related with Christian readers who thought of the book in terms wider than he had intended. Its translation into English in fact aroused great interest because, for the first time in modern Islam, it dealt intelligently with the central event in Christian experience and did not allow prejudice or superficial reading of the Qur'ān to write off that event as either unhistorical or negligible. He saw that within the Qur'ān's own terms the death of Jesus was a reality in the intentions of his hostile community, whatever might be understood by the phrase in Surah 4.157, that 'it was only apparently so to them'. This insight was very salutary, since so many, both Muslims and Christians, had failed to realise its implications. When pressed by Christian inquiry to elucidate what he thought that 'apparentness' really meant, and how we should understand the meaning of 'but God raised him to Himself', Kamil Husain preferred to offer no explicit answer but, by a comparison with Christian faith in the 'Ascension' of Christ, referred his questioners to 'the frontier between time and eternity', between history and metahistory.

Important as these aspects of *Qaryah Ẓālimah* were, and significant for Muslim–Christian discourse, they were not the primary purpose of the presentation of Jesus, his adversaries and their counsels of violence, his disciples and their reactions. The central point of *City of Wrong* was the thesis that the vested interests of collectives, of political structures, always tend towards injustice and tyranny. So tending, they demand to override the scruples of personal conscience – scruples which as corporate entities they are incapable of registering. It follows that the only check, frail as it must be, to the wrongdoing of states and parties and institutions is the resistance of individual conscience. The private person must refuse to do, in the name of some collective loyalty, what he would refrain from doing in his individual capacity. Kamil Husain felt his point was proved in the very way in which the structure with the vested interests kills off this private conscience. It does this because in massive, collective evils, like war and exploitation, the individual share is either so minuscule as to be untraceable to any particular responsibility, or so fragmentary as to be no longer culpable.[20] When you and I can no longer be linked with the guilt we can think we are absolved. Or the vested interest makes the victim anonymous. He is just the 'enemy', the person outside our pale, the non-human, the cipher we are 'justified' in killing or exploiting. He is never a fellow being whom we really 'look in the eye' or see 'face to face'. In these and other reprehensible ways, the collective literally suborns our conscience, gets its evil will done, and suppresses, in force, or propaganda, or loyalty claims, or sheer irresistibility, the personal conscience which is its only available check and curb. Conscience cannot be collectivised. Therefore collectives are prone to evil-doing.

It is important to appreciate what an unusual stance this is for a Muslim writer. For Islam historically and instinctively makes the political arm, the state structure, and the collective will, the central agents of the right society and the religious truth. Muhammad had no compunction about the legitimacy of force and called upon the private Muslim to make over his personal conscience to the common will. In the Qur'ān those who were dubious about battles and campaigns were seen as either slothful or cowardly, letting their scruples weaken their nerve or allowing their domestic love of peace to become a *fitnah*, or temptation, to them.[21] Allied to this demand for a ready personal identity with the corporate interest was a confident assumption of the innocence of power when exercised in the name of that corporate interest, understood as divinely chartered proxy for the divine will itself. There could hardly be a more questioning and questionable Islam than that of Kamil Husain, thus acutely critical of the ruling dimension of his religion.

He was concerned, too, with the parallel assumption of divine mandate implicit in the Judaic concept of a chosen people – a mandate having priority over moral considerations or assumedly immune from moral responsibility about what such mandated chosenness might involve in respect of the common humanness of those outside it. Though germane to the current political scene in which he lived, there is little evidence that Husain applied this to his country's relationship with Zionist Israel. But his choice of the trial and condemnation of Jesus makes it clear that he saw the Judaic sense of divine legitimacy analogous, in its different idiom, to the Islamic.

In either case, he saw personal purity of heart necessarily at issue with the claim of a collective invocation of rights warranted by God. The lesson, for him, was that each and all should be wary and perceptive about their 'intention', or *niyyah* (a very Islamic caution), when using the words 'In the Name of God', lest the invocation should, in fact, denote 'in the name of us'.

Another fascinating aspect of *Qaryah Ẓālimah* was the author's study of the disciples of Jesus caught in the same dilemma about the justification of force. He described them in council after the arrest of Jesus, in tense debate about a forcible rescue of their master. The argument covers familiar Islamic ground. The cause deserves what it costs; survival is the first condition of all else; the enemies are false and base; they cannot be allowed to succeed; killing is a lesser evil than *fitnah*, that is, foul conspiracy. All these points are urged in the conclave and argued throughout with Quranic support. But other disciples, wavering and perplexed, urge that Jesus had forbidden expressly all forcible action in his name. Perhaps, though, faced with mortal peril, he might change his mind. Husain contrives to have them get a message to Jesus and the answer comes back that on no account are they to shed blood, or use force, on his behalf. The cause is greater than the adversaries. God reigns. It is almost as if the writer is disqualifying basic Islamic attitudes by weighing and rejecting them in the setting of the central drama of the New Testament.

Husain believes that the continuing self-reproach and bewilderment of the disciples constitutes the traumatic event which 'defines' Christianity. The disciples cannot divest themselves of an abiding sense of guilt about what happened to Jesus and a desperate perplexity about their whole role in the crisis, somehow paralysed as they were by the will of Jesus himself and yet unreconciled to his commitment to love and to peace. This trauma he sees as with the Christian still, just as the trauma of Exodus 'defines' the Judaic spirit, and the crisis of *Hijrah* makes the Muslim soul. This, of course, is to exclude the Resurrection, as interpretation must, if it remains within the unresolved ambiguity of Surah 4.157 and 'the apparent death' of Jesus. But, in line with his moral concern about conscience, it is not Husain's purpose to resolve that ambiguity. It suffices that in the Cross of Jesus, understood as something perpetrated in evil, there is a paradigm of each man's prime temptation to let the collective interest suppress his individual conscience and pursue its evil way.

VI

To appreciate Husain's thought it is important to remember that religion is itself one of the most culpable of collectives and structures, transgressing by its vested interests no less wrongly than other organs of community. This sense, in his writings, of the institutionalised forms of religion makes for a very critical view of their traditional attitudes. He rejects all exclusivism in their doctrinal claims and believes that no religion is warranted in having universal aims. This means, in broad terms, an abandonment of the converting instinct and a rejection of *jihād*, except in the inner sense of personal struggle towards purity of heart. He is impatient with all claims, whether made by Jews, Christians, Buddhists, or Muslims, to being possessed of any unique secret about mankind, any unilateral ability to save the world. Whether it is taming man's unruliness, curbing the pride of his beliefs, coping with secularism or accommodating technology, each religion must learn humility and renounce that assurance which phrases itself, for example, 'only Islam points the way to peace', 'only the Qur'ān can guide us today'. He himself never exceptionalised Islam or the Qur'ān in this way and he was anxious that others should avoid all exclusive claims. Only so could one de-fanaticise religion.

This derived, of course, from his concept of faith, not as a truth system entailing and resisting contradiction, but as a coefficient of living, a creative response to the pull of the transcendent, the soul's echo of the divine call. Sincerity and intensity here no longer required the familiar posture by which one faith held all other beliefs false. They required a liberation from that posture. As he saw it, atheism, the extreme negation of faith as a belief system, was in fact a misreading of human nature, an insensitivity to the transcendent dimension of one's self. Indeed, faith, properly understood, belonged not to the sphere of outward fact but to the sphere of inward awareness. Its credentials were simply its presence in the soul.

Seen in these terms, faiths, for Husain, could only rightly be co-operative. He was not concerned for ecumenical relationships as a pursuit for theologians but rather as an enterprise of religious self-awareness across the whole spectrum of beliefs. But occasionally he allowed himself to interest his mind in questions which did occupy theology in the familiar usage. One such was his intriguing essay in his *Miscellany*, to which he gave the title 'Two Comparable Tests'. He compared the doctrine of the uncreatedness of Qur'ān in Islam with the doctrine of the Incarnation of Christ as the Word in Christianity. Each had occasioned controversy within the community of faith, whether Mutazilites or Arians and others. Both had come to be emphatically *de fide*, vital items of faith, question of which was heresy. Both tended to be beset by factors one might describe as political, the issues credally being taken up by partisans for other than credal reasons.

He discerned among the protagonists of the uncreated Qur'ān the same preoccupation he detected within the Christian controversy, namely the desire for certainty that what was attributed to God was truly divine. One might recognise the same impulses in thought of Mary's immaculate conception and the belief of many Muslims in the sanctity of the very letters of the Arabic Qur'ān. Both gravitated to these views in order to repel attitudes which they feared as being derogatory to divine status. Both were liable to superstitious passions which diverted many in their communities away from essentials until the real essence of the faiths was quite overlaid. Doctrine was unhappily prey to the vicissitudes of politics and power. Husain ended his essay by wondering how such comparable features could have arisen in two systems so distinctive and all collusion apart.[22] This rare foray into doctrinal fields seemed only to reinforce his view that faith, in his sense of the word, was only sadly disserved by the doctrinaire.

VII

Despite his despair of politics and his distrust of politicians, Muhammad Kamil Husain was strongly committed to the pursuit of peace. His last overseas journeys to Japan and the United States were in the interests of the Peace Movement. They were undertaken despite the increasing handicap of near-blindness. It was his sense of the demonism in power structures, in states and economic systems, which made him aware that peace was itself a battle. Like H. G. Wells his earlier optimism gave way to a much more sombre mood. He had felt, in 1940, that what he called the 'crucifixion of France' in that year would somehow redeem the world of its belief in violence and that the Second World War as a whole would finally move mankind towards pacifism by demonstrating the criminal futility of war. But realism forced him to abandon these sanguine thoughts. It was that war itself in retrospect which preoccupied him with the mystery of collective evil – the mystery which brought him to the themes of *Qaryah Ẓālimah*.

It is, therefore, the more surprising that he maintained his conviction that the Christian view of man was unduly radical, excessively concerned with sin. Perhaps his faith in personal conscience was too simple and his fear for the evil bias of institutions too despairing. For, though collective selfishness undoubtedly deepens and compounds the private selfishness, the private world is not thereby fit to be romanticised or exonerated. Likewise, may not a certain magnanimity be at least ventured, if not achieved, by bodies communal and political? Shall we serve such venture if we set the political low in our esteem?

There is a certain kinship in Kamil Husain with Buddhism, in the instinct to focus on the world within, to resolve the inward issue of purity and calm, to see the task of faith as a psychic healing. His work is almost unique in the perspective of Islam, rejecting as it does so decisively the politicisation of religion and reversing the entire direction of revelation. His work combines a desire to see all things through a scientific lens with a deep sensitivity to the religious meaning of human experience, the ache of the heart for guidance and peace. One intriguing Quranic verse might have served to capture his theme. In a setting about procreation and birth, Surah 90.4 declares: 'We have created man in *kabad*.' The term is difficult to render. 'Trouble', 'hardship', 'toil', and 'struggle' are all suggested. The reference may be to the stress of birth itself, or to the tests on which it launches the new life. There is a physical connotation and a spiritual. Man as creature must take his way through precarious trials towards the finding of his being. Life examines him, as he examines life. 'Does he think', the Surah goes on to ask, 'that there is none to whom he is obligated as a subject?' That awareness of being 'liable' to authority and power beyond the creature is the essence of Islam. The authority and power are God's, 'the Lord of the worlds'. Muhammad Kamil Husain believed so too. But he understood the Lordship and the human subject as a relationship only fulfilled in inwardness.

That 'God created man in *kabad*' was to say that man was a God-centred being, a mortal probationer whose very nature was to respond to that centre. The world and man's biography were the sphere of the response. While religion might vulgarly distort and mislead the enterprise, wisely understood and served, it was the healing, guiding, constraining ministrant to bring it to pass, when the salutation 'O soul at peace' (89.27) would come personally true. This was the Islam Kamil Husain set himself to understand and serve.

NOTES: CHAPTER 8

1   Before his death Dr Husain gave his diaries and other papers into the care of Dr Harold Vogelaar, then engaged in a doctoral thesis at Columbia University, New York, subsequently completed under the title: '*The religious and philosophical thought of M. Kamil Husain, an Egyptian humanist*' (1977). The writer is indebted to Dr Vogelaar for the opportunity to consult both the diaries and papers and the dissertation. See also Mlle Expert Bezancon, *Le Docteur Kamil Husain, médicin et humaniste Égyptien* (1982).

2   His diary of 1941 reads: 'The measure of the deceit and lies and false ideals that brought about World War II is itself a sign of the impending collapse of the falsehood . . . Our modern concept of history convinces us that the world is inevitably moving towards pacifism' (Vogelaar, pp. 30–1).

3   *Al-Wādī al-Muqaddas* (Cairo, 1968). English trans. by this writer: *The Hallowed Valley* (Cairo, 1977), p. 105.

4   The thought of Kamil Husain must not be loosely aligned with that of Rudolf Otto, for the latter had a strong emphasis on 'the numinous' and 'the holy', with which there is no clear evidence that Husain sympathised. It arose from Rudolf Otto's keen Lutheran sense of grace and from his response to intimate experience with Hindus. But there is a comparable point in the question whether the religious consciousness *is* universal and whether it remains so today. In fairness to Otto perhaps one should rather say that the sense of 'Godwardness' is 'not such as everyone *does* have . . . but such as everyone is *capable* of having'. See *The Idea of the Holy*, trans. from the German by J. W. Harvey (London, 1936), p. 181. The capability could then be fostered and nourished by prophets, by discipline and by soul direction. Of these Husain would have approved.

5   'Myxoedemia' is defined as 'swelling of the glands due to fluid in the tissues'.

6   *Mutanawwi'āt* (Cairo, 1958), vol. 2, pp. 29–34.

7   ibid., p. 31.

8   Cairo, 1972.

9   The Arabic, *tabattil īlaihi tabtīlan*, uses the absolute accusative with intensive sense: 'Devote thyself very devoutly' (Arberry). The root has the meaning of detaching from and attaching to . . . to be consigned wholly to.

10   The author of *Ṭahārat al-Qulūb* was Abd al-Aziz al-Dirini, the 13th century Sufi poet and divine.

11   *Al-Wādī al-Muqaddas*, ch. 2. See *Purity of Heart*, trans. by D. Steere (New York,

1938). The sentence comes from Kierkegaard's *Edifying Discourses*, first published in Danish between 1843 and 1844. With its later preface this address 'to the individual' has as its central theme the heightening of personal consciousness in the presence of 'the Eternal'.

12 ibid., p. 12. See all ch. 4, note 24.
13 ibid., p. 72
14 ibid., p. 74.
15 ibid., p. 105.
16 ibid., p. 29.
17 ibid., p. 26.
18 *Qaryah Ẓālimah* (Cairo, 1954), English trans. by this writer, *City of Wrong* (Amsterdam, 1958).
19 See his essay 'The Meaning of Ẓulm in the Qur'ān', trans. from *Mutanawwi'āt* (Cairo, 1958), vol. 2, pp. 3–28. A translation by the present writer appeared in *The Muslim World Quarterly*, vol. 49, no. 3 (July 1959), pp. 196–212.
20 John Steinbeck in his *The Grapes of Wrath* develops the same theme of collective wrongdoing which becomes infinitesimal when divided out among a host of private persons who can then claim either powerlessness or exoneration. Nobody is culpable where collective selfishness obtains.
21 *Fitnah* in the Qur'ān varies in meaning according to the context. The root sense of a 'trial' or 'test' entails 'persecution' when suffered by an oppressed minority, 'sedition' when occurring against a successful establishment. When the transition from oppression to victory was under way in the active campaign, post-*Hijrah*, the 'test' of Muslims was their readiness to incur the 'trials' of warfare. Among these was the fear for wives and children, for personal safety. Some Muslims in this way allowed their families to be a *fitnah* for them, that is, a test of the measure of their readiness for hardship. See Surahs 8.28, 9.49 and 64.16; cf. 25.20.
22 *Mutanawwi'āt* (Cairo, 1957), vol. 1, pp. 74–84.

9

Najib Mahfuz of Cairo

I

I became convinced that I had to find Shaikh Zaabalawi . . . I wandered off through the quarter, from square to street to alleyway, making enquiries of everyone I felt was familiar with the place. At last the owner of a small establishment for ironing clothes told me: 'Go to the calligrapher Hassanain in Umm al-Ghulām – they were friends.'[1]

It proves a fruitless quest. For the saintly shaikh whose repute has kindled a desperate seeker's urge to find him is bewilderingly elusive and defeats all efforts to locate him. The reader of the short story is impelled by its pathos and by the narrator's personal stake to realise that the writer is himself the seeker – a conclusion in line with so much that is Kafkaesque and enigmatic in his other numerous works.

It may be thought symbolic that Najib Mahfuz includes the calligrapher among a miscellany of rendezvous to which his narrator goes in *Zaabalawi* – a shaikh in the religious courts, a seller of old books on theology and Sufism such as haunt the precincts of Cairo's mosques, a musician, a returned pilgrim from the Ḥajj and a local religious notable. All are in vain. The conviction grows that though Zaabalawi has the secret and that Zaabalawi must be found, he 'brings fatigue to all who seek him', and frustration too.

A calligrapher among the guides he seeks in search of Zaabalawi would seem a very tenuous link between narrator and Qur'ān and doubtless Najib Mahfuz means it so. For there is little direct evidence in his voluminous novels and stories that he cited it – so little, indeed, that some would find it odd to include his name in these pages. Yet there is profound religious interrogation in his writing which bears directly and searchingly on the whole stance of Quranic theism. It is a sound principle in the exploration of faith to hearken to the artists and the men of letters. Precisely because they do not preach but only portray, they are often a surer index to the core of things than the official exponents of religion. Their art may not always secure them from the risk of suspicion, but it does allow them some impunity in venturing dangerous thoughts or disturbing lifeless orthodoxy. Dogma can be more readily interrogated, at a tangent, by imaginative literature than by a formal theology hostage to the very assumptions it needs to escape. There is ground for thinking that Najib Mahfuz, in his puzzling way, presents a telling plea for that *tadabbur*, or honest reflection, for which the Qur'ān calls from its readers.[2] Exegesis, whether traditional, or liberal, has its own preoccupations, grammatical, textual, marginal and erudite. The novelist, concerned with the immediacies of the soul and of society, as narration and dialogue explore and disclose them, can be taken as a commentator in a different order of scrutiny, realism and human pathos. It is for this quality, oblique as his method is, that we include Mahfuz here as a foil for all commentary, by his disconcerting probing of the human scene it is set to enlighten and to guide.

As noted in the Introduction, *zann*, or surmise, is a steady concern of the Qur'ān. The term and its derivatives occur almost seventy times. 'What is your *zann*, your supposition, about the Lord of the worlds?' it asks the pagans (37.87). 'You thought conjecturing thoughts about God,' observes 33.10 of the Muslims at Medina when beset by the battle forces of the Quraish. Surah 53.28 reproaches unbelievers who, having no sure knowledge, follow only *zann*, or unfounded conjecture. This reprehensible meaning of the term predominates. It is in evident contrast with the assurance of truth belonging to the Qur'ān and the believer, a Book 'in which there is nothing dubious' (2.2), for a people called to a sure faith.

The stories of Najib Mahfuz have the uncanny capacity somehow to reverse this confidence and to set *zann* at the heart of our experience. Zaabalawi is surely still alive. He is the loveliest of souls. All who speak of him affirm his sanctity and invite the seeker to keep on seeking, even if they themselves forbear to do so. Yet the story ends with the seeker still unsatisfied, able neither to find nor to desist. Zaabalawi, he is told, has been seated beside him in the bar, but only when the seeker slept in a wine-induced slumber (perhaps in the 'tavern' of the mystics) and in his waking urgency continues to elude him. In comparable ways, as we shall see, Mahfuz insinuates a haunting dimension of 'surmise' into his 'religious' stories, as if to turn the tables on those who would banish *zann* from godly souls. On the contrary, he will centre it in their experience and throw a dubious light into an enigmatic dark. It is as if he meant to catechise all the familiar Quranic areas of conviction as to God, His sovereignty, His attributes, His spokesmen and His ways.

Faith itself becomes the question of questions. No longer can it stay as the answer of answers. 'What is your *ẓann* of the Lord of the worlds?' may well imply a reproach. But it certainly suggests an enigma which honest puzzlement does not resolve.

Before taking stock of Najib Mahfuz's major work in this context, we must appreciate his stature in Arabic literature in Egypt today. Born in 1911, he began publishing in 1932, having graduated in philosophy from Cairo University. His first ventures were historical narratives of Pharaonic Egypt. But he turned in the forties to settings in the Cairo of his youth, bringing familiar quarters to life in stories like *Khān al-Khalīlī* (1946) and *Ziqāq al-Midaq* (1947), and his famous trilogy of titles from Cairo districts, *Bain al-Qaṣrain*, *Qaṣr al-Shauq* and *Al-Sukkāriyyah*, in which he vividly communicated both a sense of locale and changes in the flux of time, as mirrored in the generations of a single family.

Critics have detected a variety of influences from Western literature in Mahfuz's technique and themes. If there was something of Galsworthy in his trilogy, a kinship with Dostoevsky, Thomas Mann and William Faulkner can be discerned in the novels and stories of the sixties and seventies, where individuals reflect in their inner psyche the tensions in their society. The search for identity is bewildered in the chances and fluctuations of daily life, the stresses of politics and the strains of personal relationship. Decay in the soul, after the pattern of Faulkner's *Alabama*, parallels confusion and corruption in the Cairo of Mahfuz, with its petty civil servants, its university graduates, its seedy lodging houses and its restless politics, private and national. In *Mirrors* (*Marāyā*, published in 1970), he draws fifty-five individual portraits, arresting vignettes of biography, capturing a mood in lively dialogue or isolating a destiny from the welter of the Cairo scene. In a multifarious way he contrives to breathe both sarcasm and pathos into his human reporting, and to intimate the feel of the 1952 revolution and its sequel, the vagaries, extravagances and frustrations of students, conscripts, layabouts, artisans, academics, soldiers, lovers and landlords, with jostling emotions, ironies, fantasies and fears. As narrator he moves through them all, observing, puzzling, probing, commiserating and dismissing. Retrospect by his characters allows him to infuse into his stories, Proust-like, the sense of time past, haunting or distorting time present.[3]

For all his incisive realism in *Marāyā*, Najib Mahfuz contrives to avoid direct involvement in the mysteries of religious faith. He has a character, Zahrān Hassūnah, who is a religious hypocrite, making money and performing his prayers, and doing the pilgrimage annually as 'his spiritual excursion', and acting as the imam in prayers behind the bar of the café he frequented with his friends.

Religion occupied a sizeable part of their conversation. This would usually reveal a simple, sincere faith in which belief alternated with fairy tales and popular myths. But there was no doubt that it was sincere.

Yet the pressing question of integrity, of the very viability of ethics in this world, and the ambivalence of religion eloquent in these characters 'led me to fall victim to a grim, spiritual crisis which was so oppressive that I almost rejected human experience *in toto*.'[4] Elsewhere he remarks: 'I've lived through an age without precedent in which ethics and values have collapsed. I have often felt that I'm living in a huge house scheduled for demolition, not in a society at all.'[5] Some find their way out of that despair by espousing fervent communism. One such the narrator records still keeping Ramaḍān, the only element in his Muslim background which he retains with his new allegiance. 'The true greatness of religion', this man observes, 'is only obvious when you do not regard it as a religion.' The reader takes this enigmatic observation as he will.[6]

There is one character in this miscellany, Abd al-Wahhāb Ismail, an ex-Wafdist of keen intelligence, who is a member of the Muslim Brotherhood. His conversion is his response to the sense of being swamped by alien influences and materialist attitudes. The Qur'ān must be asserted to restore the world to sanity, justice and a true worship of God alone.[7]

It is the quality of sometimes sharp, sometimes wistful, scepticism impregnating his panoramic, time-oscillating survey of human society, sexuality, tragedy and cross-purposes, which Najib Mahfuz brings into studiously religious interrogation in the large work which most concerns us in respect of faith and the Qur'ān. This was *Awlād Ḥāratinā*, 'Children of our Quarter', which appeared in serial form in the Cairo newspaper *Al-Ahrām* in 1959. It was the fruit of a hiatus of some five or six years in his writing career. His earlier work had been honoured by a share in the state prize for literature in 1957. He had been employed in the Ministry of Religious Affairs and then in the Ministry of Culture. What precisely inspired his mind to employ an interlude in his characteristic concern with social immediacies in order to construct a powerful allegory of God and the world within Semitic religion must be left to conjecture. In *Awlād Ḥāratinā* the allusions and associations of his prolific *mise en scène* of modern Cairo and Cairenes are taken up into a powerful prose drama of humanity read in the idiom of prophetic agency serving divine Lordship. The same descriptive detail is there in a skilful evocation of traditional society but is made to serve a philosophic despair about the credibility of God in a retrospect of His prophets.

So radical and so explicit – for all its subtlety – was Najib Mahfuz's 'surmising' in *Awlād Ḥāratinā* that its serial publication in *Al-Ahrām* was only maintained against the outcry of the shaikhs and purists by influential support within the Abd al-Nasir regime. Its publication in book form proved too daunting for Egyptian publishers and it did not appear in a complete, or nearly complete, edition until 1967 in Beirut. It measures the full range of the doubts that are latent and elusive and surfacing only intermittently in all his other works. It brings together the people of the Qur'ān and surmise around 'the death of God'.

II

The 'quarter', with its restless, wistful population, is dominated by the great house standing on the edge of the desert and shrouded in high walls and an impenetrable silence. There, reputedly, lives Gabalawi (lit. 'the mountain man') the original ancestor from whom all the inhabitants derive their being and their history and to all of whom, again reputedly, he has given right to his estate. There are, it is true, governors and satraps who tyrannise over the people and flout what is ostensibly the will of Gabalawi. He does not, however, intervene. Indeed, the great house is wrapped in mystery and, circle round it as the author does on many a walk, in hope of a glimpse beyond its enigmatic walls and shadowing trees, it is always to no avail. The house hides in its own remoteness as if it had no relations with the world over which only legend and credence give it mastery. Its inscrutable indifference is compounded by suspicions of impotence, or malice, or decrepitude.

Symbol of an absentee Allāh, Gabalawi has nevertheless a human progeny. He has five sons, of whom Idris is the eldest and Adham the youngest. Idris emerges as a spiteful, envious Satan who tricks Adham (Adam) out of his heritage as custodian of Gabalawi's estate office where he supervises the accounts. On the grounds of brotherly assistance, Idris, who has already been cursed and ejected, persuades Adham to try to enter Gabalawi's inner sanctum and find the book in which, as Idris supposes, his fate is recorded. Caught in the act by Gabalawi, Adham, with Umayma, his wife, is expelled from his office and obliged to make his way in the world outside by pushing a barrow of sweet potatoes to sell where he can. Despite the tragic change in their fortunes, Adham still retains a wistful reverence for Gabalawi in which he is taunted and reviled by Idris, who tantalises him with gibes and scorn.

Idris is responsible, too, for the enmity which develops between Qadri and Hammam (Cain and Abel), sons of Adham and Umayma.

Qadri takes after Idris and shares something of his venom, whereas the gentle Hammam's reputation earns the favour of Gabalawi who invites him to come into the great house and belong there, with a wife and family. Gabalawi refuses Hammam's plea for his father's pardon and inclusion in the act of grace. He returns home to make his decision. But the news stirs Qadri to jealous anger and in a fit of rage he slays his brother. Qadri's act is a climax of hatred towards Gabalawi, the unforgiving, Gabalawi whose heart is hardened even against so loyal and docile a servant as his father, Adham. In a graphic narration of Hammam's burial by Qadri in the desert sand and his exhumation, at the distraught insistence of Adham, Mahfuz achieves a power of tragic irony. Father and brother carry the body home. Primal man is the father of a murderer and of a victim. It is the former's descendants who will people the alley. The central memory in their ancestry will be an expulsion, a fratricide and an unrelenting Gabalawi, secreted in ominous seclusion, his inclination for human relation buried in the grave of Hammam.

Or, one had better say, relations of gentleness and kindness. For Gabalawi, in nearer time from the 'events' thus far recorded, sends, or ostensibly sends, to the 'quarter' a sequence of three 'prophets', Gabal (Moses), Rifa'ah (Jesus), and Qasim (Muhammad). Their story Najib Mahfuz presents in a sequence of thinly veiled incidents and situations, like those already narrated of Adham and his family, making identification unmistakable, yet avoiding to state it. Every story is shot through with the theme of the elusiveness of Gabalawi and the miserable, often sordid, lot of ordinary mortals, caught in the feuds, the poverty, the crime and scandals, of the 'quarter', and never far from the dry, pitiless, barren heat of 'the desert'.

Moses is perhaps named Gabal to indicate that he is in a special way Gabalawi's man. Hamdan's people in the 'Jews' quarter' are first introduced worn down and distressed by the exactions of the Effendi's (Pharoah's) officers, while Gabal is the adopted son of the Effendi and his wife, Huda. She had seen him, twenty years before, playing around as a naked child in a pool after rain. Being herself childless and captivated by the sight, she had taken him into her own house and reared him in luxury. After a demonstration led by Hamdan against the oppression of the officers, a strict and brutal ban on movement is imposed upon the quarter. Gabal has never forgotten his origins and is torn between gratitude and affection towards Huda and concern for his persecuted folk. Wrestling one evening, out where Abel was killed, with the whole mystery of Gabalawi's world and his own dilemma, Gabal is moved to intervene against an officer chasing and beating a victim who has defied the ban and left his hovel. In mounting anger when the officer refuses to desist, Gabal fights and unwittingly kills him.

A week later, at a council in the Effendi's house called to debate measures to avenge the disappearance of the officer, Gabal resolves to join his people. They welcome him with mixed emotions. But he cannot stay. For the very man he rescued when he killed the officer betrays his secret by blurting it out in the setting of a petty quarrel of his own when Gabal intervenes. Escaping into another area of Cairo Gabal encounters the two daughters of Balqiti, the snake charmer, trying to fill their water-pots at the festival. Their father invites him to stay with him and so the reader is introduced to Mahfuz's version of the Biblical Jethro, tutor of Moses in the art of the snake. Gabal proves an apt pupil and marries Balqiti's daughter, Shafiqah. He determines to forget the dark past and settle with his new fate. But one day, charming snakes in the *sūq*, he falls in with Daabas, the man he rescued long before, learns of the deepening anguish of his people and returns with him to take up their cause. It is then he relates to them the story of his lonely encounter with Gabalawi, who 'can only be seen in the dark', and who tells him 'Your people are my people', with the promise of strength and success in doing battle for their rights.

Confused and sceptical, Hamdan and his folk are indecisive. But Gabal's confidence and calmness hearten them. The confrontation is joined when the chiefs, ordered by the Effendi, come to stifle the incipient rebellion which follows the Effendi's breaking of a promise given to Gabal after he had charmed away from the palace a plague of snakes. A pit has been prepared in their path and the officers, clutching their cudgels, fall into the mud and die cursing their erstwhile subjects in a rain of blows and stones. The Effendi yields all their rights to Gabal and to Gabalawi's people. Emboldened by their success, a neighbouring quarter lays claim to a similar emancipation. But Gabal, reluctantly, refuses to take up their cause, since his commission from Gabalawi refers to no other people but his own. They settle down to enjoy their new-found well-being.

Soon, however, quarrels break out. In a fit of temper Daabas blinds a man in a money altercation. Gabal, invoking 'an eye for an eye' and to teach the discipline which 'law and order' demand, blinds him in retaliation. Perceptibly the whole atmosphere deteriorates. Love for Gabal changes into fear or acquiescent submission. Throughout his days his achievement and his discipline avail to keep the alley righteous and loyal.

Such was Gabal, the first to revolt against oppression, the first of those to whom, after withdrawing from the world, Gabalawi appeared. He did not concern himself with other than his own tribe. He may even have despised the rest of them, as his people did. Yet he was a symbol to all. Najib Mahfuz rings down the curtain on Gabal with the comment: 'Were forgetfulness not the bane of our quarter, a fine example would not have gone to waste. But then our quarter *is* afflicted with forgetfulness.'[8]

III

The third main section of *Awlād Ḥāratinā* brings us to Rifā'ah, whose story identifies him readily with Jesus. The vigour and resolution of Gabal are replaced by a gentle, at times almost effeminate, quality to which Rifā'ah's name (refinement and honour) points. We are introduced to the young and pregnant Abdah and her husband Shafi'a on a forlorn journey from Gabal's quarter to Sūq Muqaṭṭam, where Gabal had his shelter with Balqiti, and where Shafi'a will open a carpenter's shop. They talk of Gabalawi's obliviousness of their needs and sorrows. In the next scene we find them, with their son, Rifā'ah, now a youth, back from their refuge in Sūq Muqaṭṭam and with their own folk in the alley. For all the memory of Gabal and his 'liberation' things are just as they always were. Injustice, oppression, weariness and vulgarity are rife. Rifā'ah works listlessly at carpentry but broods wistfully over what he learns about Gabalawi from Jawad, the poet. He is fascinated by the theme of evil spirits and learns something of the art of exorcism. One day he disappears and his puzzling absence sends his distracted parents into anxious search. Finally he returns from the desert where he has withdrawn to meditate and wonder. He becomes known to all the quarter as an odd sort of dreamer.

Mahfuz (ch. 50) creates a dialogue in the carpenter's shop in which Rifā'ah, his father and some neighbours discuss death and violence, the legacy of Gabal, marriage, and human misery. When they toy with nails and one remarks that 'only by force can they be driven in', Rifā'ah replies: 'Man, Sir, isn't wood. The fact is', he adds, 'that what our quarter needs is mercy.' Responding to his father's impatience with his pensive ways, his habit of desert-musing and his softness for people, Rifā'ah withholds his secret no longer but tells Shafi'a that he believes he has heard the voice of Gabalawi, entrusting him as 'a beloved son' with a task of mercy in the world, a mercy which will deliver men from evil by the power of love. His parents are confounded. Their main anxiety is to keep the puzzling thing a secret from the neighbours. There ensues a fracas in the alley about a neighbour's daughter, Jasminah, found emerging, drunken, from the house of the chief of the alley who has seduced her. The honour of Gabal's people is at stake. But they also fear the chief. To general consternation, Rifā'ah steps out from the milling crowd and volunteers to marry Jasminah to save the situation. Pity is his only motive. His people read it as stupidity.

The wedding ensues. Rifā'ah's parents try to overcome their disappointment in him at such a strange unworthy match. As Jasminah discovers to her bewilderment, Rifā'ah's is a love she will have to share with many. For it embraces all mankind and its yearning in her case is to free her from her evil spirit. Unlike Gabal who took his mission to be that of gaining his people's rights to their 'estate', Rifā'ah is not interested in rights, but in purity and inner happiness, in release from things and pride. Gabal's way avails but by its very form brings evil back again when men forget or boast. For all its disconcerting gentleness, Rifā'ah's way draws down the enmity of the chiefs, who fear the kind of strange pull his teaching has or the pity his very guilelessness evokes. For, as Jasminah demonstrates in her amours behind his back, he is easy to deceive.

Bayumi, the chief, harangues Rifā'ah, scouts his lack of interest in power and prestige, and threatens him with dire consequences. Power cannot trust or believe in those who disavow it. They are bound to be deceivers or pawns for the power-seekers.

Clearly echoing the tenor of the conspiracy against Jesus in the Gospels, Mahfuz has his own scenario. Rifā'ah is ambushed by a gang and cudgelled to death by the chief Bayumi himself. There is no intervention from the great house of Gabalawi. The body is reburied near the desert by four of his friends who remain there burdened by a sense of guilt about their cowardice.[9] His distracted parents recover slowly from their grief, while his followers keep alive his memory and try to continue the art of driving out the evil spirits, in the hope that by so doing they will be bringing Rifā'ah back to life.

But a leader among his friends, Ali (Simon Peter?), having killed Jasminah in rage and remorse over her treachery, becomes a militant force against the chiefs until finally, after much chaos and bloodshed, his group is established as an alley with rights just like Gabal's people. Shafi'a and Abdah, Rifā'ah's parents, share in the new standing and, by methods he would have himself disowned, his people find the satisfaction he disqualified. His story becomes a legend and it is rumoured that Gabalawi himself secreted his body in his garden behind those forbidding walls. We are left with another alley and another forgetfulness.

IV

And so, in the third section of *Awlād Ḥāratinā*, to Qasim – Muhammad. Again Mahfuz tells his own story with the liberties his devices admit but with clear reference to the *Sīrah* of the Prophet. Abu Talib, Muhammad's uncle and protector, is now Zakariya; Khadijah his wife is Qamar; Ali his cousin is Hasan; and Waraqah, an early mentor, is Yahya. The memory of Gabal and Rifā'ah persists but the world is still plagued with ungodliness and Gabalawi is as elusive as ever. Qasim is introduced as a lively child, then as a youth tending sheep on the edge of the desert. There he is saddened by the ways of the world and especially by the brutality of the chiefs. He reflects on the contrast between Gabal and Rifā'ah. Meanwhile, thanks to his diligence and courtesy, his affairs prosper. A romance develops between Qamar and himself, encouraged by her endearing ways which overcome his diffidence. Marriage follows and a daughter, Ihsan, is born. But dark clouds begin to pass across the sky of their peaceful domesticity, as Qasim becomes possessed of a sense of summons from Gabalawi. He is visited in a trance by Qindil (Gabriel), servant of Gabalawi, who informs him that Gabalawi has commissioned him to tell all the people that they are equal and that he is to make the quarter an extension of the great house.

Qamar is deeply troubled by this news, sensing conflict ahead, if the calling is genuine. Zakariya tries to dissuade Qasim, fearing that he is deluded or bewitched. He himself broods and ponders. But conviction grows on him and he gathers confidence, reflecting on the precedents of Gabal and Rifā'ah, steadily forming the expectation of victory in a pattern more inclusive, more decisive than theirs. 'If the Lord makes me victorious,' Qasim says, 'the quarter will never need another after me.'[10] Mahfuz does not depict scenes from Qasim's preaching but intimates the forfeiture of domestic ease and quiet as his challenge to the evil of the chiefs develops. We see him gathering a club of stalwart young men whose zeal and prowess arouse the suspicions and then the wrath of the 'establishment'. Qamar dies. Menace deepens and Qasim trains his men in fencing and combat after leaving the quarter for a mountain encampment. His followers prevail upon him to marry again and he weds Badriya (Aisha), a young girl. The band seizes the opportunity of the wedding procession of one of the chiefs to launch a vigorous attack. Surprise helps them to victory – a victory in which the justice sought by Gabal and the mercy taught by Rifā'ah will become real and the dream of Adham fulfilled in a world where human rights prevail and Gabalawi's law is done. It is only by such action that Qasim settles the doubts about Gabalawi which puzzle him, as he ponders the sight of the great house in the setting sun.

But he is old with the years and like this sun declining to the horizon the fear of him falls away. Where are you? How are you? Why do you seem as if you were no longer there? Those who are false to your commandment are just here, an arm's length from your dwelling place. Are not these women and little ones far away on the mountain the folk nearest to your heart? You will come again into your proper role when the conditions that go with your sacred benefaction are fulfilled, without some supervisor being slain or some bully running amok, a return sure like the sun rising into its zenith in the sky. But for you we would have no father, no quarter, no sacred estate and no hope.[11]

Qasim's adversaries are angry and confounded by this narrative equivalent of the Battle of Badr and they debate barricading themselves in against further attacks, or sallying forth to capture him. More bitter fighting follows and Qasim's band prevails. Many of his followers leave the quarter and join him in the hills, fearing the vengeance of the defeated pagans. A mysterious murder sets them against each other. Finally Qasim's band breaks into their midst, the leaders are cut down and peace ensues. Qasim is victorious. He announces the full implementation of Gabalawi's charter. The satraps have been liquidated for ever with their tyranny, their drunkenness and their dissensions. The human estate will be equitably divided. Some of Gabal and Rifā'ah's people murmur in disgruntlement. But they acquiesce. Harmony reigns as long as Qasim lives. His character enshrines all the virtues. Even his way with many wives demonstrates both his political sagacity and his human quality.

Many people said that if forgetfulness had been the bane of the quarter, then the time had come for it to be rid of that bane for good. They said it would get rid of it for ever. So they said! So they said, *Haratina!*[12]

V

With the passing of the age of Qasim, Najib Mahfuz comes to the end of Gabalawi's 'prophets'. The fourth section of *Awlād Hāratinā* belongs to Arafah, the modern scientist. He occupies the last twenty-three of its one hundred and fourteen sections.[13] At once we are into a situation where Gabal, Rifā'ah, and Qasim have become little more than legends, stories told from the past, in a world still rife with the oppressions they were said to have banished. It is a world now the more sceptical because of their very remoteness and their seeming futility. Things, indeed, deteriorated very soon after Qasim's demise. Intrigues and quarrels divided his followers and made barren his legacy.

Mysteriously, Arafah emerges from the desert and takes up his abode in a basement in the Rifā'ah quarter. There he begins work on a laboratory workshop making medicines and remedies. He senses in his science a power more effective, more decisive, than Gabalawi's messengers ever achieved. His determination is to apply his skills to the liberation of the alleys from their miseries and their pointless obsession with the stories of the prophets. He woos and marries a girl of the quarter, whose old father, seemingly demented, has inveighed against Gabalawi and been struck down by a leading citizen. In their nuptial happiness he forms the idea of penetrating into the great house to seek out Gabalawi, to discover why he is so oblivious of his domain, to confront him with his evasiveness, to see, indeed, if he is there at all. His bride is appalled, but also fascinated, and he is not to be deterred. He wants to apply his workshop assumption to the biggest question of all which is the question of Gabalawi. If he succeeds in finding him, well and good. If not, at least matters are clarified. Confusion and surmise will be ended. The risk he decries in the very spirit of the prophets who had decried risks also.

With his brother Hanask, Arafah goes into the desert, the place redolent with memories of Hammam, Gabal, Rifā'ah and Qasim and their encounter with Gabalawi's servants. He tunnels through the wall and emerges within the walls, inhaling the very perfumes which were the paradise of Adham. Stealthily, he creeps across the garden and reaches the terrace where Gabalawi had once banished Idris from his presence. Arafah survives an alarm from a servant relieving himself outside, and gropingly arrives at what must be the bedroom, as the smell of incense seems to proclaim. He is transfixed with fear when an old negress stirs and goes out of the door and returns. She is presumably on guard. Arafah, aching to lay hands on Gabalawi's book of magic (for such it is), strikes a match and sees a pair of watching eyes. They belong to a negro whom, in a paroxysm of fear, he strangles to death. Unnerved by his crime and distraught in the darkness, he slinks away, retraces his steps down the terrace, across the garden and through the tunnel.

He tells his story to his brother and his bride. Sleep eludes him. In his agitation, he avows there is no Gabalawi and that only in his, Arafah's, science is there reality and hope. Somehow news breaks out of a murder in the great house, the murder of the negro. But the populace believe a rumour that the shock of it has caused the death of Gabalawi and the quarters almost come to blows about who shall conduct his funeral. It is finally agreed that he be laid to rest within a little mosque inside the estate office in the great house. Only the servants are present at the washing of the corpse and at sunset the body of 'Gabalawi' is laid to rest.

Consternation oppresses Arafah, the murderer. He vows to use all his magic to bring Gabalawi back to life. It had been easier to kill him than to see him or to verify him. Embroiled in another killing of a brutal chief, Arafah unleashes against his pursuers a magic bottle with a lethal destructiveness hitherto unknown (the atomic bomb?). Another wily chief bargains with Arafah for possession of the weapon as the price of securing him from vengeance. He accepts. But his wife and brother urge upon him the bitter truth of his captivity. His magic, thus purloined by the powermongers, will become a universal curse.[14] Arafah is tempted to believe that he can always go further in invention and out-threaten the bosses. For 'magic has not limits'.

Arafah and his wife move into a palatial residence in league with the powerbase, in relations of deepening suspicion. Magician and chief know each needs the other. Rapidly Arafah's character degenerates. His wife finds him out in guilty liaisons. Life disintegrates in suspicion, remorse, perplexity, and drugs, until one morning he encounters the old negress who had stirred that night when he penetrated Gabalawi's bedroom. She tells him she was commissioned by her master, Gabalawi, as he died in her arms, to go and inform Arafah that he was 'pleased with him'. Arafah is suspicious and incredulous. His brother, despite Arafah's angry protest, is convinced it is all hallucination and tells Arafah so. The uneasy partnership between Arafah, man of magic, and the trustee, man of power, finally breaks down. Fearing for his life, Arafah flees but he and his wife are captured and buried alive. All Arafah's magic is now at the disposal of the man of power, whose tyranny grows to unbridled brutality. The story closes with the people dimly hoping for Arafah's surviving brother to appear with the book in which are secreted the mysteries of his science – a science perhaps now irretrievably locked in an irrecoverable dossier, so that the power it has conferred on tyranny perpetuates itself against all hope. Yet hope is precisely what the alleys of long-suffering humanity continue stolidly to cherish – a hope, however fragile, surviving even the demise of Gabalawi and the receding memories of Gabal, Rifā'ah and Qasim, his celebrated messengers.

VI

It would be easy for an angered orthodoxy to turn from the concluding Chapter 114 of *Awlād Ḥāratinā* to the concluding Surah 114 of the Qur'ān and identify Najib Mahfuz's portrayal of human existence with 'the evil of the whispering insinuator who whispers in the hearts of men' from which that final Surah 'seeks refuge' with 'the God of men'. For it might be read as the most radical calling in question of the confidence of traditional religion. Its haunting, wistful, scepticism presents a searching challenge to ordinary believers. Served by eminent narrative skill and literary art, it invites them to look into a void, to think themselves stripped of their familiar securities, to divest themselves of assumptions about God and His messengers which have

always been instinctive to their minds and culture. It confronts them
with the unthinkable, with the implication that everything on which
they had relied might need, for its own sake, to be called in question.
Its tests of faith are not those of orthodoxy, but of existence. A reaction
which banishes them with a shudder as none other than 'the evil of the
whispering insinuator' suborning the soul will have failed to
understand how faith must be able to contain a doubt of itself – once
life or literature have given doubt a shape.

Awlād Ḥāratinā is the shape of doubt, as Cairo formed it in the
life and writing of Najib Mahfuz. It is a splendid interrogation of 'the
Lord of men, the God of men, the King of men', to whom Surah 114,
like its predecessor, 113, repairs for 'refuge'. It interrogates only
because it has explored so sombrely and depicted so sharply the very
evils of human society from which the two Surahs yearn to be
delivered. By his sustained and vivid picture of how evil they are,
Mahfuz is thoroughly loyal to the Qur'ān in reading the human
predicament as a vacancy for God.

That may seem an almost scandalous position to be held within the
enveloping God-consciousness of Islam and Muslims. Yet, paradoxic-
ally, it may be one of its truest forms. For how is that consciousness of
God, on our human part, alive and authentic, if it protects itself
fearfully from contrary evidence, if it fails to relate divine ethic with the
real world, if it refuses to believe in God sufficiently to be puzzled, even
desperate, about His seeming absence, His elusiveness, His silence?
How will it be loyal to God Himself if it has no demands on Him
commensurate with His sovereignty, if it dismisses what the old writers
called 'theodicy' and merely pretends that He is all He needs to be
when the seeming is so largely otherwise? Will such suppression of
thought, such insensitivity about what worship means, be truly
confessing Him? If we confess God too readily, too meekly, too
acquiescently in face of evil, are we not confessing Him the less? Are we
confessing Him at all?

These are the probing questions which Najib Mahfuz is raising.
Must we not say that he is a better Muslim for doing so? Has it not
sometimes seemed to many that it is man's tenacity on behalf of God
that really keeps His credibility alive? So Mahfuz at least appears to
suggest in laying the accent, for example, on Adham's steady cleaving
to awe of Gabalawi, despite the taunts of Idris and Qadri, and against
the evidences of near malignity in 'the great house'. Do not these
'negatives' in the reckoning of loyal faith, these non-fulfilled
expectations as to God, have their place if faith is to be both honest and
justified? One might perhaps even link this line of thought, hauntingly
sketched in *Awlād Ḥāratinā*, with the Islamic *Shahādah* itself. It

has a negative before it has a positive. 'There is no god . . . except God.' The negation there has the idols in view, the pseudo-deities of paganism. These have to be excluded before the true confession can be made. The great positive, *Allāh*, turns on their elimination. There is no 'both/and' under divine sovereignty. Similarly, must we not be able to negate, ethically and essentially, those 'disqualifiers' of God – indifference, neglect, irresponsibility, incapacity – if we are truly to affirm 'but God'? Must we not first repudiate, as the *Shahādah* does, before we can confess? For faith in God, properly to be held, must 'see off' suspicions of inadequacy no less than errors of pluralism. For they are no less incompatible with a right faith than the idols of the heathen. That is no faith in 'the God of men, the Lord of men, the King of men' which, while disowning the idols men make, will not own the doubts and fears they suffer.

In concluding so, are we reading theology too explicitly into what Mahfuz presents to us as literature? Perhaps too explicitly, but not improperly. For literature is the way in which he gives theology currency, indeed, in the Cairo world, makes theology expressible. The fact that it is not professional explains its very feasibility, not to say its incisiveness. It does not explain away its meaning and significance.

The whole question of God in *Awlād Ḥāratinā* is closely bound up with His special representatives. In that the author is loyally Islamic. He stands squarely in the Semitic tradition, where Gabalawi and the great house relate to the alleys of humanity, if at all, via the chosen leaders He has mysteriously commissioned. These Mahfuz presents in very simple, even reductionist terms. Gabal is the snake charmer, Rifā‘ah the exorcist, and Qasim the vigilantes' leader. Though there are associations, in each case, with the Biblical and Quranic scenes, there are whole dimensions of the impact and import of each which are left to total silence. His interest throughout is the unruliness of humanity, the avid hopes so quickly dissipated and overtaken by futility. He sees the 'prophets' as only availing for a while, unable after their demise to ensure any abiding salvation for mankind from the burden of being human. That preoccupation engrosses him so that he ignores the kindred issues that belong with the contrasts between the three 'Semite' figures in his panorama. To be sure, he characterises Gabal as the man for his tribe, Rifā‘ah as the man of compassion, and Qasim as the man of robust action. Perhaps it is his location of them all in the quarters of Cairo which occasions his neglect of the rich complexity behind these simple pictures. The mystique of exodus and land possession, of seed and territory, in the Gabal cycle; of *hijrah* and *qiblah*, prayer and pilgrimage, in the Qasim cycle – these are left to silence. Rifā‘ah's gentleness, his scarcely credible 'marriage', his languid disposition bear no relation to the decisive, urgent figure in the Gospels. We could well desire that the strong narrative power of Najib Mahfuz had been employed in a more adequate, rounded reckoning with the subtle, manifold significance of his chosen heroes for Gabalawi.

Doing such riper justice to Moses, Jesus and Muhammad would doubtless have taken him beyond his chosen focus on human futility and puzzlement about God. But it would also have taken him into a more penetrating and perhaps more hopeful analysis of the human meaning and its salvation. There was much more to Muhammad's struggle against *Shirk* and for a divinely amenable society than the recruiting, training and leading of a tough band of cudgelling fighters. The very despair *Awlād Ḥāratinā* conveys about the human scene might have inspired the artist to probe the factors in the Messianic decisions of Jesus, their deliberate acceptance of suffering and their role in the healing of the human hurt, as achieving the answer for which such despair so ardently yearned. What evidence do we have elsewhere that Najib Mahfuz has been open to that logic?

VII

There are several novels and short stories in which Najib Mahfuz ponders the quest for salvation, or reflects on the cynicism and lovelessness which tragically frustrate it. One such is *Al-Liṣṣ wa-l-Kilāb*, 'The Robber and the Dogs',[15] in which a robber, released from prison by an amnesty, strives to become an honest man. He finds temporary shelter and consolation with a Sufi. But the way of mysticism does not 'save' him, unable as he is to comprehend its meaning or its discipline. Making no headway to lasting 'salvation' within a rejecting world, he undergoes a reaction and becomes bent on avenging himself on society for his imprisonment. He murders but later finds himself outcast even from his own gang. His wife forsakes him and marries the new gang-leader. He himself is finally shot by the police.

Where, then, is life to be found? Mahfuz has stories which propose 'commitment', work and a wife. In *Al-Samman wa-l-Kharīf*, 'Quail and Autumn',[16] a Wafdist politician, dismissed from his politics, is presented with the option, where 'all are aliens on a foreign land', of seeing marriage as an act of faith, a remedy for the rootlessness of life. A Muslim Brother and a communist elsewhere provide another of Mahfuz's characters with an object lesson in commitment as a way of salvation.[17] He is an intellectual who has abandoned belief in God and who senses, like Arafah in *Awlād Ḥāratinā*, the prostitution of

science by power. His lostness both to God and technology is
contrasted with the drive and devotion of the Muslim Brother and the
communist. But neither carries conviction for the seeker. He finds their
zealous 'causes' illusory. They are deceived by mere collective fervour.
The man who wants to be obligated and committed can find no sane
authentic way to what he seeks. Is the alternative only aimlessness?

Nor are the mosque professionals possessed of the answer even for
themselves. In 'The Street Mosque', we meet Sheikh Abd Rabbihi,
imam of a lowly mosque which stands at the crossing of two lanes in a
red-light district of Cairo.[18] The imam has a scant following: the
audience for his sermon one evening, on purity of conscience, is only
one solitary street salesman. The next morning he is summoned, with
other imams, to the Inspector General for Religious Affairs. They are
all instructed to preach in their mosques about obedience to the regime.
They react differently, some deploring this politicising of their sacred
tasks, others pleading how Islamic it is to obey rulers. With hopes of
promotion, Sheikh Abd Rabbihi dismays his Friday audience by a
brazenly political sermon, with police eavesdropping in the mosque.
He is killed in a bomb attack disputing with his 'parishioners' over
using their mosque as a bomb shelter. Is there any secure identity, any
true integrity, even in the custodians of the faith?

In the same *Dunyā Allāh*, however, there is another story, *Kalimah
fī-l-Lail*, 'A Word in the Night',[19] which brings Najib Mahfuz closest
to an ultimate answer to the human dilemma of doubt, alienation and
significance. It is the story of a government official at the point of
retirement after a long and busy career in which he has got ruthlessly to
his goals, neglecting family, scorning scruples, distressing friends, in a
selfish drive to realise himself. But when the office ends, everything
turns to pointlessness and dismay.[20] He has thrown away everything
for his career and now life, likewise, has discarded him. Consumed
with apprehension and restlessness, he is arrested one morning by the
words of the *Fātiḥah*, the opening Surah of the Qur'ān, words he had
never before really taken in.

For the first time he found himself face to face with the words: 'In
the Name of God', with nothing to distract him from their meaning.
For the first time in his life he discovered them. He felt a strange
tremor as he asked himself how it could have been thus so long.
Deeply moved he went out of his house into the street, walking not
into the public highway as he had been used to do every day through
the decades past, but into his own inwardness. He had had no mind
ever to go that way for long years . . . 'In the Name of God.' That
was how every Surah began. Truth to tell, that was how everything

should begin. Perhaps this truly was what he was seeking for. As he went along new beings became evident to him that had never entered his thoughts. On either side stretched green gardens, in tidy array, and fields beyond them. Trees of staid beauty stood along the sidewalks, as if they were whispering in a silent language expecting someone to reveal their secret just as he himself had penetrated other secrets.

The road seemed to stretch into infinity. He was overcome with wonder, asking himself why all this magnificence had been created? It came to him that he would be highly embarrassed by the disclosure if he were to come clean to anyone. But who was there to whom he could confess himself? His heart knew no composure. It was altogether desolate.

The truth of your fate is that you will find life has abandoned you. It was so from the first day of retirement. What profit had there been in his past life? What but emptiness and pointlessness? You exerted yourself more than man could bear, but it was all in the name of mad ambition, in the name of greed and selfishness, in the name of enmity, of envy and combat. Not one deed was 'in the Name of God'.

Wondering at the peace and beauty and guilelessness of nature, he returns deeply moved, to his home and the following conversation ensues with his wife:

'I had never realised how beautiful our street is.'

What has happened to him? she asked herself – street new, tidy and clean, with trees and greenery? Then she said with surprise: 'It has been like that all your life.'

'But I never saw it till today!'

She gave him only a listless glance but it spoke the bitterest reproach and disapproval. Then he kissed her meekly. He was asking himself anxiously whether there was any time remaining in life to reform the past with its corruption, to find pardon from every fault, atonement for all the evil done, and to turn enemies and victims into friends? He pondered a long time and then he said with a child's eagerness: 'Is it not possible for man to begin a new life even when he is as old as I am?' 'What life?' 'A new life, in every sense of the word. Please answer me whether it is possible?' An intense curiosity possessed her, mingled with misgiving as she said: 'I do not understand what you mean.' 'You will understand . . .' New in every sense of the word. Otherwise how is the rest of life to be borne? . . . He closed his eyes like someone recalling distressing things, while she followed him with furtive glances. But ere long she was saying to herself: 'Did he ever have a smile like that?' For smiling he was, an altogether new smile, there was nothing false about it, nothing malign. It was not a cunning, nor a drunken, nor a crafty, nor a threatening smile. Nothing of those.

It was the smile of a pure heart.[21]

It is fitting to leave Najib Mahfuz and his radical despair, his characters and their harassed, restless, bewildered report on humanity, with this picture of redemption through a spirit opened on to nature, to love, and to 'the Name of God'.

NOTES: CHAPTER 9

1 The story is translated by Denys Johnson Davies in *Modern Arabic Short Stories* (London, 1967), pp. 137–47.

2 *Tadabbur* means the alert, intelligent pondering which the text invites and requires. The question comes in 4.82 and 47.24. Surah 38.29 describes the Qur'ān as 'a blessed Book which We have sent down upon you in order that the thoughtful may ponder its signs and have them in mind'. Such *tadabbur* is responsive on man's part to the *tadbīr*, or 'ordering', which, on God's part, lies behind the created world and the Quranic revelation.

3 *Al-Marāyā* (Cairo, 1971) was translated into English by Roger Allen as *Mirrors* (Minneapolis, 1977). The Arabic was originally a series of items in a radio and TV journal in Cairo.

4 ibid., pp. 78 and 80.

5 ibid., p. 76.

6 ibid., p. 235.

7 ibid., pp. 175f.

8 *Awlād Ḥāratinā* (Beirut, 1967), p. 210. Translation by this author. An English trans. by Philip Stewart was published in London, in 1981, under the title *Children of Gebelawi*, and also in Washington DC.

9 His friends are named, perhaps significantly, 'Alī and Husain, the two tragic figures in the history of Shī'ah Islam. Najib Mahfuz also alludes elsewhere to the idea that Gabalāwi himself retrieved the body and buried it himself within the bounds of the great house, as a signal mark of honour to Rifā'ah.

10 *Awlād Ḥāratinā*, p. 364.

11 ibid., p. 410.

12 ibid., p. 443.

13 It may be entire coincidence that Najib Mahfuz gives 114 chapters to his masterpiece, a number identical to the Surahs of the Qur'ān. 'Seeking refuge' is the one theme of the two final Surahs, just as it is the long quest of the people of 'our quarter'. The human atmosphere of those two concluding Surahs is akin to the whole 'feel' of *Awlād Ḥāratinā*.

14 The exchanges here are uncannily close to those in Bertholt Brecht's *Galileo*, between Galileo and Andrea in scene 14, in which he foresees how progress in science will be progression away from mankind, and scientists will surrender their knowledge to those in power to use, or not to use, or to misuse, as suits their purpose.

15 Cairo, 1961.

16 Cairo, 1962.

17 In *Al-Sukkariyyah*, 'The Sugar Bowl' (Cairo, 1957). Mahfuz leaves us in no doubt that this story of a radical, yet wistful, sceptic, whom 'religion has left empty-

handed', reflects his own spiritual crisis and that of his generation. The only value is that which derives from human commitment itself. He is 'like a tourist in a museum', a non-participant looking in on the irrelevant.

18   In *Dunyā Allāh*, 'God's Lower World' (Cairo, 1963), pp. 62–78. A translation of this story is in Mahmud Manzalaoui (ed.), *Arabic Writing Today: The Short Story* (Cairo, 1968), pp. 117–28.

19   *Dunyā Allāh*, pp. 190–203.

20   There is an intriguing resemblance in this story to the novel of John Braine, *Room at the Top* (London, 1957), p. 256 in which a callous go-getter succeeds in his drive for selfish ends but concludes in futility and despair. He is told, by an intending comforter: 'Don't worry: nobody blames you.' To which he replies: 'That's just the trouble.'

21   *Dunyā Allāh*, pp. 202–4.

10

Conclusion

I

Readers of these brief reviews of Qur'ān interpreters may well have been developing along the way the sense, or the charge, that the selection is not representative. They may be right, since what is 'representative' is itself at issue. No single choice about what should be chosen can presume to be a final verdict. Minority voices sometimes deserve a careful hearing precisely because they are *not* traditional. The Prophet himself at the first crucial stage in the *Risālah* was in a minority of one. The vitality of faiths has sometimes turned on the queried and querying fidelity of those who were least conventional.

Those, however, who are minded to conclude that only Sayyid Qutb, among our eight figures, is truly representative of Islam will have much in history to commend their opinion. He certainly embodied, in his own bold and sacrificial re-enactment of the logic of the *Sīrah* itself, a contemporary expression of Islamic identity, while his long and detailed Commentary on the Islamic Scripture exemplifies both the erudition and the temper of mind in which generations of Muslims would wholeheartedly recognise themselves. Sayyid Qutb's life and writing enshrine what generations have taken Islam to be and mean. So any attempt here at a conclusion, as we take leave of our mentors, will be wise to let that shape of Muslim loyalty inform any final reflections on their significance.

The central note in this expression of Quranic revelation and Islamic obedience is that of absolute authority. Acknowledged by a full and firm surrender, which in Sayyid Qutb's case was deeply aware of its own quality, Islam itself conditions and determines the personal will and the human reason which receive it, so that the mind and spirit of the adherent stand under an unquestioned – indeed unquestionable – authority. The believer lives by, and within, a religious 'positivism' which is self-authenticating by virtue not of an open activity of faith but of a guarantee of truth grounded in its system and structure of doctrine and *Dīn*. He is possessed, absolutely, of truth, to which, hence-forward, both thought and conduct are surrendered. Such, in these terms, *is* Islam. Other than such it cannot be.

In a quite different context, T. E. Lawrence, early in his *Seven Pillars of Wisdom*, in characteristic vividness of metaphor, described this quality of the Arab Muslim spirit:

> In the very outset, at the first meeting with them, was found a universal clearness or hardness of belief, almost mathematical in its limitation, and repellent in its unsympathetic form. . . . They were a dogmatic people, despising doubt, our modern crown of thorns. They did not understand our metaphysical difficulties, our introspective questionings. They knew only truth and untruth, belief and unbelief, without our hesitating retinue of finer shades. . . . Their thoughts were at ease only in extremes. They inhabited superlatives by choice.[1]

'Revolt in the Desert', which was Lawrence's context for these assessments, is not one which should be transposed artificially into the different realm of Scripture and scholarship. But something in the counterpart belongs to all spheres, both of thought and action. In the partnership of will and certainty, the understanding of religion as certitude, Sayyid Qutb reflects the long and instinctive posture of Islam: God as absolute; transcendent; presiding majestically, even – for some – implacably, over creation, humankind and history; legislating; ordaining; prohibiting, from on high; requiring a total obedient conformity; and arbiter of final destiny – such is the pattern of much Islamic theology, excluding as inappropriate the sort of 'theodicy' or 'justification' which theologies elsewhere have laboured to discern.

Implicit in this measure of the divine–human situation is the necessary 'dissociation' of God from the world. 'Dissociation' is, unhappily and confusingly, what Muslims normally derive from the central concept of *Tauḥīd*, conceived and defined in opposition to *Shirk*, of which it is the antithesis. *Shirk*, understood in the original setting of the Qur'ān contending against the *Jāhiliyyah*, necessarily meant 'dissociation' of God from idols and *their* representation. *Tauḥīd*, in that context, required a total, forthright denunciation of the pagan 'association' of what was only God's with the things of nature or of man. Islam has all religion in its debt for that firm exclusion of idolatry, that resolute dissociation of God from plural 'sacrilisation' and natural phenomena.

But the tragedy in those origins was that this urgent 'distancing' of God from the world as an arena of deifications and idolatries was perpetuated in a distancing of God from the world as an arena of human partnership (with Him) in the doing of the divine will. In spite of the evident 'association' of God with mankind in the fact of creation, in the mission of prophethood, and in the obligations of worship (all of which idolatry distorted), theology, by and large, remained under the tyranny of its – otherwise legitimate – preoccupation with idolatry and, so doing, obscured the full significance of its own faith in the Creator, the Revealer, 'the merciful Lord of mercy'. Can any of these aspects of divine activity be rightly or fully confessed unless a divine involvement with mankind is also acknowledged? That God creates, entrusts the world to man, and charters that entrustment via *Waḥy* in *Sharī'ah* surely means that there is a divine stake in the human response – a stake which prophethood supremely attests by its urgency and its travail.

We have, therefore, to uphold divine 'dissociation' from man and the world wherever and whenever human idolatries impugn and deny it. But that obligation does not warrant us in failing to perceive and to confess the wondrous divine 'association' with the world and ourselves, as it is implicit in our witness to His Lordship and our knowledge of ourselves. Indeed, it constantly obliges us to cry praise and adoration at the mystery and benediction of the ever-associating Lord, as mercy and truth engage Him with the world and engage us with His grace and purpose.

Kamil Husain liked to interpret the three great monotheisms as having received in traumatic events at their genesis the characteristic mark of their identity, whether Exodus and special peoplehood, the Cross and preoccupying evil and forgiveness, or the Battle of Badr and manifest success.[2] Perhaps it would be truer to see the Islamic hallmark not at Badr, however crucial that victory, but in this besetting ambiguity whereby a valid necessity to dissociate God from pagan plural worship notions was perpetuated into a theology of transcendent aloofness and indifference, hard to reconcile with the Qur'ān's own firm witness to man and nature, mercy and law.

II

What then emerges as perhaps the most significant feature in our eightfold review – and the one which most bears on the query whether it was 'representative' – is the evidence it offers of an Islam, *pace* Sayyid Qutb, moving away from sheer transcendence and divine aloofness or distance from the human, towards a faith as to divine engagement with man and in the world. Clearly this development, if such indeed it be, is deeply relevant to all the four major concerns, both of life and exegesis, in our time. It is the surest response to the menace, and mistake, of

secularisation. This is so not only because a starkly authoritarian concept of God is the most exposed to existential doubt and repudiation
from within the current sense of human autonomy which technology
releases and pursues. It is so also because the sense of human trusteeship through *khilāfah* and dominion, as divinely given and divinely
risked, in one way corroborates the undoubted 'lordship' which mankind exercises and which current technology maximises. But such
corroboration implies no licence to exploit unworthily, no mandate to
assume ourselves our own law, no warrant to think ourselves
unobligated beyond our own undoubted autonomy. On the contrary, a
sense of the divine stake in our pursuit of humanness disciplines, as
well as commissions, our competence. It is then possible, and
necessary, to see our very ability to exclude God from our human
self-sufficiency as in fact the very form of His presence. And what
volumes such a conclusion speaks as to His generosity, His patience,
His magnanimity, the sheer awesome extent of His risk in our being.
Will such convictions mean that transcendence is 'compromised', or
that 'greatness' is somehow impaired? Will they not rather deepen and
authenticate just those very convictions so central to Islam? Is there any
other way either to tame or to trust all those efficiencies our scientists
have attained and which our politicians and our economists translate
into power, into markets and structures, into tension and conflict? For
they cannot be disinvented. Nor can the history which contains them
be exempted from a theology of providence in their sequences and their
consequence. If, as we must, we are to go on asking, and caring, how
God is Lord, it can only be *within* and *about* the human order He – as all
Muslims and Christians believe – has willed, enabled and divinely
risked.

Divine 'dissociation', then, will be the last prescript by which to
hope to retain a theology, or a worship, to interpret, consecrate and
control a juncture in our humanity which many read, whether
arrogantly or painfully, as constraining us inescapably to secularity.
Such a theology and worship will live and move only in a keen
assurance of divine 'association', in which the will for God, on our part,
matches initiatives of grace and love on His part, consistently with
what, as we believe, *has* been given in trust to us in our humanity, and
with what, from such entrustment, we believe remains altogether His
in sovereignty and will. Those initiatives, relating as they do to an
entrustment, will not be only those of authority and direction, of law
and decree, but of condescension, grace and reconciliation, and an
energy of Holy Spirit in a mutuality of divine and human purpose.

Mamadou Dia, among our thinkers, comes closest to this vision of a
divine engagement with mankind. He allows it, as we saw, to open out

his Islamic allegiance to the relationships of Christianity. From the occasions of *rapport* with Senghor and de Chardin, he reaches his social and political position by what is a partially reciprocal Muslim–Christian theology. That enables him to put behind him all the instinctive vetoes on a theology of 'the Word made flesh', inasmuch as the Christian sense of 'God in Christ' plainly presents itself as a feasible, if not yet approved, realisation of just that divine engagement with the burdens, entailed upon mankind in the world as it is, of fulfilling the divine intention. With Dia, authentic social action requires, as a spiritual prerequisite, this faith in the co-activity of God with men and in man as co-present with God. That conviction means the end of a concept of divine transcendence that is only sovereign in being remote and sublime.

Hasan Askari must be invoked broadly in the same sense, except that he would not see such affirmation of divine–human inter-engagement as disallowing a view of transcendence which could also disown it. This is so because of his feeling that a proper sense of ultimacy may require us to reserve negation for what we also affirm, lest God should somehow be within the constraints of *any* formulation under which we, and our faiths, conceive Him. This, for some minds, may be a necessary reservation, keeping faith in an Islamic way with the negative theology. But, in practical terms, and philosophy apart, it need not deter us. The patterns of action will be the same. Praise will be our consecration of God's name within the sanctuary of the world. Monotheism will be the corollary of the will to a just society, and, read in these terms, it must be open to interact with all faiths, even if they do not comparably 'name His Name', because they are, by intention, with us and we with them, the disparities belonging with symbol and culture rather than with essence and meaning.

III

By his insistence, if it is sustained, on an exclusively 'functional' role of God within the human scene, Fazlur Rahman would take the course of thought back towards a Sayyid Qutb position, large and deep as are the convictions that otherwise divide them. For an exclusive accent on divine command, on God as law and moral necessity, reduces the human stature and leads it away from the autonomy which modernity likes to assume and which a full doctrine of creation acknowledges. It also disallows just those aspects of divine relationship to man – solicitude, grace, pathos, yearning – which, as we have seen, transcendence must include.

However, the emphasis Fazlur Rahman also firmly brings, in respect of responsible obedience to revelation by authentic 'translation' of its there-and-then incidence to its here-and-now implementation, does something to redress the balance towards a 'transcendence of risk' for which we are pleading. For, if the time factor entails on human judgement such a crucial responsibility as the faithful custody of a historical revelation needing such 'translation', that situation must surely indicate a vital divine reliance upon man and a necessary human co-operation with God. *Taqwā* also, by his insights into its social and personal meaning, presupposes a degree of divine stake in mankind implicit in the obligation on us to bring it, but also to realise existentially what it entails. In contemporary terms education, as Fazlur Rahman insists, is the clue to both. May it not then ripen into an awareness, on our part, of divine relatedness, not merely in respect of what is enjoined and prohibited, but of what is awaited and left humanly at risk? The Qur'ān may then cease to be merely a programmatic revelation, and Muhammad may be found often returning to the 'cave' of communion. In turn, the obligation to 'succeed' may be changed into a more patient, more creative vocation to love and to serve where fidelity is the only issue.

That would seem to be the lesson of Maulana Abu-l-Kalam Azad's life experience and we will return in conclusion to one of his favourite Qur'ān verses. His sense of *Rubūbiyyah* may have been arguably naïve in some of its teleology within nature. But his career was a long commentary on travail in what he believed to be 'the way of God' as human tribalism impeded it. Contemporary history certainly exhibited the actuality, and the tragedy, of social choice within the freedom of decisions that make and motivate the structures through which those decisions have their way. Could one involve the divine purpose within the actual political partitioning of India except as something entrusted to, and as Azad believed violated by, the option of men? If God was *not* an absentee, then the form of His presence must have been the liberty of the human factors, and thus a suffering patience within all the further liabilities the human choices entailed. What at least can be discerned in that 'theological' conclusion from Azad's personal significance is an ongoing divine–human partnership in redemption and in the retrieval of situations which our own undoubted responsibility is seen to be creating, aggravating and compounding. Something like the New Testament thought of 'the God of patience', served by human partnerships capable of retrieving their tragedies, would seem to be inseparable from any sustainable theism as explored and commended by careers like that of Maulana Azad, with their ambition to be 'godly' and their experience of tragedy. If we believe in neither an indifferent nor an interventionist divine sovereignty, the only other manner of sovereignty left for faith must be one of redemption in engagement with human servants of redeeming purposes that are both God's and theirs.

IV

It is hard to comprehend Kamil Husain within these terms. On the one hand he is acutely conscious, via *ẓulm* and *Shirk*, of the perversity present within social history and the collective organs of human culture, including religion itself. But so aware is he that he tends to leave the outer world of politics and conflict and withdraw to the inner self and to the healing grace of purity and peace as faith may attain these in the personality. Truth itself being constituted by its work in the psyche, he would find our concern for doctrines of transcendence, whether immune or engaged, as having no point. Faith is significant only in the cure of souls.

Do we not have to ask whether this admirable search for inner *iṭmi'nān* has not also duties of mind to the external world, to nature in its independence of, and hospitality to, man, to the stars in their courses, and the vast immensities which majestically and enigmatically house our sentient selves? Theology can hardly be simply a psychic study within this total context. Though obviously a ready solution to the disparities between faiths, this comprehension of them all within the healing function in the soul does little justice to their intellectual reconciliation or their spiritual obligations as 'institutions' in history. And for some, even the therapeutic virtue we seek from them could not avail unless they were also authentic ventures of interpretation on a wider scale. For a truth which is consciously employed or cherished only as a means to peace of mind will need to be deepened into conviction of mind about the cosmic whole. Even so, Kamil Husain's service in the hospital of life suggests how a Muslim humanism might derive itself from the Qur'ān.

Ali Shariati is in direct antithesis. His concerns are passionately social and revolutionary. Far from withdrawing into the search for personal 'truth', he plunges with passion into the disturbance of the private world on behalf of the recruitment of the masses. For him it is only social *Jihād* which gives authenticity to the private world, which, in that *Jihād*, will be private no longer. The individual must lose himself in the goal and the struggle towards it. Here what we can mean by the 'transcendent' is, indeed, immersed in the human scene. But it is so in terms of radical strife towards liberation from oppression and the achievement of justice. God is, indeed, *Ilāh al-Nās* – God, as grammarians have it, 'in construct' with another noun, and that 'the masses'. It is the people who themselves in *Hijrah* project Muhammad himself on the path of power which necessarily succeeds the task of preaching. That same sequence has to obtain today. 'God' is the dynamic of the masses. Transcendence becomes immanence in the will of the people. The religious hierarchy, custodians of the transcendent Lord within the Shī'ah system, must realise and serve the dynamism of the masses as the revolutionary intention of the divine will. Here theology is wholly taken up into liberation and the springs of faith and action arise from the stresses of society.

V

All these are voices from within Islam. We find most of them moving away from a rigorous transcendence 'dissociated' from man, towards a sense of the divine engagement within the human predicament, its struggle and its tragic dimensions. Most of them, too, we find responding to a lively debate within the house of Islam and also between faiths, and doing so in recognition of the problematics of secularising attitudes in the wake of accelerating technology.

If any such review of recent mentors of Islam is to be rightly Islamic there is only one place where it can conclude, namely with the central question of Surah 7.172, a question at the heart of the entire theme of the divine–human relationship. 'Am I not your Lord?'

Why need the question be asked at all? Should sovereignty in God be a subject of doubt, or of inquiry? Is God not sublimely and altogether Lord? Surely so. Yet the question must be asked. For this Lordship waits to be recognised. God's is a power which, all-powerfully, makes itself reciprocal to human assent. His is a Lordship to be acknowledged in submission. There is no question about God: only the question to man. But, in that loving, responsive sense, question it remains. Otherwise, why Islam, or any other faith, to bring the answer?

It is not a question without the human pronoun. 'Am I Lord?' would leave open the sort of philosophical perplexity, the kind of barren speculation which the Qur'ān firmly excludes. God is not a theme of academic debate. Nor is His being such as to await proof. The real question is expectant. It is asked in the negative form: 'Am I not . . . ?' Bare omnipotence would not speak this way. Love may and does. It is the sort of question which expects the answer 'Yes!' Transcendence has a seeking heart. There is perceptibly a yearning, even a pathos, in the very shape of what is between man and God. His is an expectant Lordship whose rule and grace, being inviolate, yet await the crucial consent of our whole being.

The words of the question do not speak of God's decreeing, God's commanding, nor even of God's doing. '*Am* I not your Lord?' is about God's being. That of which He will say 'I am' is a Lordship linking itself with a human pronoun. The intelligent conclusion of all we find and undergo in mortal life and history, in nature and in time, is surely towards our consent in the awaited 'Yes!' Such response is the meaning we can understand in that human *fiṭrah* which, according to Surah 30.30, is God's shaping of our humanness. The closer we can all come to the reality of the question, the surer and purer will be the integrity of the answer.

NOTES: CHAPTER 10

1 T. E. Lawrence, *The Seven Pillars of Wisdom* (London, 1921), ch. 3.
2 Kamil Husain, *City of Wrong*, trans. from the Arabic *Qaryah Ẓālimah* (Amsterdam, 1959), appendix.

Bibliography

MAJOR WORKS OF MAULANA AZAD

Tarjumān al-Qur'ān, trans. Syed Abdul Latif, Volume 1 (Bombay, 1962); Volume 2 (Bombay, 1967).
India Wins Freedom: an Autobiographical Narrative, edit. Humayun Kabir (Bombay, 1959).
Speeches of Maulana Azad, 1947–55 (Delhi, 1956).
Tarjumān al-Qur'ān (Urdu text), Volume 1 (Lahore, 1931); Volume 2 (Delhi, 1936).
Baqīyat Tarjumān al-Qur'ān, edit. Ghulam Rasul Mehr (Lahore, 1961).

See also:
Humayun Kabir (ed.), *Maulana Azad: A Homage* (Delhi, 1958).
Humayun Kabir (ed.), *Maulana Abul-Kalam Azad: A Memorial Volume* (Delhi, 1959).
M. M. Siddiqi, *The Religious Philosophy of Maulana Azad* (Hyderabad, 1965).

MAJOR WORKS OF MAMADOU DIA

Essais sur l'Islam, Volume 1, *Islam et Humanisme* (Dakar, 1977).
Essais sur l'Islam, Volume 2, *Socio-Anthropologie de l'Islam* (Dakar, 1979).

Mamadou Dia's Senegal setting may be studied in:
L. C. Behrman, *Muslim Brotherhoods and Politics in Senegal* (Cambridge, Mass., 1970).
Vincent Monteil, *L'Islam Noir* (Paris, 1964).
Peter Clarke, *West Africa and Islam* (London, 1970).
R. S. Morgenthau, *Political Parties in French-speaking West Africa* (Oxford, 1964).
J. C. Froelich, *Les Musulmans d'Afrique noire* (Paris, 1962).

MAJOR WORKS OF SAYYID QUTB

Ṭifl min Qaryah (Beirut, 1967): 'A Village Child' (autobiographical).
Al-Naqd al-Adabī (Beirut, 1972): 'Literary Criticism'.
Al-Taṣwīr al-Fannī fī-l-Qur'ān (Cairo, 1963): 'Literary Artistry in the Qur'ān'.
Ma'ālim fī-l-Ṭarīq (Cairo, 1981): 'Signposts on the Way'.
Social Justice in Islam (Washington, 1953), trans. by J. B. Hardie.

Fī Ẓilāl al-Qur'ān, 30 vols (Cairo, 1972): 'In the Shade of the Qur'ān'. Vol. 30, covering Surahs 78 to 114 translated into English by M. D. Salahi and A. A. Shamis (London, 1979).
Mustaqbal Hādhā-l-Dīn (Beirut, n.d.): 'The Future of this Religion'.
Al-Salām al-'Ālamī wa-l-Islām (Beirut, 1965): 'World Peace and Islam'.
Mashāhid al-Qiyāmah fī-l-Qur'ān (Beirut, n.d.): 'Aspects of the Re-surrection in the Qur'ān'.
Ṭarīq al-Da'wah fī-Ẓilāl al-Qur'ān (Cairo, 1963): 'The Way of the Call to Faith in the Shade of the Qur'ān'.
Fiqh al-Dīn (Beirut, 1970): 'Law and Religion'.

MAJOR WORKS OF ALI SHARIATI

On the Sociology of Islam (Berkeley, 1979), trans. by Hamid Algar.
Marxism and Other Western Fallacies (Berkeley, 1980), trans. by R. Campbell.
The Visage of Muhammad (Tehran, 1981), trans. by A. A. Sachedin.
Civilization and Modernization (Houston, 1979).

MAJOR WORKS OF FAZLUR RAHMAN

Prophecy in Islam (London, 1958).
Islam (London, 1966).
Islamic Methodology in History (Karachi, 1965).
Major Themes of the Qur'ān (Minneapolis, 1980).
Islam and Modernity (Chicago, 1982).

See also:
'The Sources and Meaning of Islamic Socialism', in D. E. Smith (ed.), *Religion and Political Modernization* (New Haven, 1974), pp. 243–58.
'Islamic Modernism, Its Scope, Methods and Alternatives', in *International Journal of Middle East Studies*, volume 1 (1970), pp. 317–33.

MAJOR WORKS OF HASAN ASKARI

Inter Religion (Aligarh, 1977).
Society and State in Islam, An Introduction (New Delhi, 1978).
'The Sermon on the Mount', in C. D. Jathanna (ed.), *Dialogue in Community* (Mangalore, 1982).
'Islam and Modernity', in S. T. Lokhandwalla, *Technological Revolution and Indian Muslims* (New Delhi, 1971).

MAJOR WORKS OF MUHAMMAD KAMIL HUSAIN

City of Wrong (Amsterdam, 1959), trans. by Kenneth Cragg.
Mutanawwi'āt 2 volumes (Cairo, 1957–8): 'Miscellanies'.

The Hallowed Valley (Cairo, 1977), trans. by Kenneth Cragg.
Al-Dhikr al-Ḥakīm (Cairo, n.d.): 'The Wise Mentor' (Quranic studies).
Wiḥdat al-Maʿrifah (Cairo, n.d.): 'The Unity of Knowledge'.
Al-Taḥlil al-Biʾūlūgī li-l-Tārīkh (Cairo, 1955): 'Biological Analysis of History'.

MAJOR WORKS OF NAJIB MAHFUZ

Children of Gebelawi (London, 1981), trans. by Phillip Stewart.
Mīrāmār (London, 1972), trans. by Fatma Musa Mahmud.
Midaq Alley (Beirut, 1966), trans. by T. LeGassick.
Mirrors (Minneapolis, 1977), trans. by Roger Allen.
Al-Liṣṣ wa-l-Kilāb (Cairo, 1961): 'The Robber and the Dogs'.
Thartharah fauq al-Nīl (Cairo, 1966): 'Chatter on the Nile'.
Bidāyah wa Nihāyah (Cairo, 1949): 'Beginning and Ending'.
Khān al-Khalīlī (Cairo, 1946).
Dunyā Allāh (Cairo, 1963): 'God's Lower World' (an English trans. by Akef Abadir and Roger Allen, Minneapolis, 1973).

Index

Qurānic Passages cited.

Surah 1 18, 20, 21, 24, 25, 26, 30, 48, 79, 135, 161
Surah 2.2 69, 84, 134, 146
2.143 117, 123, 125
2.152 133
2.191 76
2.213 84
2.217 62
2.251 59
Surah 3.7 2, 23
3.42 133
3.55 133
3.103 114
Surah 4.157 138, 140
Surah 5.32 86
5.41 134
5.44 58
5.49–50 58, 59, 62
5.56 18
5.64 24
5.99 81
Surah 6.91 114
Surah 7.157–8 97
7.172 24, 119, 172, 173
Surah 9.103 134
Surah 10.3 24, 46
10.37 69
Surah 11.44 132
11.114 136
Surah 12.2 80, 132
12.53 136
Surah 13.2 46
13.11 19
13.28 135
Surah 16.35 81
Surah 17.44 30
Surah 20.12 134
20.113 80, 132
Surah 21.11 137
21.16 83
21.30 66
21.105 46
Surah 22.26 133
22.44 59
22.74 114

Surah 24.54 81
Surah 27.88 31
Surah 28.88 83
Surah 29.18 81
Surah 30.30 25, 69, 83, 123, 173
Surah 32.2 69
32.6–7 30
Surah 33.10 46
33.33 134
33.42 133
Surah 37.87 46
Surah 38.27 83
Surah 39.38 28
39.67 114
Surah 41.3 80
Surah 42.7 132
Surah 43.4 80, 132
Surah 49.12 2, 8
Surah 50.37 93
50.45 21
Surah 53.19–23 99
Surah 54.1 72, 82
Surah 56.60 8
56.79 73
Surah 58.22 18
Surah 59.7 103
Surah 64.12 81
Surah 70.41 8
Surah 73.1–2 91
73.5 94
73.8 133
Surah 74.1–2 91
74.4 133
Surah 75.2 136
Surah 78 57
Surah 87.15 133
Surah 89.14 102
89.27 135, 143
Surah 90.4 67, 142
Surah 94.1–4 82, 94
Surah 96.4 1
Surah 105 67, 68
Surah 113 158
Surah 114 82, 157, 158